The Civil Service Today

The
Civil Service
Today

GAVIN DREWRY

and

TONY BUTCHER

Basil Blackwell

Copyright © Gavin Drewry and Tony Butcher 1988

First published 1988
Second edition first published in paperback 1991

Basil Blackwell Ltd
108 Cowley Road, Oxford, OX4 1JF, UK

Basil Blackwell, Inc. 1054668 5
3 Cambridge Center
Cambridge, Massachusetts 02142, USA

British Library Cataloguing in Publication Data

A CIP catalogue record for this book is available from the British Library.

Library of Congress Cataloging in Publication Data

Drewry, Gavin.
  The civil service today/Gavin Drewry and Tony Butcher.—2nd ed.
     p. cm.
  Includes bibliographical references and index.
  ISBN 0–631–18172–5 (pbk.)
  1. Civil service—Great Britain. I. Butcher, Tony. II. Title.
JN425.D7 1991
354.41006—dc20   91–16907
                                                                CIP

Printed on acid free paper

Typeset in 11 on 12½ pt
by Alan Sutton Publishing Ltd.
Printed in Great Britain by
T.J. Press Ltd, Padstow

17/08/92   Latest Ed 08/03

Contents

Acknowledgements

This book has had a long period of gestation. It was conceived in 1982 when Gavin Drewry, long frustrated, in common with many teachers of British public administration, by the surprising absence of an up-to-date textbook on the civil service, approached the publishers (then Martin Robertson Ltd) with a proposal to produce such a book. Our first acknowledgement is to the then editor, Sue Corbett, for her encouragement and helpful advice, and for her patience in the face of a succession of excuses for non-delivery. Although the early chapters were written to schedule, the author allowed himself to be side-tracked into other commitments, and the project sank into the sand.

Phase two of the saga began in 1986, when Gavin Drewry approached his colleague, Tony Butcher, to help reactivate the book. Apart from the need, by then, to update material already written, several chapters had to be written from scratch, and to a tight deadline. To Gavin Drewry's relief and gratitude, Tony Butcher agreed to undertake the bulk of this. The publishers, by now transformed into Basil Blackwell Ltd, suspended their disbelief and agreed to the new arrangement. We are grateful to Sean Magee, of Basil Blackwell, for his confidence in us, and for his help and encouragement.

We have gratefully received a lot of helpful advice and information from official sources, and would like also to thank successive librarians of the Royal Institute of Public Administration for their assistance. The burgeoning literature of British public administration has still not thrown up another student textbook on the civil service, but the authors have benefited from reading Geoffrey Fry's stimulating interpretive essay, *The Changing Civil Service* (Allen and Unwin, London 1985). Thanks are due to Charlotte Lawrie for converting our untidy manuscript into a polished typescript. Above all, we owe much to our families for their support and patience.

Material in many of our figures and statistical tables is adapted from official publications and is used here by permission of the Controller of Her Majesty's Stationery Office. Some material is also reproduced from *The Complete Yes, Minister* by Jonathan Lynn and Anthony Jay with the permission of BBC Enterprises Ltd.

Gavin Drewry
Tony Butcher

Note on the Second Edition

This second edition of *The Civil Service Today* takes account of developments since the beginning of 1988, when the first edition went to press. The most important of these – a landmark in the modern history of the UK civil service – has been the launching of the 'Next Steps' initiative, which holds out the prospect that three-quarters of all civil servants will be working in newly-created departmental agencies by the end of the 1990s. This is discussed in a completely new chapter, chapter 12.

We have also taken the opportunity – in some cases by making textual amendments, in others by adding postscripts to the original chapters – to note other recent changes that have affected the civil service. However, we have left most of the original statistical tables unaltered: the aggregate size of the civil service has continued to diminish (at the beginning of 1991, the total number of civil servants in post was about 570,000), but considered in relative terms most of the figures tell much the same story in the early 1990s as they did in the late 1980s.

In July 1988, the Department of Health and Social Security (DHSS) was split into two separate departments. We have not altered either the text or the tables to take account of this, partly because the new Department of Social Security is undergoing a major upheaval, with most of its functions being transferred to Next Steps agencies – so any updating would quickly be overtaken by events. Most of our references to the Thatcher years are still expressed in the present tense; the implications for our subject-matter of Mrs Thatcher's replacement by Mr Major, towards the end of 1990, have yet to become clear, though we would hazard a guess that the relationships between the civil service and governments of the 1990s will prove to be less strained than they sometimes were in the 1980s.

We would like to thank the many academic colleagues, officials and reviewers from whose encouraging and constructive comments we have benefited in undertaking this revision.

Gavin Drewry
Tony Butcher

Prologue: Some Crises of the 1980s

At the beginning of this century, the prospect of a growing civil service was regarded with alarm in some quarters as a harbinger of collectivism – even of socialist revolution. This unease has never wholly been dispelled and, indeed, the Thatcher government's continuing determination to question the scope of state intervention and cut the civil service down to size (literally and figuratively) echoes in some respects this kind of thinking. However, the civil service survived and grew steadily not only in size but also, by and large, in stature; it was an essential instrument in the post-war establishment of a welfare state and a managed economy. Throughout the prosperous Butskellite 1950s, commentators were almost unanimous in extolling the virtues of the civil service.

But such complacency did not survive Britain's post-war decline as a world power and her recurrent affliction with economic ills that neither of the main political parties seemed able to tackle. The 1960s were a period of major institutional reappraisal, much of it long overdue, but some of it tainted with the feeling that scapegoats were being sought. By the mid-1960s, there was mounting criticism that the civil service was 'amateurish' and incapable of tackling the problems of the modern state. Criticism also focused on the allegedly excessive power possessed by civil servants, especially their negative capacity to obstruct ministerial policies of which they disapproved.[1] Some commentators spoke of a 'crisis' in the civil service.[2] Such attacks were given formal recognition in the Report of the Fulton Committee in 1968.[3]

Today, nearly 20 years after Fulton, the debate on the civil service still includes charges of inefficiency and excessive power. Much of that debate has revolved around a set of concerns relating to the nature of the relationship between elected ministers and non-elected civil servants, an area of the constitution which has come increasingly into the spotlight since the election of the Conservative government in 1979. The British civil service has been passing through an era in which civil servants have been both forcibly reorientated and 'deprivileged', and in which some familiar constitutional landmarks have changed significantly.

These issues will be raised again, in various guises, in the chapters that follow. Meanwhile, by way of a prologue, we outline three particularly significant and dramatic episodes of the 1980s that illustrate some of the constitutional tensions that form the backcloth to our discussion of the civil service today: the prosecution of the senior civil servant, Clive Ponting, for breaching the Official Secrets Act; the constitutional and political issues arising out of the government's involvement in the financial plight of Westland plc; and the implications of the government's civil action in the Australian courts to prevent publication of Peter Wright's account of the activities of the British security services.

The Ponting Case

On 18 August 1984, Clive Ponting appeared at Bow Street Magistrates' Court charged under Section 2 of the Official Secrets Act 1911 with communicating information to an unauthorized person on or about 16 July.[4] Ponting was at that time an assistant secretary in charge of Defence Secretariat 5, a division of the Ministry of Defence dealing with naval operations. The communications that were the subject of the charge were departmental documents, one unclassified, the other originally designated 'confidential' but subsequently declassified, concerning proposed ministerial responses to parliamentary inquiries relating to the sinking of the Argentinian cruiser, the *General Belgrano*, during the Falklands campaign in May 1982. The 'unauthorized person' was Tam Dalyell, a Labour MP who had been fighting a long battle to expose what he believed to be serious government mis-statements about the sinking of the *Belgrano*. The offending items had been sent anonymously to Dalyell, who passed them to the House of Commons Foreign Affairs Committee, which had begun an inquiry into the future of the Falkland Islands. After some disputatious deliberation within the committee, the chairman returned the leaked documents to the Secretary of State for Defence, Michael Heseltine.

Committal proceedings were completed in October, and the trial, described by Ponting's counsel as 'the most political trial of the century' opened on 28 January 1985. The jury had been vetted, although the prosecution had acknowledged from the outset that national security was not at issue; and some of the proceedings were held *in camera*. Defence counsel observed that this was 'not a case about spying. It's a case about lying, or misleading Parliament.'[5] Ponting claimed that his motives for leaking the documents stemmed from his view that he was being required to assist ministers to evade, through deliberate deceit, legitimate parliamentary scrutiny. His defence rested on the provision in Section 2 (1) (a) of the 1911 Act that the information had been communicated 'to a person to whom he is authorised to communicate it, or to a person to whom it is in the interests of the State his duty to communicate it'. As the defence conceded that Dalyell was not an 'authorized' person, the case turned upon the second part of the provision. Thus the arguments centred on the definition of the terms 'duty' and 'in the interests of the State'.

The judge, Mr Justice McCowan, directed the jury that 'duty' meant official duty, meaning the duty imposed upon Ponting by his position. As for the words 'in the interests of the State', the judge said:

> I direct you that those words mean the policies of the State as they were in July of 1984 when Mr. Ponting communicated the information to Mr. Dalyell and not the policies of the State as Mr. Ponting, Mr. Dalyell, you or I might think they ought to have been. The policies of the State mean the policies laid down for it by its recognised organs of government and authority . . . while it has [the support of the majority of the House of Commons] it is the government, and its policies are for the time being the policies of the State.[6]

On 11 February, in the face of a summing-up that appeared to amount to an implicit direction to convict, Ponting was acquitted. He resigned from the civil service on 16 February. The whole affair was dug over once more on 18 February in a Commons debate on the sinking of the *Belgrano*, during which ministers revealed further, hitherto confidential, information purporting to show serious inconsistencies in Ponting's account of his actions and motives.[7]

As we shall see in chapter 9, the Ponting case was the culmination of a series of incidents involving the leaking of official information. A fortnight after Ponting's acquittal, the Head of the Home Civil Service, and Cabinet Secretary, Sir Robert Armstrong, issued a *Note of Guidance on the Duties and Responsibilities of Civil Servants in Relation to Ministers* (now known as the 'Armstrong Memorandum').[8] The *Note* starkly reasserted the principle that 'the civil service has no constitutional personality or responsibility separate from the duly elected Government of the day.' The duty of the individual civil servant, it said, was first and foremost to the minister in charge of the department in which he or she was serving. The minister was answerable in Parliament for the conduct of the department's affairs and the management of its business.

The debate surrounding the Armstrong Memorandum – which gave rise to critical comments both inside and outside the civil service – prompted the House of Commons Treasury and Civil Service Committee to set up a sub-committee to inquire into the duties and responsibilities of civil servants and ministers. During the course of the sub-committee's inquiry, the exercise acquired added momentum from the Westland affair which came to a head at the beginning of 1986.

The Westland Affair

The Westland episode, which has been described as the biggest British political scandal for a quarter of a century, concerned a relatively small aircraft company in the West Country.[9] The only British firm engaged in the manufacture of military helicopters, Westland faced a difficult financial situation in 1984, stemming partly from a decline in the market for civil helicopters and partly from the lack of large orders from the British armed services. The company's financial situation deteriorated with the collapse of annual profits from £26.1 million to £2.75 million, and the withdrawal of a takeover bid by Bristow Rotorcraft in June 1985. Following the withdrawal of the Bristow bid, Sir John Cuckney was appointed chairman on 26 June, and the rest of the summer was taken up with a search for a way out of the company's difficulties.

In the early autumn, Westland put forward proposals for the company's financial reconstruction, which included the raising of new capital from a new large minority shareholder, either Sikorsky, an American company with whom Westland had a long-standing relationship, or a European company. The then Secretary of State for Trade and Industry, Leon Brittan, recognized that the company most likely to take a large minority shareholding was Sikorsky, but considered that Westland should be encouraged to pursue the possibility of a European alternative. It was agreed that the then Secretary of State for Defence, Michael Heseltine, should explore the European option, but it was the government's frequently stated view that it was in the end for the Westland Board to decide. Heseltine, who was concerned at the possibility of the UK becoming dependent on the USA as its sole supplier of military helicopters, favoured an association with European-based companies, and subsequently arranged a meeting of the National Armaments Directors (NADs) of France, West Germany, Italy and the UK. On 29 December the NADs recommended that the helicopter needs of their amred services should be covered solely by helicopters designed and built in Europe, a move which, according to Sir John Cuckney, would preclude the Sikorsky deal.

Two weeks later, the Westland Board received a bid from a European consortium, which was rejected in favour of Sikorsky who, meanwhile, had brought the Italian automobile company, Fiat, into the deal. Brittan was later to argue that Heseltine's enthusiasm for a European solution had 'caused him to take action going beyond what was consistent with the Government's policy in relation to the handling of Westland'.[10] Heseltine, however, continued to support the European option, and canvassed support from the House of Commons Defence Committee, which had decided to investigate the defence implications of the future of Westland.

On 19 December a Cabinet meeting restated the government's policy of showing no preference between the two rescue packages and allowing the company to reach its own decision. Despite this, the crisis came to a head in the early new year, when Heseltine sent a letter stating the disadvantages of the Sikorsky–Fiat deal to Lloyds Merchant Bank (advisers to the European consortium). On 6 January 1986, the Solicitor-General, at the Prime Minister's instigation, wrote confidentially to Heseltine, referring to 'material inaccuracies' in the letter to the bank. The substance of the Solicitor-General's letter was promptly leaked by Department of Trade and Industry (DTI) officials to the Press Association, the apparent motive for the leak being to undermine the credibility of Heseltine's advocacy of the European rescue package.

The long-threatened political and constitutional storm over the government's handling of the crisis finally broke on 9 January, when Heseltine resigned from the Cabinet, unable to accept the requirement for Cabinet Office clearance of any future public statements on the Westland affair. Five days later, under pressure from her law officers, the Prime Minister instructed Sir Robert Armstrong to investigate the circumstances of the leak. He reported to her on 22 January. On the same day, it was revealed that the Director of Information at the DTI, Miss Colette Bowe, although having grave reservations about the form of disclosure, was responsible for the leak, leading to speculation about whether it had been authorized.

The Prime Minister's statement to the House of Commons on 23 January confirmed that the leak had been authorized by Brittan, after obtaining 'cover' from Bernard Ingham, the Prime Minister's Press Secretary, and Charles Powell, the Prime Minister's Private Secretary specializing in foreign and defence matters. The following day, Leon Brittan resigned his Cabinet office.

The Defence Committee, which was continuing its inquiry into Westland, sought oral evidence from the DTI officials concerned in the leak, as well as Bernard Ingham and Charles Powell, all of whom had already been questioned by Sir Robert Armstrong. However, the Committee was denied the opportunity to cross-examine any of these key witnesses, the Prime Minister defending the refusal on the grounds that for private secretaries and personal staff to give evidence had 'major implications for the conduct of the government and for relations between Ministers and their Private Offices'. This was a significant setback for the Committee, but there was a consolation prize in the shape of two separate sessions of evidence from Sir Robert Armstrong, who had in effect to speak for the Prime Minister and the Cabinet system and (in his capacity as Head of the Home Civil Service) to defend individual civil servants into whose conduct he had already carried out an inquiry.

On 12 February the Westland shareholders voted 2:1 for the Sikorsky–Fiat rescue package, but the political controversy surrounding the Westland affair rumbled on. On 23 July the Defence Committee published two reports, one on the defence implications of Westland's financial crisis,[11] the other entitled *Westland plc: The Government's Decision-Making*.[12] The latter report was highly critical of the procedures adopted by the participants in the episode, and found it 'extraordinary' that no disciplinary action was being contemplated against any of the five officials involved in the leak.[13] The report also condemned the failure of the government to allow officials to be cross-examined by the Committee, echoing criticisms made in the report of the parallel inquiry on *Civil Servants and Ministers* by the Treasury and Civil Service Committee (TCSC), published in May, which had urged the government to produce specific proposals on how the crucial question of accountability should be dealt with in the future.[14] The government made no direct response to this in its reply.[15] In its reply to the Defence Committee's report, the government repeated earlier expressions of regret about the method used to disclose the contents of the Solicitor-General's letter, but insisted that those concerned acted in good faith and that no disciplinary action was called for.[16] It roundly condemned the Committee's attempts to investigate the conduct of individual civil servants, pointing out that accountability to ministers, reinforced by conventions of confidentiality, meant that civil service witnesses were unable to speak freely in their own defence. It went on to say that it proposed to make it clear to civil servants giving evidence to select committees that they should not answer questions which concern their own, or their colleagues', conduct. Not surprisingly, this dismissive reply caused great concern amongst MPs, and the TCSC returned to the subject of civil service accountability in a further report in December.[17] December also saw the publication of a report from the Liaison Committee, which considered general matters relating to select committees, demanding that select committees should be able to examine civil servants about conduct.[18] The government's reply in February 1987 refused to concede this demand, and new guidelines to officials appearing before select committees stated that civil servants questioned about conduct should consult their minister before answering.[19]

The Wright Case

A key figure in the Westland affair, Sir Robert Armstrong, also figured prominently in another *cause célèbre* in 1986: the Thatcher government's attempts to prevent the publication of a book, *Spycatcher*, by Peter Wright, a former counter-espionage officer in MI5, now living in Australia. The book included allegations that the late Sir Roger Hollis, a former head of MI5, had been a Soviet agent, and that MI5 had carried out unlawful and criminal acts, notably a plot to destabilize the Wilson government in the mid-1970s. Although the Thatcher government had declined to take action to prevent publication of Chapman Pincher's *Their Trade is Treachery* and Nigel West's *A Matter of Trust*, both of which contained allegations similar to those made by Wright, the government took civil action in the Australian courts to prevent publication of the Wright book on the grounds that, as a former MI5 officer, Wright had an obligation of confidentiality to the Crown which bound him to permanent silence about his intelligence work. The government had already successfully obtained a blanket ban on the publication, in any part of the British media, of the allegations made by Wright.[20]

The case was heard in the New South Wales Supreme Court during November and December 1986, and the government's chief witness was not a government minister but the Cabinet Secretary, Sir Robert Armstrong, who spent an embarrassing two weeks in the limelight. Much of Armstrong's evidence was treated with considerable scepticism by the judge in the case, Mr Justice Powell, who described parts of it as 'baloney' and a 'mere form of words'. Sir Robert was not helped by having to admit during evidence that he had inadvertently misled the court by statements concerning the circumstances in which the government had declined to take action over the Pincher and West books; that he had been 'economical with the truth' in a letter to the publisher relating to the publication of the Pincher book; and that he had unwittingly misled the court by claiming that the Attorney-General had taken the decision not to take action to prevent publication of Pincher's book.[21]

Mr Justice Powell's judgment was delivered on Friday, 13 March 1987, and demolished the government's case. While accepting that Wright had a duty of confidentiality to his former employers, the judge argued that this was overridden by the fact that most of the information in the Wright memoirs was no longer secret. The British government had surrendered its claim to confidentiality by acquiescing in the publication of other books about MI5, and by doing nothing to prevent television interviews with former MI5 officers. The judge was highly critical of the way the British government had conducted its case, and particularly of Sir Robert Armstrong, much of whose evidence, the judge said, 'must be treated with considerable reserve'.[22] The Cabinet Secretary's role in the affair was also criticized in Britain, the leader of the Liberal Party describing Sir Robert Armstrong as a 'garbage disposal operator for the Thatcher Government', a role which reflected badly on his high office.[23] In September 1987, the New South Wales Court of Appeal upheld the trial judge's decision by a two-to-one majority. Meanwhile, in August, the House of Lords had upheld, by a three-to-two majority, a decision of the Court of Appeal in London that the public interest required the continuation of temporary injunctions restraining English newspapers from disclosing or publishing material from *Spycatcher*.[24]

Thus the Wright case in some respects picked up where the Westland affair left off in raising fundamental questions about the association of senior officials with the government of the day. It also reinforced disquiet about the secretive nature of British central government, an issue highlighted by the Ponting case. All three cases are of profound importance in attempting to understand the position of the civil service, and the context in which it operates in the 1980s, and we will encounter them on many occasions throughout the book.

1

Charting the Territory

When a cartoonist wants to draw an instantly recognizable sketch of a British civil servant he will quite probably draw a middle-aged man in a pin-striped suit, walking along Whitehall, equipped with a bowler hat and a furled umbrella. The civil servant thus portrayed will often be presented in an unflattering light, as being stuffy and arrogant and possessing a world-weary cynicism, an insensitivity to ordinary people's feelings and a remarkable thirst for cups of tea. The archetypal civil servant or 'mandarin', depicted in so many political cartoons and newspaper articles, works rigidly 'according to the book' and is bound up in time-consuming 'red tape'. The words 'bureaucracy' and 'bureaucrat' (common but misleading synonyms for civil service and civil servant) are implicitly terms of abuse, suggesting something both inefficient and antithetical to electoral democracy. It is taken more or less for granted (and not just by journalists and cartoonists) that this 'bureaucracy' has grown, is growing and ought to be diminished, in its size and in the amount of influence it exercises on public affairs.

Caricatures can be a useful shorthand way of making a perfectly serious and valid point. And they can be fun. But they can also – as in this case – be both unfair and a reflection of ignorance and prejudice, endowing dangerous half-truths with a status they do not deserve. Let us consider some aspects of the caricature described in the preceding paragraph:

1 Civil servants do not, of course, match a single sartorial or physical stereotype. How could they, given that there are some 600,000 of them, of both sexes and of all shapes and sizes, spread across the age spectrum of the working population? Bowler hats are nowadays a rarity, even in Whitehall. (Tea, however, is not.)

2   The word 'mandarin', used originally with reference to officials of Imperial China, is commonly used in the context of the British civil service, usually to describe the small percentage of top officials concerned with formulating policy and advising ministers (the 'higher civil service', see below). It is not helpful to use it as a synonym for civil servants in general; an administrative officer (formerly clerical officer) in a local office of the Department of Health and Social Security, a telephonist in the Ministry of Agriculture and a civilian welder in a naval dockyard – all of these are civil servants, but none could sensibly be called a mandarin. It is important to grasp at the outset that the civil service employs people in a vast range of different jobs, and that only a tiny proportion of these jobs give any direct access to the levers of governmental power.

3   It is also a mistake to think of the civil service exclusively, or even predominantly, in terms of 'Whitehall'. Only about one-sixth of all civil servants work in Inner London and not all of these are actually in Whitehall itself; the Department of Health and Social Security, one of the largest departments, has its London headquarters at the Elephant and Castle, and the great majority of its staff work in numerous local offices, or in its huge office complex in Newcastle. However, many of the most senior advisory posts do tend to be concentrated in central locations simply because the ministerial heads of government departments need frequently to attend both Parliament and meetings with other ministers, in Cabinet and Cabinet committees. London, like all capital cities (particularly in unitary states, where power is not shared between federal and state tiers of government), is the nerve centre of government, and is the place where, for example, overseas embassies are situated and where many influential pressure groups have their headquarters.

4   Some civil servants are inevitably, if only by the law of averages, arrogant, aloof, cynical and so on. The reports of the Parliamentary Commissioner for Administration (commonly known as the Ombudsman), who deals with alleged maladministration in central government, regularly disclose instances where members of the public have suffered at the hands of high-handed and/or inept officials. But sometimes the fault lies more with the system (e.g. unclear legislation or understaffed departments) than with the individuals who are the 'public face' of a department. And the number of abuses reported (we can only guess at the size of the submerged portion of the iceberg in relation to its tip) is minute in relation to the vast volume of civil service activity.

Inevitably, parts of a large bureaucratic machine will sometimes cause frustration to the consumer of its services by moving ponderously and inflexibly. As in many complex organizations, disharmony between management and staff (the latter backed in the civil service, as elsewhere, by powerful trade unions, see chapter 6) can work against the interests of the consumer; restrictive practices and overmanning may afflict the civil service as they afflict many commercial undertakings. But while faults and failings of bodies financed out of the public purse and responsible for the formulation and implementation of public policy are obviously a matter of legitimate public concern, it is absurd to tar the whole of the civil service and every individual civil servant with the same disparaging brush.

5   It is even more absurd to indulge in blanket condemnations on the basis of emotive slogans about the inherent 'evils of bureaucracy'. 'Bureaucracy', as defined by the German sociologist, Max Weber, at the beginning of the century, is a term which usefully describes a form of organization which in its 'pure' form (i.e. what sociologists call an 'ideal type', providing a yardstick against which to measure phenomena in the real world) exhibits a cluster of characteristics such as hierarchical structure, routine procedures, staff employed under contract, an ordered career structure and codes of conduct.[1] Used in this sense, the term bureaucracy is entirely neutral and carries no emotive charge. Weber, building on work done by earlier scholars, showed how bureaucracy is endemic to advanced, complex societies as the most rational form of administrative organization. And not just for national governments: civil servants are bureaucrats, but so too are administrators in local government, in the National Health Service, in universities and perhaps even in Marks and Spencer.

Subsequent students of organizational structure and behaviour have developed and criticized Weber's analysis. They have also looked at other aspects, such as the circumstances in which it is desirable for bureaucracies to adopt more flexible, less rigidly formalistic and hierarchical working arrangements in order to optimize their capacities to realize their objectives, e.g. the virtues of loosening 'red tape' in order to provide a quicker and friendlier service to the public, and of encouraging junior members of staff to learn about and identify with the organization's aims. Virtually all the vast and growing literature on organizations accepts, implicitly or explicitly, that bureaucracy is an inevitable feature of advanced societies, even of Communist countries where, according to classic Marxian theory, bureaucracy ought to have melted away in the heat of the proletarian revolution. It also acknowledges the risk that the sheer size of public bureaucracies, and the dependence of politicians upon the expert advice of officials when they are faced with difficult decisions, may indeed pose a threat to that comforting but Utopian model of democracy which regards the minister as being 'on top' and his civil servant as merely 'on tap'.[2] This is a major area of controversy to which we shall return in chapter 8. But the point is that 'bureaucracy' is not *in itself* a problem, and it is wasteful of a valuable noun to use it carelessly and as a term of general abuse. It is crudely tautological to redefine bureaucracy to mean, in effect, 'the rule of non-elected officials' and then to condemn such bureaucracies for being anti-democratic.

6   As for the size of the civil service, this has long been an item on the agenda of political debate and has become entangled with partisan ideology. Politicians, never slow both to exploit and to reinforce public concern about the 'evils of bureaucracy' (see above), know that easy political capital can be made from promises to cut the numbers of civil servants. This may form part of a wider commitment to cut back the scale of state intervention, something that Mrs Thatcher's government, first elected in 1979, has pledged itself to do. Lady Young, minister with day-to-day responsibility for the civil service, observed in 1982 that: 'It costs £14,000 million a year to run government. That is a huge sum and our aim is to cut it by having less government and greater efficiency.'[3]

There are two strands to the argument. The first concerns the extent to which the state ought to be interfering with the operation of free market forces and regulating the lives of its citizens. After all, even as recently as the turn of the century, when early Victorian dogmatism about the virtues of economic *laissez-faire* and a tardiness in facing up to the social problems thrown up by the industrial revolution had steadily been giving way to a widespread acceptance (albeit still a grudging one in some quarters) of a more interventionist or collectivist role for the state, there was as yet no welfare state, Keynesian theories of economic management were undreamed of, income tax was 8d (about 3.25p) in the pound and the total civil service (a much larger proportion of which comprised industrial staff than is the case today) was only about one-sixth of its present size. A government can therefore cut the civil service by eliminating ('hiving off' or 'privatizing') some of the jobs that it has been doing; but there may well be high political costs in pursuing such a strategy, given that citizens will have become accustomed to a given range and quality of state-run services. Tax reductions may sugar the pill for some, but the low-income consumers of many expensive welfare services do not earn enough to pay much or any tax.

The second, less contentious, argument has to do with efficiency. Most big organizations have some surplus 'fat' that can be 'sweated off'. Civil service numbers may in some areas be cut without reduced output by making the remaining workforce more productive per capita. Some recent discussion of effectiveness and efficiency in the civil service is considered in chapter 10.

Having said all this, however, we must remember that this 'numbers game' is played according to very complicated and opaque rules. From about the mid-1950s until the early 1980s, the overall size of the civil service remained more or less constant while the volume of public sector activity and the overall number of public sector employees expanded; this was achieved by allocating more and more responsibilities to local government and other bodies;[4] 'quasi-governmental' and 'quasi-non-governmental' bodies (quangos), not staffed by civil servants and not usually directly accountable to Parliament, have proliferated, though probably not to the extent that some critics have alleged.[5] In 1969 the Wilson government cut the civil service by one-third when it changed the status of the Post Office from a government department to a public corporation. These matters are discussed elsewhere, particularly in chapter 3. But part of the difficulty in this area stems from the fact that the accepted definitions of 'civil servant' (as distinguished from other public officials) are both narrow and unclear.

What is a Civil Servant?

The most widely used definition of a civil servant is that suggested by the Tomlin Commission in 1931: 'Servants of the Crown, other than holders of political or judicial offices, who are employed in a civil capacity and whose remuneration is paid wholly and directly out of moneys voted by Parliament'.[6] The term was first used in the late eighteenth century to distinguish the covenanted civilian employees of the East India Company (through which India was governed, until the Indian Mutiny of 1857–8) from military personnel. This use of the adjective 'civil' to connote 'non-military' carried over into the context of the early nineteenth century British civil service, but was gradually displaced by another meaning intended to convey the crucial distinction between holders of *permanent* posts and those whose jobs changed hands when there was a change of government.[7]

However, it was not until well into the nineteenth century that political and permanent officials (i.e. ministers drawn from Parliament and their non-political staffs) clearly emerged as two separate and distinct species of public servant. Departments remained mutually autonomous and diverse in their structures and their practices. In such circumstances the term 'civil servant', and any notion of a coherent entity called a 'civil service', had and could have had no useful meaning. Even after the major reforms in central administration that took place in the middle of the nineteenth century, and are outlined later in this chapter, the expressions only gradually crept into common currency. Until 1870, as Chapman and Greenaway point out, 'statesmen and leading administrators were reluctant to talk of the "Civil Service"; they used instead such terms as the "public offices" or the "public establishments"'.[8]

So, the terminology is of quite recent origin. And, even in the hundred years or so that 'civil servant' has been part of the day-to-day vocabulary of public affairs, the underlying meaning of the term has been elastic. We have already considered some weaknesses in the popular stereotype, and pointed out that there can be no such thing as a 'typical' civil servant. The impossibility of stereotyping is emphasized when we add a historical or comparative dimension. The civil servant of late Victorian Britain was a very different animal from his modern counterpart. He was, after all, the product of a very different social and political order. The state that employed him has subsequently changed greatly in size and shape. Similar problems arise when we try to draw international comparisons, using the familiar vocabulary of the British 'civil service' with reference to the central bureaucracies of France, West Germany or the United States. The neutral 'ideal type' of bureaucracy devised by Weber gives us some helpful guidelines for undertaking basic comparison across tracts of time and space. However, we must be very careful not to fall into traps of over-ambitious comparison.

Can we even be confident, in an age when public services are so extensive and so diverse, and are provided by such a variety of organizations, and when concepts like 'Crown' and 'departments of government' are themselves surrounded by a penumbra of definitional uncertainty, that we really do know precisely what a civil servant is? In stark contrast to the confident words of definition cited at the beginning of this section, Mackenzie and Grove open their authoritative account of British central administration with the discouraging observation that:

We are met at the outset by the fact that there are no precise criteria, either legal or historical, by which to determine the scope of the Civil Service.

There is a central core which is unmistakeable, but at the margin no sharp line divides those public servants who are within the Civil Service from those who are not.[9]

Some 20 years later the Expenditure Committee of the House of Commons (whose report on the civil service, published in 1977, we will encounter again in later chapters) reached much the same conclusion, in an interesting Appendix which is reproduced at the end of this chapter.

Defining civil servants became of considerable importance once patronage was eliminated in 1870 (see chapter 2). It is no good preventing politicians from nominating their own candidates if they can still insert their nominees under a different definitional guise.[10] This problem has re-surfaced with the continuing debate about the appointment of temporary 'political advisers'.

For most practical purposes, the definition cited above will suffice perfectly well, though there is need for greater precision when (as in chapter 3) we start to look at civil service statistics, or when politicians themselves start to play the civil service 'numbers game' (see above and chapter 10). The absence of firm definitions is symptomatic of the reluctance of British administrative reformers to place central bureaucracies within a coherent framework of public law (see chapter 6). The Superannuation Acts, dating from the early nineteenth century, and providing a rare instance of statutory intrusion into the operation of the civil service, are often taken as a basis for an official definition of the scope of the civil service for statistical and other purposes, though in fact the definition they provide is somewhat tautological.

Rather than indulge in semantic games about anomalies and marginal cases, let us try to clarify the issue by considering some categories of public servant who, by general consensus, must *not* be regarded as civil servants:

1 Ministers and MPs are public servants who receive remuneration from public funds, but they are *political* officers and therefore definitely not civil servants. By virtue of the House of Commons (Disqualification) Act 1975, MPs who enter defined categories of public office, including the civil service, forfeit their eligibility for membership of the House of Commons. Even the number of ministers eligible at any one time to sit in the Commons is strictly limited by statute. Conversely, civil servants who wish to stand as parliamentary candidates are obliged by regulations of the service to resign before doing so.

2   Members of the armed forces are Crown servants, but are not serving in a *civil* capacity, using that adjective in its original sense (cf. reference to the East India Company above).[11] But extensive civilian support is provided for the three branches of the armed services by the civil servants who work in the numerous divisions of the Ministry of Defence, which is by far the largest government department.

3   Judges and chairmen of administrative tribunals are public servants whose independence from government is safeguarded by special rules and conventions. In the case of the higher judiciary these special rules are of great constitutional weight and historical importance. No one in any of these categories is a civil servant. But the courts are administered by civil servants.[12] In some contexts – for example, the work of the inspectors in the Department of the Environment who resolve planning appeals – the work of civil servants may have a strong judicial flavour. In any case, the line between 'judges' and 'administrators', though constitutional purists may take it very seriously, is an arbitrary one. In many continental countries, like France, the judges are to all intents and purposes specialized civil servants, serving in a Ministry of Justice – a department which has no equivalent in Britain. And overseas district officers in the former British Colonial Office, not to mention the nineteenth-century civil servants of the East India Company, used routinely to combine administrative tasks with high-level judicial work, and no one seems to have thought this a constitutional outrage.

4   Employees of Parliament are not servants of the Crown. They may belong to civil service unions; the Clerks of the two Houses, and their supporting staff, are recruited through the Civil Service Commission and enjoy terms of service more or less indistinguishable from those prevailing in the civil service, but they are not civil servants.

5   Local government employees are certainly public servants but they are not civil servants. A high proportion of local authority income (much of which is spent on staff wages and salaries) comes from central government grants approved by Parliament. But local authorities are constitutionally (if not in political reality) autonomous bodies, and those who work in them are not servants of the Crown. This excludes from our definition many categories, such as school teachers and policemen, who in other European countries would be classed as civil servants.

6   Public corporations, the bodies that run what now remain of the nationalized industries and other services such as broadcasting,

though subject to ministerial directives and in some contexts supported by central government funds, are also constitutionally autonomous; those who work in them (coal miners, steelworkers, train
drivers, BBC newscasters etc.), or who are appointed to their
governing Boards, are neither Crown servants nor civil servants.

7 Quasi-governmental bodies. There are many organizations
operating on the fringes of central government, performing ancillary
administrative tasks, sometimes in association with government
departments, but staffed for the most part by non-civil servants.
These range from formal institutions (like the Arts Council and the
Commission for Racial Equality) appointed by ministers and
accountable in varying degress to Parliament, to more or less
independent 'quangos' (such as the National House Builders Registration Council and the British Board of Film Censors), used by
government as instruments of administration. This is a subject beset
both with political controversy (the Thatcher government having
pledged itself to cut back on the number of quangos) and definitional
uncertainty, and we do no more than note its existence for the
purposes of this preliminary discussion.[13]

The Universal 'Secretary'

In the BBC's television comedy, *Yes, Minister*, the permanent
secretary (i.e. the principal civil servant in charge of a government
department), Sir Humphrey Appleby, enlightens the newly
appointed minister, Jim Hacker, with the following helpful words of
explanation:

Briefly, sir, I am the Permanent Under Secretary of State, known as the
Permanent Secretary. Woolley here is your Principal Private Secretary. I,
too, have a Principal Private Secretary, and he is the Principal Private
Secretary to the Permanent Secretary. Directly responsible to me are ten
Deputy Secretaries, eighty-seven Under Secretaries and two hundred and
nineteen Assistant Secretaries. Directly responsible to the Principal Private
Secretaries are plain Private Secretaries. The Prime Minister will be
appointing two Parliamentary Under Secretaries and you will be appointing
your own Parliamentary Private Secretary.[14]

Hacker himself, as a minister of Cabinet rank, bore the title of
Secretary of State. He was no doubt as bewildered by this torrent of
secretaries as the mischievously urbane Sir Humphrey intended him
to be. And the reader may be forgiven at this point for feeling
similarly bemused.

In his history of English government, K. B. Smellie aptly observes that 'our system of government is haunted by the ghosts of extinct offices and confused by a terminology which might have been deliberately designed to confuse appearance and reality.'[15] Here the confusion is compounded by our modern habit of equating 'secretary' with 'shorthand typist'. At one time, secretaries were confidential advisers (as 'permanent secretaries' are, in more modern terminology, the confidential advisers of ministerial 'secretaries of state', and secretaries of state remain, constitutionally, the confidential advisers to the Crown).[16] A secretary who served the Tudor and Stuart monarchs was a person of considerable social rank and political influence. Consider the case of the ill-fated Thomas Cromwell who served (and in 1540 was executed by order of) Henry VIII. Sir John Craig writes thus:

Cromwell, though he made some attempt to organise a faction of personal supporters in the House of Commons, can be regarded . . . as an exaggerated head of the Civil Service, completely responsible to a superior, the King, who would neither be bored by detail nor forgive even those errors that he had approved. He had the Clerks of the Signet, the Privy Seal and the [Privy] Council for routine work, but depended largely on his private office, many members of which were rewarded sooner or later with posts in the Royal Service.[17]

We must remember that Craig is not, of course, using 'civil service' in its modern sense; the passage cited includes an oblique but significant reference to the fact that sixteenth-century government was as yet sufficiently uncomplicated for the King to interest himself in the details – something that a twentieth-century monarch would be unwise to attempt. And although there is a hint of some parliamentary politicking in Cromwell's activities, in an era of autocratic monarchical government there could be nothing resembling the modern convention of ministerial responsibility to Parliament. At the accession of James I in 1603 two officers were formally invested with the title of the King's Principal Secretary. According to Craig's account, 'one was to sit in the Lords and the other in the Commons, and they were to change places weekly unless some special matter required the attendance of both in a single House'.[18] They were the King's appointees, safeguarding the royal interest, and answerable to no one but the King. It was only after the constitutional upheavals of the seventeenth century, in which Parliament wrested power from the monarchy, that the foundations of the modern system could begin to be laid; and only when 'constitutional monarchy' was established at the end of the eighteenth century that a permanent and apolitical 'constitutional bureaucracy' first emerged.

How did the descendants of Thomas Cromwell fit into the new scheme of things? Some time before 1830 a crucial division of functions occurred. A number of senior subordinate officials at the level of under secretary, who had hitherto combined the tasks of modern permanent secretaries with those of junior ministers, while at the same time sitting in Parliament, began to separate into two distinct streams – civil servants and ministers. In the words of Henry Parris, 'as it became increasingly difficult for a man with a seat in the Commons to deal with a heavy burden of office work also, some went one way, some the other.'[19] The official stream spawned today's permanent under secretaries (not to be confused with under secretaries, a later invention, situated a couple of rungs from the top of the civil service ladder), usually known by the abbreviated title of permanent secretary. The political stream became the parliamentary under secretaries, who are the most junior members of the ministerial teams which head each department. Although it is hazardous to compare the relative capacities for influence possessed by officials on the one hand and ministers on the other (their respective roles are in fact quite different), there can be little doubt that permanent secretaries have evolved into far more formidable engines of public policy than their distant cousins, the parliamentary under secretaries.

Thus the word 'secretary' has remained part of the vocabulary of government, applied today to the main posts in the higher ranks of the civil service: permanent secretary, deputy secretary, under secretary, assistant secretary, secretary to the Cabinet; it is also applied to the top ministerial post of secretary of state.

Her Majesty's principal secretaries of state are the ministerial heads of most of the major government departments. Most members of the Cabinet are secretaries of state, though there are exceptions: a *minister* heads the Ministry of Agriculture, Fisheries and Food (MAFF); and Cabinets normally contain members bearing the antique titles of Chancellor of the Exchequer, Lord Chancellor, Lord Privy Seal and Paymaster-General. Secretaries of state can also be traced back through the long line of principal royal secretaries, but the office only began to take its modern form at the end of the eighteenth century, was shaped by the emergence of the Cabinet system and party government in the nineteenth century, and diversified in response to the growth of the interventionist state in the twentieth century.

In the eighteenth century the functions of central government were limited, more or less, to national security – defence and diplomacy and keeping a grip (a tenuous one as it turned out) on the colonies. The functions of the King's principal ministers, the secretaries of state, revolved around these preoccupations. In the years immediately preceding 1782 there were two Principal Secretaries of State for Foreign Affairs, one of whom was responsible for business relating to northern Europe, while the other, the Southern Secretary, dealt with France, Switzerland and the southern European countries, as well as with Irish and colonial affairs. This inconvenient division was based originally upon the fact that the offices had once been assigned to officers sympathetic to the Protestant and Catholic European powers respectively. In 1782 the Northern Department became the Foreign Office while the Southern Department became the Home Office, retaining Irish business and the colonies (a third, Colonial, Secretaryship, created in 1768, being abolished). In 1794 an additional Secretary of State, for War, was appointed, and in 1801 he took over responsibility for colonial affairs. We must, of course, remember that all this happened before the emergence of collective Cabinet government and the convention of ministerial responsibility to Parliament, and while the scope of public business was tiny by today's standards. A modern civil service was still in embryo. So the job specification of a Home Secretary at the beginning of the nineteenth century bears no resemblance to that of his twentieth-century namesake.

Hereafter, the story of the development of the office of secretary of state becomes increasingly complicated as government functions have grown and diversified. Constitutionally, there is still only *one* such office, and concurrent holders of part-shares of it are, in theory, entirely interchangeable. As the range of state activity has expanded, so the number of secretaries holding office at any one time has grown. Nowadays we are accustomed to seeing Cabinets containing 14 or 15 secretaries of state with portfolios covering such functions as Energy, the Environment, Education and Science, and Social Services – aspects of state intervention which were undreamed of two centuries ago and the prospect of which might have startled many observers even at the beginning of the present century. And most secretaries of state will be assisted in their diverse duties by subordinate colleagues – middle-ranking ministers of state, and junior parliamentary secretaries (see above). On the other hand, the break-up of the Empire has seen the rise and fall of the Department and Secretaryship for India (1858–1947) and the absorption of the old Colonial Office into the Commonwealth Relations Office in 1966, the latter being merged in turn with the Foreign Office two years later.

Thus the political and the official head of a modern department – the secretary of state and the permanent under secretary of state – have the same distant ancestors, though their respective functions have developed along divergent evolutionary paths. Where their functional relationship now stands is a matter of both constitutional importance and political controversy, and this is a subject to which we will return.

The Higher Civil Service

The crucial interface between politicians and officials, among whom public policy is ground out, is much more complicated than the one-to-one relationship between a secretary of state and his permanent secretary. Ministers themselves work as part of a team (though some are more team-minded than others) both intra-departmentally and inter-departmentally via the Cabinet and its many committees. On the official side, too, there is an endless round of inter-departmental activity in committee and elsewhere.

Although permanent secretaries are the main filter through which departmental business is purified, reduced and made palatable for ministerial consumption, they are by no means the sole link between department and minister. The minister has his private office, staffed by bright, middle-ranking 'high-fliers'. Other senior civil servants will have frequent access to ministers, others less senior may have intermittent access. Some ministers are more anxious than others to talk directly to relatively subordinate officials immediately responsible for particular areas of business or possessing appropriate specialist expertise; some permanent secretaries are more anxious than others to encourage their ministers to do so. Many civil servants lower down the hierarchy will contribute written briefs which pass upwards into the higher reaches of the policy-making apparatus. But below the top few grades the breadth of the hierarchy spreads exponentially. Thus in 1986 (see table 3.5, p. 64) 659 senior civil servants occupied the top three 'open structure' grades of permanent secretary, deputy secretary and under secretary; just two or three rungs lower down the ladder were some 77,000 senior executive officers, higher executive officers and executive officers; and at the base of the non-specialist grades were about 143,000 administrative officers (then clerical officers) and administrative assistants (then clerical assistants), plus a multitude of telephonists, typists, cleaners and messengers.

It is just not possible in the real world to draw hard and fast distinctions between (or even to agree firm definitions of) the inter-related processes of 'policy-making' and 'administration'. And clearly the 'success' of a given policy is contingent, not just upon the very small body of people (ministers and top civil servants) who dream up ideas and translate them into policy instruments (Acts of Parliament, statutory instruments, policy directives etc.), but also upon the actions and qualities of subordinate public servants (not always civil servants) who execute those policies and deliver them as services to the public.

Thus, whenever we think or talk about the civil service we must retain a full awareness of the massive labour force that constitutes its rank and file. Nevertheless, for many purposes we inevitably tend to focus attention upon the tiny minority of officials at the top of the hierarchy who operate in the rarified atmosphere of policy-making and ministerial briefings, and who also take charge of top-level managerial functions so vital to the effectiveness and the cohesion of a vast organization like the civil service. But how close to 'the top' does an official have to be to be counted in this category? Given the enduring distinction between 'generalist' civil servants and various kinds of 'specialist' (see below), there surely can be no single 'top', merely a lofty 'open structure', surrounded by slightly less lofty specialist peaks.

It may be helpful in this context to adopt the concept of a 'higher civil service', as used in a book by H. E. Dale published in 1941 and echoed by others, including the Priestley Commission on the Civil Service a decade later (see chapter 6).[20] Dale observed that when an official becomes an assistant secretary 'he begins to breathe a rather different air', and took the view that no one of lower rank 'exercises a real and distinct influence in important matters'. His higher civil service therefore began at the rank of assistant secretary (i.e. grade 5 in today's 'open structure', a category not invented at the time when Dale was writing). He added to the list a few others in lower grades (e.g. principals serving as private secretaries to ministers, then and now important staging posts for many 'high-fliers' in the civil service) and some senior specialists, particularly departmental legal advisers who are in a particularly crucial position to know what is happening in their departments. On this basis, he arrived at a total of about 500–600 top officials out of the total of 450,000 civil servants (a much higher proportion of whom were in industrial posts than is the case today). Dale offers comfort to those who might be alarmed 'by the thought that there are as many as five or six hundred matured

bureaucrats surrounding and advising ministers' with the observation that most of them, at the level of assistant secretary or principal
assistant secretary (the latter grade has since disappeared), are
qualified to offer policy advice only within the limited sphere of their
respective divisions.[21]

The concept of a 'higher civil service' is blurred at the edges, and
this paradoxically enhances its utility, for its starting point is not
people but *process* – namely the process of policy formulation and
advice. It enables us to break out of the managerial constructs
(grades, occupational groups, open structure etc.) used by the civil
service itself and focus instead upon the swirling tides of bureaucratic
pressures that flow through and around ministers who are the
political stewards of a democratic policy-making process, and are
answerable to Parliament and ultimately to the electorate. This is a
recurrent theme in this book and is, indeed, the central focus of much
of the study of public administration.

The useful imprecision of the term 'higher civil servant' militates
against accurate quantification. But using Dale's arithmetic, we
arrive at a total of about four to five times the one calculated by him.
That is to say, a figure of the order of 3,000 out of nearly 500,000
non-industrial civil servants; a total very much larger than the 40 or
so permanent secretaries (grade 1 of the 'open structure', see below)
with which we began this discussion, but amounting, none the less,
to a very small area of interface between the political and the official
grindstones.

Some Official and Semi-official Terminology

As with most complex subjects, discussion of the British civil service
involves the use of some technical words and phrases which need to
be explained at the outset. This explanation also forms a useful
trailer for some of the issues we will be considering later.

Groups, classes and grades

The organizational structure of the civil service, a body which has
evolved in a disjointed fashion, is dauntingly complex. As we shall
see later, some simplification of the grading structure took place in
the wake of the Fulton Report;[22] one important change was the
combination of the main 'generalist' classes (clerical, executive and
administrative) into a single linear 'administration group', from

clerical assistant (administrative assistant since January 1987) up to assistant secretary; another was the creation of a new 'open structure' at the elevated level of under secretary and above (since considerably extended). But the picture remains complicated, and the terminology is not calculated to elucidate matters. The following terms are particularly important:

The open structure now comprises the top seven civil service grades, from permanent secretary down to principal, each of which is filled, in theory if not in practice, by the most suitable person available, regardless of academic background or of previous service in a 'generalist' or 'specialist' stream of the service.

Occupational groups (e.g. administration group, statistician group, librarian group, legal group) are the basic groupings used by the civil service for the purposes of pay, recruitment and personnel management.

Categories comprise one or more such groups having a common pay and grading pattern. The biggest category is the General Category (containing the administration, economist, statistician, information officer and librarian groups). In some cases an occupational group contains a single staff category, e.g. the groups/categories covering office secretaries, scientific officers and security officers.

Classes mostly disappeared in the post-Fulton rationalization, the Fulton Committee having argued that 'the word "class" and the structure it represents, produce feelings of inferiority as well as of restricted opportunities',[23] but the terminology lives on. Thus there are various 'general service classes', covering personnel employed in more than one department, ranging from high-ranking professional staff (such as accountants, actuaries, medical officers and psychologists) down to low-ranking supporting staff (such as cleaners, messengers, stores officers and telephonists). There are also various 'departmental classes': prison officers and immigration officers employed by the Home Office; tax inspectors, who work for the Inland Revenue; schools inspectors in the Department of Education and Science; and driving examiners employed by the Department of Transport.

Grades are the titles and ranks attached to a particular job within a given group or class: e.g. executive officers, higher scientific officers, security officer IV, prison governor – the list is almost endless.

Vertical sub-divisions

Horizontal boundaries divide civil servants into different grades, vertical ones separate them into groups and classes. But the most important vertical boundaries are those which apportion civil servants among the various *government departments* (organizational units that we will examine in chapter 4). And within the departments there are important sub-divisions. The nature and extent of these and the terminology associated with them varies from department to department; but probably the most important units correspond to the major responsibilities assigned to a *branch* (headed, usually, by an under secretary, and sometimes called, confusingly, a 'department'), which are in turn sub-divided into a number of *divisions*, each headed by an assistant secretary. Some branches (e.g. a legal branch or an architects branch) will be headed and staffed by specialists belonging to the relevant occupational group, many will be manned entirely by generalist administrators, some will be a mixture. Some branches and divisions provide managerial and professional services, rather than being assigned part of the department's substantive business. Occasionally such services may be shared between departments: the Department of Transport, for example, has its establishment, research, legal, information and various other services provided for it by the appropriate divisions of the Department of the Environment, of which it was once a part. Some departments exercise a common service role, with other departments as clients: the Treasury Solicitor provides litigation and property conveyancing functions for many departments, and legal advisory services for some that do not have legal advisers of their own; Her Majesty's Stationery Office provides common printing and publishing services.

Specialists and generalists

These terms, and the distinctions they imply, are well recognized within the civil service, though they are not strictly part of the official vocabulary. For reasons which we will consider in chapter 2, the centre of gravity of the British civil service has always been the generalist administrator, with specialists (such as scientists, lawyers, accountants and economists) playing a supportive and subordinate role. This contrasts with the relative dominance of specialists in the central bureaucracies of other countries, in Europe and elsewhere. There are some exceptions (e.g. the lawyers who occupy the strategic posts in the Lord Chancellor's Department, responsible for the administration of the courts) but they are the exceptions that serve only to prove the general rule. The merits of preserving generalist dominance in the economically and technologically advanced society of Britain today have been the subject of lively debate. The Fulton Committee's recommendations (see chapter 2) stemmed from its conclusion that a more prominent role ought to be accorded to specialists.

These are matters to which we must turn in due course, but for the moment we are concerned only with definition. One key to the distinction lies at the point of recruitment. Specialist posts are filled only by those possessing stipulated academic and/or professional qualifications, and those recruited will be required to exercise their special skills as an integral part of the job to which they have been appointed. A generalist is one whose prior training is not considered relevant to the job he or she has been recruited to do. Qualified economists and lawyers are recruited to specialist posts in the economist and legal groups; but some graduates with economics or law degrees may also enter the service as generalists in the administration group, along with graduates in other subjects.

Thus the main (though not the only) consideration in recruiting specialists is whether applicants are of a high calibre in their particular field. The philosophy underlying generalist recruitment is that you pick the best people regardless of subject specialism, and then mould them into versatile all-rounders. Inevitably, however, the distinction breaks down inside the service. Senior specialists may exercise managerial functions and find themselves having to give policy advice that goes wider than their specialist expertise: the mixing of specialists and generalists (albeit with more of the latter than the former) in the open structure implicitly recognizes the blurring of the distinction at this high level. Conversely, many civil servants who have been recruited without reference to the subject matter of their previous training find themselves doing highly specialized tasks for most if not the whole of their careers. Some – for example, executive officers doing technical work in the Land Registry, or district valuers employed by the Inland Revenue – may be encouraged, or even required, to obtain professional qualifications by part-time study. And are highly trained tax-inspectors, recruited though they are from diverse academic backgrounds, specialists or generalists?

The Home Civil Service and the Diplomatic Service

Constitutionally distinct from, but closely related to, the civil service is the diplomatic service, whose staff are separately recruited by the Civil Service Commission for service in the Foreign and Commonwealth Office and in diplomatic missions abroad. In 1986 the size of the diplomatic service stood at nearly 5,000 staff. The service has its own grading structure (with its own terminology) linked for salary purposes with that of the home civil service. With the steady diminution in Britain's status as a world power there have been a number of recent proposals for drastic cutbacks in the diplomatic service, and the possibility of merging it with the home civil service has been mooted.[24] The distinction has in any case been blurred by the fact that civil servants in many domestic departments often have to spend much of their time abroad, liaising with, for instance, the institutions of the European Community or of NATO.

Established and Unestablished Civil Servants

Established civil servants are those who have received certificates of eligibility for superannuation from the Civil Service Commissioners and who hold an established post, i.e. a post approved by the Treasury, which is the body responsible for civil service manpower. The enactment of the Superannuation Acts in the early nineteenth century, the allocation of the power to grant or withhold certificates of eligibility to the Civil Service Commissioners, and the development of Treasury control over establishments, are all crucial elements in the history of the modern civil service.

Industrial and Non-industrial Civil Servants

The civil service still employs a large body of blue-collar industrial workers who do a variety of manual jobs, for example in Ministry of Defence fire services, the HMSO and the Royal Mint. Their pay and conditions of service are largely administered separately from those of non-industrial staff, and they generally belong to non-civil service trade unions appropriate to the kind of work in which they are engaged. Industrial staff comprises about one-sixth of all civil servants, but this represents a steady and continuing decline in the proportionate strength of this part of the civil service, a matter to which we will return in chapter 3.

Appendix: Definition of Civil Servant

From the Eleventh Report from the Expenditure Committee, 1976 – 77: *The Civil Service*, HC 535–1 (HMSO, London, 1977)

1   Apparently, the only legal definitions of 'civil servant' are those contained in Superannuation Acts. The Superannuation Act 1965, s.98(2), reads as follows:

> 'In this Act "civil servant" means a person serving in an established capacity in the permanent civil service, and references in this Act to persons ceasing to be civil servants, to persons retiring from being civil servants to retired civil servants shall be construed accordingly.'

'Civil service' upon which the above definition depends is defined in s.98(1) of the same Act as:

> 'In this Act "civil service" means the civil service of the State.'

This is by no means a clear definition since 'the State' (as distinct from the Crown or various other institutions) does not seem to be an entity known to the law in the United Kingdom in any other context and 'the State' is not the employer of any civil servant. The Act itself seems to recognise this because it goes on to say in s.98(3):

> 'For the purposes of this Act no person shall be deemed to have served in the permanent civil service unless he holds his appointment directly from the Crown or has been admitted into the civil service with a certificate from the Civil Service Commissioners.'

This definition, though it is no doubt satisfactory for pension purposes, is most unsatisfactory in many other respects. It implies, for example, that there is an impermanent civil service the members of which are not civil servants and there are in fact many people commonly regarded as civil servants who do not fall within it. However, for what it is worth, there seem to be about 746,000 people who are civil servants in law.

2   Because of the difficulties mentioned above previous enquiries into the civil service have adopted a different definition, described in 1931 by the Tomlin Commission in the following words:

> 'Servants of the Crown, other than holders of political or judicial offices, who are employed in a civil capacity and whose remuneration is paid wholly and directly out of moneys voted by Parliament.'

Though it was adopted in 1968 by the Fulton Committee this definition too is, however, an unsatisfactory one since it implies that whether a person is a civil servant or not should be determined by whether he or she is paid out of monies voted annually by Parliament. Thus members of the Royal Household, for example, seem to be civil servants under the Superannuation Act but were not so regarded by the Tomlin Commission or the Fulton Committee, though it is difficult to imagine anyone who is more of 'a servant of the Crown' than such members of the Royal Household. This Tomlin definition embraces 725,000 people.

3　The full difficulties of defining 'civil servant' are perhaps best realised by considering who in the working population is primarily paid for his employment directly or indirectly from the Exchequer. That includes all local government employees and indeed in many countries, eg France, such employees – even including teachers – are regarded as civil servants, though they are not so regarded in Britain. Such a definition, if adopted in the UK, would add another 3 million people.

4　Even restricting the definition to exclude local government employees does not solve all the problems. There are also, under the central government, organisations with employees not paid from the Exchequer, eg nationalised industry corporations (1.9 million employees) and companies in the beneficial ownership of the Crown (400,000 employees). If an individual is employed by a subsidiary of, say, ICI, he usually regards himself as an employee of ICI as a whole and, although this may not be technically correct in law, it has an element of common sense about it since his salary will form part of ICI's consolidated accounts. Yet an employee of say, British Leyland, probably does not regard himself as a civil servant and is not so regarded by others and in any case the UK has no consolidated accounts as such.

5　Apart from employees of organisations which are corporate persons in law, there are also employees of various other organisations the precise status of which is unique and even doubtful. The largest case of this is the National Health Service (1 million people) whose remunerated staff are not regarded as civil servants, although the head of the NHS is a Secretary of State. That staff also seems to be technically the employees of a variety of bodies, whilst general medical practitioners, for example, contract with the Family Practitioner Committees. It is by no means clear to us why some at least of the administrative staff of the NHS should not be regarded as civil servants.

6   The importance of all this is that the vagueness of definition has given scope for a fruitless juggling of statistics in which numbers of 'civil servants' are bandied about which are really meaningless for the purposes of sensible discussion. For example, until 1974 there were about 33,000 'civil servants' in the Department of Employment of whom 18,000 were transferred to the Manpower Services Commission and its agencies in that year and thus disappeared from the statistics of civil servants. In 1976, the employees of the Manpower Services Commission and *its* two agencies, by then 21,000 strong, were all transferred back to the civil service thus reappearing in the civil service statistics (Civil Service Statistics 1975 and 1976).

7   We recommend that an agreed definition of civil servant which would continue to be applicable irrespective of such changes in organisational structure should be worked out jointly by the CSD and our General Sub-Committee.

2

How Things Came to Be

It has already been implied that the civil service today cannot be understood without constant reference to its past. Many of the mysteries and apparent incongruities of our central bureaucracy stem from the stubborn resilience of old forms and modes of description. Were we to design from scratch a new civil service to suit today's needs (assuming we could even agree upon what those needs are), we would surely not re-invent the untidy edifice bequeathed to us by our forefathers, though we might borrow some features of it. And were we to undertake such a rash enterprise, no doubt our descendants a hundred years hence would view the products of our labours with the same mixed emotions with which hindsight imbues our feelings about the efforts of the Victorian reformers.

In any event, we should not deceive ourselves that the real shortcomings of today's civil service lie in the survival of superficial archaisms. Nor must we exaggerate the extent to which the present-day service is the prisoner of its past – see, for instance, the famous but facile half-truth that begins the Report of the Fulton Committee (1968): 'The Home Civil Service today is still fundamentally the product of the nineteenth century philosophy of the Northcote–Trevelyan Report. The tasks it faces are those of the twentieth century. This is what we have found; it is what we seek to remedy.'[1] Nor, indeed, should we commit the historical solecism of regarding the evolution of this or any other institution teleologically as the 'progressive' unfolding of some grand design.

Lawrence Lowell, in his major study of British government published at the beginning of this century, suggested that 'the history of the permanent civil service would be one of the most instructive chapters in the long story of English constitutional development', adding that 'unfortunately it has never been written.'[2] Since then, a great deal of material has appeared in print, but no one has claimed to tell the whole story.

There are two main explanations for the absence of a comprehensive history of the civil service. First, there is the enduring problem of 'departmentalism', a problem which not only militates against coherent description but which also, in the eyes of many critical observers, is a major obstacle to coherent and co-ordinated policy-making (see chapter 4). The civil service is distributed across an enormous range of semi-autonomous departmental and sub-departmental empires, linked, it is true, by a common framework of recruitment, grading etc. and by the formidable centripetal forces exerted by the Treasury and its satellites, but still for many practical purposes self-contained. Yet this fragmented picture of the civil service in the 1980s is a model of unity and coherence compared with its counterpart in the 1880s; as for the 1780s, there was then no civil service in anything like its modern form. The process of gradual and partial unification of the civil service since the middle of the nineteenth century is, in itself, a story worth telling in any history of British administration. But, ultimately, there can be no all-embracing history of the civil service, only a series of inter-related histories of the separate bodies in which civil servants have been employed. And, as K. B. Smellie has pointed out, 'in England the history of every government department is almost as complex as the constitution itself.'[3]

The second problem arises from the fact that it is very hard to isolate the civil service from its wider context. Its history is bound up with countless other constitutional developments – electoral democracy, parliamentary government, the party system, local government, public corporations. Obviously the line has to be drawn somewhere – but where? If one draws the boundaries of relevance too tightly, then the civil service is artificially isolated from its constitutional context. (This problem has afflicted many official inquiries into the civil service, which have tended to be hemmed in by narrow terms of reference.) If the boundaries expand too far, however, then the volume and complexity of the material quickly become unmanageable and the story loses its civil service focus. The same difficulty faces the historian of any institutional area of government.

Our own, necessarily brief, excursion into this territory begins with a tabular chronology of 'landmarks' in civil service development, intended as a checklist or an *aide-mémoire* (see p. 33). There is, of course, an element of arbitrariness in designating some items as worthy of inclusion and others as not; much has been left out, and each item must be set in a much wider context. It is no coincidence, for example, that many of the items cluster around periods of international conflict (particularly the Crimean War and the two World Wars) which provided the stimulus for major reforms.

We must also remember the march of technological development, something which has increased the complexity of life and added new dimensions to the role of the civil service (and to the continuing debate about whether sufficient scope is given to the expertise of 'specialists'). At a more mundane level, technological progress has had a profound effect on office routine and ultimately on the structure of the civil service. The invention of the typewriter in the late nineteenth century heralded the end of the 'copyists' in government departments; the advent of the telephone revolutionized communications in Whitehall and elsewhere. Both were resisted as new-fangled nonsense when they first appeared:

The Board of Inland Revenue, which was in touch with the facts of life, introduced typewriters very shortly after they were invented. They were so successful that Sir Algernon West, Chairman of the Board, tried a sales talk on his friend Sir Reginald Welby, Permanent Secretary to the Treasury. He was not successful at first, but experience with Inland Revenue had taught him persistence, and in April 1889 he induced Sir Reginald to admit a carefully selected typist, with her machine, to the Treasury building. In May, another one was let in to keep the first one from pining, and then the whole Treasury sat back and confidently waited for disaster. It waited three years, but all that happened, apart from a noticeable speed up in routine business, was that in 1892 one of the old copyists retired on pension. His place was filled, after no more than the usual amount of minute-writing, with a third typist and her machine.[4]

Wars do not appear in our chronology, nor do telephones and typewriters; nor for that matter do the ebbs and flows of political life, which provide the atmosphere which civil servants constantly breathe. Readers should use the list in close conjunction with the items cited in the bibliography. Having absorbed this bird's-eye view, we can then consider in more detail a number of inter-related themes in the development of the modern civil service, up to and including the Fulton Report.

Landmarks in the Development of the Modern Civil Service, 1780 to 1968

N.B. Most, but not all, of the items listed here are referred to in the text, in this chapter or elsewhere: see the index.

1780   Edmund Burke's speech on 'economical reform'. Parliament sets up the first of a long series of commissions of inquiry into public accounts and the administration of public offices.

1782   Offices of the secretaries of state re-organized: origins of Home Office and Foreign (and Commonwealth) Office. Separate Secretaryship for War established in 1794.

1806   The Directors of the East India Company establish Haileybury College to educate nominees to the Indian Civil Service for their subsequent duties. Charles Trevelyan an early product of the College.

1810   An Act concerning civil service pensions: no pension or compensation for loss of office without Treasury approval. First direct parliamentary concern with the running of the civil service, and an early landmark in Treasury control.

1834   Superannuation Act gives statutory force to a Treasury Minute of 1829, establishing contributory pensions scheme for civil servants.

1848   Committee on Miscellaneous Expenditure. Trevelyan's scheme for reform of Treasury establishment, followed by further inquiries by Trevelyan into departmental organization, 1848–57.

1853   Act directing that recruitment to the Indian Civil Service to be by open competitive examination. Northcote–Trevelyan inquiry into the civil service.

1854   Macaulay Report on the Indian Civil Service.

1855   Order in Council establishing the Civil Service Commission.

1859   Superannuation Act, requiring certificate of the Civil Service Commissioners to qualify for a pension on retirement. Non-contributory pension scheme. First statutory reference to 'the permanent Civil Service of the State'. First major open competition held by Civil Service Commission to fill eight clerkships in the newly established India Office.

1860   Select Committee, chaired by Lord Stanley, to inquire into methods of appointing candidates to junior posts in the civil service. Cautious support for open competition.

1866   Exchequer and Audit Departments Act establishes office of Comptroller and Auditor-General. (Commons Public Accounts Committee had been established in 1861.)

1870	Order in Council giving Civil Service Commission general control over entry into the civil service, subject to agreement with individual departments and with the Treasury. Some exclusions, notably Foreign Office and Home Office. Subsequent Treasury regulations distinguishing between examinations by Regulation I (graduate recruitment for higher posts) and Regulation II (examinations for junior posts).
1871	Order in Council defining terms on which unestablished clerks ('writers') could be employed. Subsequent discontent over conditions.
1872	Treasury Minute establishing principle that departmental accounting officers should be the permanent heads of departments. Many loopholes, and principle re-stated more firmly in 1920.
1875	Playfair Report. Endorses open competition. Proposes re-grading into higher and lower divisions, and improvements with respect to position of 'writers'. Stronger co-ordinating role for Treasury. Extended employment for women. Easier transfers from one department to another.
1876	Order in Council creating a Lower Division, common to most departments; but Higher Division still organized on a departmental basis. First appearance of civil service unions.
1884	Civil servants required to resign when standing for Parliament.
1886–90	Four reports by the Ridley Commission on Civil Establishments. Recommends open competition to a unified Higher Division on the basis of examinations linked to subjects of final schools in universities. Lower Division to become Second Division. Latter recommendation accepted (by Order in Council 1890), but no common salaries for Higher Division until 1919. Thus higher posts remained departmentalized.
1901	Cabinet Committee of Imperial Defence. Acquires a Secretariat, which is forerunner of the Cabinet Secretariat set up in 1916.
1910	Order in Council empowering Treasury to inquire into the pay and number of officers employed by any department at intervals of not less than five years.

1912–15 Six reports by the MacDonnell Royal Commission on the Civil Service. Recommends system of open competitions for professional posts; a Treasury Establishments Division; unification of main grades of the civil service in three service-wide classes.

1918 Report of Haldane Committee on Machinery of Government. Underlines the negative character of Treasury control, and the friction it causes.

1918–19 Bradbury Committee on the post-war civil service. Endorses idea of Treasury Establishments Division.

1919 Treasury institutes common salary scales throughout the service for administrative staff below level of deputy secretary. Treasury Establishments Division set up as part of a major re-organization of the department. Establishment officers appointed in all major departments.

1920 Prime Minister's consent required for appointments or removals of permanent and deputy secretaries, principal establishment officers and principal finance officers: to be advised by Head of the Civil Service. Order in Council empowering the Treasury to regulate the civil service. Re-organization Committee of the newly established National Whitley Council endorses MacDonnell's recommendations concerning service-wide classes. Order in Council sets up clerical, executive and administrative classes, also typist classes.

1929–31 Tomlin Royal Commission on the Civil Service.

1943 Barlow Report on Scientific Staff results in establishment of service-wide scientific classes.

1944 Report of Assheton Committee on the Training of Civil Servants. Education Division set up in Treasury in 1945.

1946 Marriage bar for women civil servants abolished.

1948 Report of Masterman Committee on the Political Activities of Civil Servants.

1952 Government concedes principle of equal pay for women civil servants.

1953–5 Priestley Royal Commission on the Civil Service enunciates principle of pay scales based on 'fair comparison' with outside employment. Pay Research Unit set up in 1956.

1961 Report of Plowden Committee on Control of Public Expenditure includes recommendations on management, training etc.

1962	Following Plowden, Treasury divided into 'Finance and Economic' side and 'Pay and Management' side.
1963	Treasury Centre for Administrative Studies set up following report of the Morton Committee.
1965	Government Economic Service established.
1965	Commons Estimates Committee calls for inquiry into structure, recruitment and management of the civil service.
1966–8	Fulton Committee on the Civil Service.

The Emergence of 'Constitutional Bureaucracy', 1780–1830

We have already noted the emergence of an embryonic concept of the 'civil service' in the early part of the nineteenth century, and the crucial bifurcation between ministers and permanent officials at the level of under secretary that took place around 1830. Before 1780, that amorphous collection of functionaries that some writers have incautiously termed a civil service was in fact no such thing: in the words of the administrative historian, Henry Parris, 'it was not permanent, it was not civil and it was not a service.'[5]

Permanency is now the main criterion for distinguishing civil servants from ministers. But eighteenth-century ministers often remained in office for as long as they felt they retained the King's confidence, even when the Prime Minister (a designation which did not then have the meaning it has acquired today) had resigned; collective ministerial responsibility, underpinned by cohesive and disciplined political parties, did not emerge until the second half of the nineteenth century, accompanied, as we shall see, by the incremental modernization of central bureaucracy. It was not 'civil' (i.e. non-political, see chapter 1) in so far as ministers, until at least the first quarter of the nineteenth century, personally administered their departmental affairs, while their subordinate officials performed tasks which nowadays would be considered political and therefore taboo for neutral civil servants (see chapter 8). And it was certainly not a 'service', in the sense intended by Parris: 'a body of full-time salaried officers, systematically recruited, with clear lines of authority, and uniform rules on such questions as superannuation' (shades of Max Weber's 'ideal type' bureaucracy, associated with the modern industrialized state). The nineteenth-century debates about civil service reform reflected the need for institutional adjustment in a society that had been undergoing an extensive industrial revolution.

So far as Parris's criteria are concerned, rules about salaries and superannuation were not consolidated until the 1830s, and systematic recruitment did not become the norm (and even then with many exceptions) until after 1870 (see below).

In the latter part of the eighteenth century it became usual for an out-going ministerial team to resign *en bloc* and go into opposition. This established a pattern of 'government' and 'opposition' which made it necessary to distinguish permanent from temporary (i.e. ministerial) servants of the Crown, and it quickly became established that the great majority of posts must be permanent (there were, of course, fewer departments and far fewer officials than is the case today). It could, of course, have happened very differently. Why, for example, did Britain not acquire a 'spoils' system as in the United States, where many top jobs in Washington change hands whenever there is a change of President? Part of the explanation lay in the view of government posts (many of them sinecures to which no real duties were attached) as inalienable items of freehold property. Thus Emmeline Cohen quotes William Pitt, speaking in the House of Commons in 1797:

sinecure offices are given in the nature of a freehold tenure. Parliament has expressly said, they will respect them as freehold property: and if, in answer to this solemn declaration, it is urged, that Parliament may rescind their former resolution, I say they may, by a parity of reasoning destroy every kind of property in the country.[6]

Crown sinecures were, nevertheless, gradually abolished following a series of parliamentary inquiries inspired by mounting concern in the first half of the nineteenth century about wasteful public expenditure. And the death knell of patronage was sounded by the Northcote–Trevelyan inquiry of 1853, considered below.

Administration became separated from politics, partly in consequence of the campaign begun in the 1780s to diminish the influence of the Crown, and partly because the growing volume and complexity of government business forced a division of labour between ministers, increasingly busy in the House of Commons and elsewhere, and their officials. A non-political and permanent (the two are almost synonymous) civil service evolved alongside a non-political monarchy: in Parris's words, 'as the monarchy rose above party, so the civil service settled below party. Constitutional bureaucracy was the counterpart of constitutional monarchy.'[7]

The Rise and Rise of Treasury Control

An unbroken and ever-thickening thread running through the otherwise disjointed history of the civil service is the increasingly pervasive influence of the Treasury in matters of staffing. This originated in the movement for 'economical reform', begun in the late eighteenth century. As we will see in chapter 4, the recent history of Treasury control has had several notable episodes, including the rise and fall of a separately constituted Civil Service Department from 1968 to 1981. But for the moment we will concentrate on an earlier period.

Parliament's growing concern, from 1780 to the 1850s, with public economy gave rise, as we have seen, to a series of select committees to investigate separate departments. These committees encouraged the abolition of sinecures and tighter control over staffing. The Treasury, as the department holding the public purse strings, was naturally required to give evidence to these inquiries, and to see that recommendations were implemented. It was also in control of the patronage of Customs and of Excise, then two of the three largest departments (the third being the Post Office), and thus had a direct interest in a major aspect of staffing.

Sir Edward Bridges (a former permanent secretary to the Treasury) posits three main stages by which Treasury control of the civil service grew out of the long campaign against waste.[8] First, an Act of 1810 laid down a general pensions scheme for the employees of public departments, and stipulated Treasury sanction for the grant of any pension. This legislation (and later Superannuation Acts) marked the beginning of general Treasury responsibility for pensions and pay, and was an early stage in the eventual (though never quite complete) unification of the civil service. The second landmark was the inquiry into the civil service, in 1853, by two Treasury officials, Charles Trevelyan and Stafford Northcote, discussed in the next section. This ultimately led to a system of open competition under the supervision of the Civil Service Commission. Bridges observes that, although the selection of individual candidates lay in the unfettered discretion of the Commission, 'Treasury Ministers were answerable to Parliament for the work of the Civil Service Commission, and the approval of the Treasury was necessary for the regulations in which the Civil Service Commission prescribed the qualifications required of candidates and the methods by which the competitions were to be conducted.'[9] Thirdly, there was the development, from 1876 onwards, of 'Treasury classes', employed throughout the civil service according to common conditions of service centrally determined by the Treasury.

Ultimately, control of most things hinges upon power over money, and we must take account of crucial changes in the system of public audit which took place in the first half of the nineteenth century and were consolidated and extended in the Exchequer and Audit Departments Act 1866. In 1861 the Treasury acquired the power of vetting all departmental estimates before they were submitted for approval by Parliament. The Act of 1866 placed responsibility for auditing departmental accounts in the hands of an independent officer, the Comptroller and Auditor-General, who reported to a select committee of the House of Commons, the Public Accounts Committee. For the first time, the Treasury acquired a means of discovering *how* the departments were spending the money voted to them annually by Parliament. In Smellie's words:

After 1866 the reports of the Comptroller and Auditor-General told the Treasury what the departments were doing and subjected the Treasury itself to the same supervision as was applied to them. The Treasury was now informed, controlled and responsible. The co-operation of the Public Accounts Committee, the Comptroller and Auditor-General and the Treasury secured the development of an efficient code of financial procedure.[10]

The triangular relationship between Treasury, Public Accounts Committee and Comptroller (recently up-dated by the National Audit Act 1983) remains to this day one of the most powerful instruments for securing departmental accountability; it forms part of the background to our discussion of civil service efficiency and effectiveness in chapter 10. As for Treasury control of the civil service, by the Act of 1866 'an enlightened tyrant replaced a capricious despot'.[11]

But Treasury control over departments remained, in essence, negative, based as it was on criticism of profligacy rather than encouragement of enterprise. The Treasury tended (and perhaps still tends) to niggle away at proposed expenditure, including the cost of staff, without much sympathy for innovation and strategic planning. The Gladstonian traditions of rigid economy came under increasing attack as the scope of government activity widened, and the central department which should have been leading the civil service into a new era found itself branded by many critics at the turn of this century as a hotbed of reaction.

The whole apparatus of government, including the civil service, came under stringent scrutiny during the First World War, and influential official inquiries (notably the MacDonnell Commission and the Haldane and Bradbury Committees) recognized the pressing need to do something about the Treasury's position *vis-à-vis* the other departments.[12] The immediate aftermath of the war produced several major landmarks in Treasury, and civil service, history.

In 1919 the Treasury was extensively re-organized, and acquired an Establishments Department to deal with civil service pay and organization; establishment officers were appointed in all the major departments to share responsibility with the Treasury for personnel matters. At the same time, the service-wide 'Treasury classes' (see above) were extensively rationalized, and the familiar pre-Fulton generalist career grades in the administrative, executive and clerical classes were established.

A Treasury circular of September 1919 designated the Permanent Secretary to the Treasury (then Sir Warren Fisher) as 'Permanent Head of the Civil Service', with the task, among other things, of advising the Prime Minister about civil service appointments. In March 1920 it was decreed that the Prime Minister (acting on the advice of the Head of the Civil Service, who would in turn consult his senior civil service colleagues) must consent to the appointment or removal of all permanent secretaries, deputy secretaries, principal finance officers and principal establishment officers. Subsequent Prime Ministers, including Mrs Thatcher, have been accused of using this power to 'politicize' the upper echelons of the civil service (see chapter 8).

Then, in July 1920, an Order in Council laid down that: 'the Treasury may make regulations for controlling the conduct of His Majesty's Civil Establishments, and providing for the classification, remuneration, and other conditions of service of all persons employed therein, whether permanently or temporarily.' Cumulatively, these measures were of momentous effect. In Henry Roseveare's words, 'at no time in the past had the relationship of Treasury control with the machinery of government been so logically formulated or so clearly enunciated.'[13] The Treasury was now indisputably the core of a reformed and largely unified civil service. And so it has remained, with occasional challenges and setbacks, ever since.

The Northcote–Trevelyan Report, 1854

In 1848 the long series of piecemeal parliamentary inquiries into aspects of efficiency and economy in the public departments culminated in the setting up of a Committee on Miscellaneous Expenditure.

The chief permanent official (then designated Assistant Secretary) to the Treasury, Charles Trevelyan, submitted evidence which was highly critical of wasteful and antiquated administrative practices. He deplored, in particular, the unconstructive use of junior officials with superior qualifications on routine copying work, and submitted a detailed scheme for the reform of his own department, including the drawing of a clear division between the duties of superior officers and those of copying clerks. His ideas were ahead of their time and received scant support from other departmental heads. The Committee itself declined to endorse his proposals; but there followed a series of inquiries into departmental organization, headed (except for those concerned with Irish departments) by Trevelyan, and in many cases including in their membership Sir Stafford Northcote.

Trevelyan and Northcote – an almost legendary double-act in administrative history – were contrasting figures. Trevelyan had been a pupil in Haileybury College, founded in 1806 by the East India Company to provide a prescribed course of education for young men intending to enter the Company's civil service. After a period of service in India (to which he was later to return as Governor of Madras), Trevelyan came back to England, and was soon offered the top post in the Treasury. His awareness of the relatively high quality and prestige of the Indian Civil Service undoubtedly contributed to his critical views about the system (if such it could be called) in which he was now employed. Trevelyan was, moreover, the brother-in-law of the celebrated historian and public figure, Thomas Babington (later Lord) Macaulay, who himself presided, in 1854, over an influential inquiry into the Indian Civil Service; the relationship reinforced and helped to shape Trevelyan's strong views about the need for administrative reform, as well as helping him to gain influential access to leading political figures.

Northcote, a rising protégé of the then rapidly rising politician, William Gladstone (architect, among other things, of the transformation of the system of public audit, discussed earlier), was later to become a prominent politician and statesman in his own right. But he was ten years Trevelyan's junior, and is generally regarded as having been in the present context a compliant subordinate to his more forceful and experienced associate.

In April 1853 the Treasury asked Trevelyan and Northcote to consider all the public departments with a view to ensuring 'that none but qualified persons will be appointed, and that they will afterwards have every practicable inducement to the active discharge of their duties'. Six months later their report was signed; it was eventually published with a letter written by the celebrated Oxford scholar and architect of university reform, Benjamin Jowett, which discussed the kinds of examination that might best be used as the basis for civil service recruitment.[14]

The report strongly condemned recruitment by patronage for its failure to procure appropriately qualified and competent entrants into public offices. 'Admission into the Civil Service is indeed eagerly sought after', it said, 'but it is for the unambitious, and the indolent or incapable, that it is chiefly desired.' Its main conclusions and recommendations were:

1   Civil service posts should be divided between superior and inferior categories, corresponding to a distinction between 'intellectual' and 'mechanical' tasks.
2   Entrants into the service should, in general, be young men, who would then receive on-the-job training for their duties; it rejected the alternative of recruiting 'men of mature age who have already acquired experience in other walks of life'. The recruitment age for superior posts should be 19 to 25, and for inferior posts, 17 to 21.
3   Recruitment should be by way of open competitive examination. There should be an independent, central Board to conduct the examinations; all candidates (with very limited exceptions) should 'pass a proper examination before the Board, and obtain from them a certificate of having done so'.
4   The examination 'should be in all cases a competing literary examination' (i.e. in liberal arts rather than professional or technical subjects). Competitive examinations for the superior posts should be 'on a level with the highest description of education in this country' (i.e. the universities).
5   Promotion within the service should be on the basis of merit, with appropriate safeguards against 'favouritism'.
6   The report noted (as we have done) the 'fragmentary character' of the civil service, and suggested that placing the mode of appointment upon a uniform footing would help to remedy this. It also proposed a facility for staff to be promoted to posts in other departments, and endorsed the principle of appointing 'supplementary clerks', on uniform salary scales, who could be transferred from one department to another 'according as the demand for their services may be greater or less at any particular time'.

The Report had strong backing from the Chancellor of the Exchequer, Gladstone, who had already persuaded Northcote and Trevelyan to re-draft an early version of the document which would still have left considerable scope for Treasury patronage; he saw civil service reform as an essential adjunct to parliamentary control over an executive which was assuming an ever-expanding range of functions.[15] But when the Report was published, in February 1854, it met stiff opposition from top civil servants and hostility from Gladstone's own Cabinet colleagues. There was much implicit apprehension at the prospect of a class of gentlemen administrators being displaced by middle-class, meritocratic clerks, though the proposed linking of higher posts to the university system effectively preserved upper-class dominance (a modern shadow of which, the so-called 'Oxbridge bias' in civil service recruitment is nowadays grist to the mills of critics of the service). On the fall of Lord Aberdeen's coalition government, Gladstone himself was succeeded at the Treasury by Sir George Cornwall Lewis, a declared opponent of open competition.

But in the circumstances of Gladstone's temporary departure lay the seeds of at least slow and partial reform of the civil service. Fed by vivid despatches from *The Times* correspondent, W. H. Russell, there had been mounting public agitation about administrative incompetence in the conduct of the Crimean War, and it was the parliamentary backwash from this that had brought down the coalition. It remained as a matter of grave concern to Palmerston's new ministry. Although the growing popular movement for administrative reforms bore no direct relationship to the Northcote–Trevelyan proposals, the government accepted a compromise course which would at least defuse parliamentary concern, while preserving the control of ministers over departmental appointments. An Order in Council of May 1855 authorized the setting up of a three-man Civil Service Commission empowered 'to examine young men proposed to be appointed to any of the junior situations in any of Her Majesty's Civil Establishments'.

The Commission was given the task of ensuring that candidates were within the prescribed age limits, were physically fit and were possessed of the 'requisite knowledge' for their duties. All examinations were to be conducted by the Commission, in consultation with the nominating department. The early reports of the Commission graphically reveal the appalling low calibre of many nominees. But despite the introduction of this welcome element of quality control, and notwithstanding the subsequent reinforcement of the Commission's position by the Superannuation Act of 1859, which laid down that all civil servants must have a certificate from the Commission to qualify for a pension, ministerial nomination remained more or less the norm. Limited competition was often a thinly disguised form of patronage, if only because favoured nominees could be put into a spurious competition with others chosen only for their convenient inferiority.

The principle of open competition was not established until 1870, and then only because, as Chapman and Greenaway observe, Gladstone (now Prime Minister) and Robert Lowe (his Chancellor of the Exchequer) were no longer willing to tolerate a situation which had been improved only marginally by the reforms of 1855:

Of the 9,826 certificates of fitness issued [by the Commission] between 1855 and 1868, no less than 7,033 (over 70 per cent) went to men appointed without any competition; 2,76[5] went to those appointed after *limited* competition; and a mere 28 to the victors in a completely open competition. The system, far from being, as was popularly supposed, 'limited competition', was really 'limited nomination'.[16]

An Order in Council of June 1870 provided that virtually all clerks seeking entry into the civil service must have a certificate of fitness from the Civil Service Commission before entering, and that a system of competitive examination, administered by the Commission, was to be applied to all departments, save where the minister rejected such an arrangement. In the result, only the Home Office and the Foreign Office took temporary advantage of the facility for exemption. Thus open competition, roughly as envisaged by Northcote and Trevelyan, became the norm, though even at the time of the First World War the MacDonnell Commission was to find lingering pockets of old-fashioned nomination.[17]

Another major theme of the Northcote–Trevelyan Report, already touched upon in the context of our discussion of Treasury control, was unification. In 1875 an official inquiry, chaired by Lyon Playfair, and consisting mainly of civil servants, recommended, among other things, a radical reform of the grading structure.[18] Many of its proposals (some of which contradicted Northcote–Trevelyan) were ignored, but its efforts did lead, in February 1876, to the establishment of a new Lower Division of men clerks and boys 'engaged to serve in any department of the State to which they may, from time to time, be appointed or transferred'.

This step towards the creation of a service-wide grade was consolidated in the wake of a later Royal Commission on Civil Establishments, chaired by Sir Matthew Ridley (and set up largely because of the discontent among civil servants themselves about their conditions of service).[19] The Commission recommended that the service be re-organized into First and Second Divisions, the former to be a small class, in three grades, filled by open competitive examination related to the final honours schools of the universities, and having common salary scales. The idea of common salaries was not implemented until 1919, and the Higher Division, the forerunner of the administrative class, remained fragmented on a departmental footing. But an Order in Council of March 1890 did re-constitute the Lower Division into a Second Division, divided into two grades, and thus secured some advance towards unification. The next stages were to occur in the aftermath of the First World War, as already described. As we shall see in chapter 3, separate 'departmental classes' survive to this day, particularly in the specialist and semi-specialist categories.

The Northcote–Trevelyan Report was undoubtedly an important factor in the crystallizing of a new set of conceptions and assumptions about the nature of a modern civil service. But it was not a blueprint for reform. The rhetorical reference to it in the Fulton Report, cited earlier, proves on closer examination to be wholly misleading (unless we detach the 'philosophy' of Northcote and Trevelyan entirely from their actual proposals). The civil service in the 1960s was the product of many things, but very little of it can be traced clearly and directly back to the Report of 1854.

The Generalist Tradition

In marked contrast to the rest of Western Europe, the British civil service is firmly rooted in a generalist tradition which has scarcely been dented by the modern counter-movement on behalf of the down-trodden specialist, epitomized by the Fulton Report. C. H. Sisson observed over 30 years ago that 'in general, the continental administrator, of the type which corresponds more or less to our Administrative Class, is a lawyer, specialising in that branch of law – namely administrative law – which is most directly concerned with the function of government.'[20] In Britain, lawyers, economists, scientists, engineers and doctors have come to occupy important positions in central administration, but even the more senior among them generally ply their skills at one step removed from the levers of power. The 'higher civil service' (see chapter 1) is essentially a generalist elite serving a generalist minister; the permanent secretary is, almost by definition, the generalist *par excellence*.

We have noted the 'liberal arts' emphasis in the Northcote–Trevelyan Report. Emmeline Cohen aptly observes that the Victorian reformers hoped to select young men of superior talent, 'who excelled in whatever it was the fashion of the age to teach'.[21] And Mackenzie and Grove quote Macaulay's dictum that 'the youth who does best what all the ablest and most ambitious youths are trying to do well, will generally prove a superior man.'[22] Civil service reform was intertwined with university reform (mainly via the influence of Jowett); and the exclusive fraternity of the old universities (there were few new ones) constituted a reassuring filter to maintain the upper-class basis of the new-style civil service.

V. M. Subramaniam (drawing upon the work of others, such as Ernest Barker) notes also the influential views of the seventeenth-century political philosopher, John Locke, on the importance of 'the generally educated gentleman who avoided pedantry as well as manual labour', which counteracted a natural tendency evident elsewhere in Europe to promote scientific education at the expense of the humanities.[23] Subramanian explains the rise of the generalist tradition in terms of the peculiar two-stage evolution of British representative democracy. First, in the seventeenth century, power is wrested away from the monarchy by enlightened aristocrats and the landed gentry. At this stage the administrative structure remains rudimentary; the eighteenth century sees the consolidation both of a 'lay' tradition in government and a decentralization of power to the local squirearchy. Then, in the mid-nineteenth century (an industrial revolution having meanwhile taken place without government assistance, and certainly without the aid of technocratic civil servants), there is an expansion of governmental functions, together with the rise of organized parties; ministers turn for advice, and for assistance with burdensome detail, to generalists from the same social and educational mould as themselves. The First World War brought more specialists into government, but by then the generalist hegemony was entrenched.

This two-stage process is contrasted with the single-step transition from absolute monarchy to representative democracy that occurred in France and Prussia, and occurred more abruptly and much later than in Britain. Monarchs buttressed their position with a powerful, technically skilled administrative apparatus, which was taken over by their democratic successors. There was no cult of enlightened gentlemen, nor of deference towards a liberal arts-based education, and hence no predisposition to reserve a special place for the generalist administrator. Ministers seeking to run this high-powered machine and to communicate with technocrats surrounded themselves with *cabinets* of their own staff – a model still found in France, and one which has in recent years been advanced in some quarters as a possible means of enhancing ministerial control (and hence responsibility) in Britain (see chapter 8).

The Growth of Government

The size of the civil service at any given time is a function of (among other things) the scale of government activity; and the latter is, in its turn, a function of (among other things) varying fashions in political philosophy – often summed up in beguiling but ambiguous expressions like '*laissez-faire*', 'interventionism' and 'collectivism'. And these, in their turn, are responses to social, economic, industrial and constitutional developments, all of which are, of course, interrelated. So the task of the analyst, seeking to unravel these tangled threads of change, growth and development is not an easy one.

TABLE 2.1   *The size of the civil service: 1797–1989*

Year	No. of civil servants	Year	No. of civil servants
1797	16,267	1901	116,413
1815	24,598	1911	172,352
1821	27,000	1914	280,900
1832	21,305	1922	317,721
1841	16,750	1939	387,400
1851	39,147	1943	710,600
1861	31,943	1950	684,800
1871	53,874	1979	732,300
1881	50,859	1986	594,400
1891	79,241	1989	569,200

Sources: W. J. M. Mackenzie and J. W. Grove, *Central Administration in Britain* (Longman, London, 1957); *Annual Abstract of Statistics*, 1990

The rate of growth of the civil service does provide at least a rough index of the growth of government (see table 2.1). Such figures do, of course, need to be interpreted with caution, if only because their sources cannot be standardized, and because the definition of a civil servant has always been slightly blurred at the edges. We need in any case to look behind the figures to see what *kinds* of staff are being talked about (noting the different proportions of industrial/non-industrial, senior/junior and specialist/generalist staffs at different stages): we return to this in chapter 3. In the present context, moreover, we must bear in mind that central departments are by no means synonymous with 'government', 'the state' and 'the public sector' (nor, indeed, are these terms necessarily synonymous with one another). A large proportion of state activity at the beginning of the nineteenth century was conducted through local agencies (based upon counties and parishes, and superintended by Justices of the Peace); today, local government manpower is about four times as great as that of the civil service, and a lot of government activity is transacted via semi-autonomous boards and quasi-governmental bodies.

Nevertheless, the figures clearly show the slow nineteenth-century expansion of the civil service in response to the experimental and gradual (though ultimately revolutionary) reforms of the Victorian period, and the acceleration of the rate of growth around the two World Wars. The years before the First World War saw the foundations of the welfare state; the years following the Second World War saw the consolidation and expansion of that process, and a massive increase in the size of the public sector.

At the beginning of the nineteenth century the central departmental structure was rudimentary, but appropriate to a government whose activities were largely confined to foreign policy and defence of the realm; transactions with the colonies; support for overseas trade; dispensing justice (through local justices and an independent higher judiciary); and collecting revenue to pay for these functions. The largest departments were Customs, Excise and the Post Office.

But gradually, over the next three or four decades, the concept of 'national' policy broadened in scope. General (as opposed to local) Acts of Parliament became a larger part of the parliamentary agenda.[24] Following the first Reform Act, important, if initially tentative, innovations occurred in the use of central inspectorates; these itinerant officials were initially conceived as coercive instruments of policy enforcement with reference, for example, to the new Poor Law and the Factories Act, but eventually they emerged as substantial policy innovators in their own right. Central boards (notably the Poor Law Commission 1834, and the General Board of Health 1848) were established, and worked initially through single-purpose local authorities; but they were superseded (they sometimes remained 'boards' at least in name – note, for instance, the survival

of the Board of Trade until 1970) by departments, headed by
ministers who were responsible to Parliament. Single-purpose local
authorities eventually coalesced into the multi-functional bodies we
know today.

Many of the new functions, and variants upon older ones,
devolved upon the Home Office, which worked through its own
specialized inspectorates. Jill Pellew, in her historical study of the
department, recalls late nineteenth-century frictions which foreshadowed today's 'specialists versus generalists' controversy: she
notes that Home Office inspectors tended sometimes to act almost as
partisan pressure groups on behalf of their own administrative
sectors, while the Home Secretary 'turned instinctively for advice to
his permanent under secretary rather than to his chief inspector of
factories'.[25] She notes also another significant index of increased
government activity (or at least of the internal growth of a well-
established department towards which new functions tended to
gravitate): between 1862 and 1872 the number of registered papers
coming in to the department increased from 18,659 to 30,047; by
1880 the number was 44,541, by 1906, 62,624, and by 1909,
71,153. Probably the advent of the typewriter fits somewhere into
the story.

Readers might usefully contemplate the following list of departments which were represented in Lord Salisbury's Cabinet of 1900,
and consider what has since been added and subtracted from the list
(the Cabinet today is much the same size as it was then). Eleven of the
21 offices (those marked with asterisks) were occupied by members
of the House of Lords.[26]

*   Prime Minister (combined with office of First Lord of the Treasury
    when Balfour succeeded Salisbury in 1902)
*   Lord President of the Council
*   Lord Chancellor
*   Lord Privy Seal
    (Chancellor of) the Exchequer
*   Foreign Office (held briefly by the Prime Minister)
    Home Office
    Admiralty
    Board of Agriculture and Fisheries
    Colonial Office
*   Board of Education
    India Office
    Chief Secretary of Ireland

* Lord Chancellor of Ireland
* Lord Lieutenant of Ireland
* (Chancellor of) Duchy of Lancaster
  Local Government Board
  Post Office (initially not in Cabinet)
* Scottish Office
  Board of Trade
* War Office

Throughout this century the number of ministers (including non-Cabinet ministers) has, at most, doubled; the number of civil servants for whom those ministers are (at least nominally) responsible has multiplied by about five – non-industrial civil servants by much more. The income in taxes and duties required by government has grown in real terms by a factor of nearly twenty. All this has important implications both for the shape of the public sector and for matters of accountability and control to which we will return in due course.

The Fulton Report, 1968

Over the years there have been many official inquiries into aspects of the civil service (our chronology lists several of them). Probably the most ambitious of these exercises was undertaken by the Fulton Committee of 1966–8, set up by Harold Wilson in the light of growing political and academic concern about whether a civil service imbued with powerful generalist and conservative traditions was equal to the tasks expected of it by a technically advanced and increasingly complex society. The exercise can be seen as part of a wider institutional reappraisal, which was at that time exerting pressure for change in parliamentary procedure, in the apparatus of economic planning, in local government, in the nationalized industries, in the National Health Service and in the machinery of central government.

The Fulton Report (see prologue, note 3) dominated the debate about the civil service in the early 1970s, and generated a large quantity of critical and descriptive literature (see bibliography). The diagnoses, prescriptions and outcomes of the exercise are outlined in table 2.2. The Report has been condemned for its tendentious use of language (e.g. its equation of 'general administrator' with 'amateur'); for its tendency to draw misleading parallels between the civil service and private sector organizations; for its failure to break out of its

TABLE 2.2 *The Fulton Report on the civil service, 1968*

What it found	What it recommended	What happened
Dominant philosophy of the 'amateur'	Preference for 'relevant' degrees when recruiting	Preference for 'relevance' rejected
Insufficient scope given to specialists	Administrators to specialize in one of the broad areas of economic/financial administration or social administration	Not implemented. Dominance of generalists little affected by 'open structure', which was extended to cover the top seven civil service grades in the mid-1980s
Too few civil servants trained in management	Civil Service College (courses to include management training for specialists)	Set up (but most training still done in departments)
Staff management inadequate. Not enough career planning; over-frequent movement from job to job. Promotion too dependent on seniority. Treasury should not combine management with its financial and economic functions	Civil Service Department to be set up, headed by Prime Minister, to absorb the Civil Service Commission	Established, but abolished in 1981. Some evidence of greater concern with up-to-date management techniques
'Rigid and prolific departmentalism' arising from proliferation of classes	Unified grading, following job evaluation exercise	Some rationalization. Most civil servants in occupational groups. 'Open structure', but still separate hierarchies and some departmental classes

Not enough contact between the civil service and the community it serves	Greater mobility (and capacity for two-way transfers on temporary basis) between civil service and other employment	Civil service pension rules modified to facilitate mobility, but little evidence of much effect
Too much secrecy	Inquiry into the Official Secrets Act	Franks Report (1972) on Section 2 of the Official Secrets Act 1911. Not yet implemented
Social and educational exclusiveness	Inquiry into methods of recruitment. Larger graduate entry	Davies Report (1969) on 'Method II'. Administration Trainee grade, and enlarged entry. Drastically cut in 1981.
Deficiencies in aspects of departmental structure relating, for example, to accountability and policy planning	Various recommendations, e.g.: (a) 'Hiving off' some departmental functions (b) Promotion of 'accountable management' (c) Planning units, headed by senior policy advisers	(a) Some functions hived off (e.g. in employment area) (b) Not much – but continuing debate on accountability – and some later developments, e.g. FMI (c) Some planning units – but not on Fulton's model

rather narrow terms of reference, which restricted its capacity to
examine machinery of government and ministerial responsibility; for
the superficiality of its research; and for its opportunism – both in
telling politicians what they wanted to hear and in seizing upon
existing trends and dressing them up as something new.

The civil service was re-examined by the General Sub-committee
of the House of Commons Expenditure Committee in 1976–7, which
found that many of Fulton's proposals had been watered down or
abandoned.[27] Some critics have argued that this was inevitable,
given that the task of implementing the Report was entrusted to the
civil service itself. The generalist ethos, the main target for Fulton's
criticisms, remains largely intact. In the early 1980s two of the most
notable products of the Fulton exercise – the administration trainee
scheme for expanded graduate entry (see chapter 5) and the Civil
Service Department (see chapter 4) – became casualties of the
Thatcher era.

The Fulton Report, like the Northcote–Trevelyan Report, was the
product of its time, and is now part of the modern history of the civil
service. However, it did spark off a vigorous debate, and set the
agenda for much of the discussion that took place in the 1970s and
1980s. As we shall see in chapter 12, the central philosophy behind
the important Next Steps programme, which promises to transform
the structure and management of the civil service, carries strong
echoes of Fulton.[28] Much of the vocabulary of debate about today's
civil service and its functions derives from or was highlighted by the
Fulton Report, and we will encounter it (or its spirit) on many
occasions in the chapters that follow.

3

Some Facts and Figures

Mr Justice Streatfield deserves immortality of a kind not commonly accorded to a High Court Judge for his gnomic observation (recorded in 1950 in one of the *Observer*'s 'Sayings of the Week') that 'facts speak louder than statistics'. So far as the civil service is concerned, some 'facts' are easy to come by, while others (particularly the really intriguing ones relating, for instance, to the interplay between top civil servants and ministers) are not. Statistics may not speak particularly loudly in this context, but they do provide an economical and coherent way of presenting a large body of factual information about a very complex organization.

Thus this chapter presents a statistical profile of the modern civil service (we have already encountered in table 2.1 the growth of the civil service over a much longer period) as an aperitif to a number of items on our menu, for instance the much-discussed 'Oxbridge bias' in recruitment to higher posts. The drawbacks of separating statistics from discussion are more than offset by the advantage of giving a succinct bird's-eye view of the subject before looking in more detail at particular aspects of it. In particular, this body of quantitative material usefully underlines what has already been stressed about the sheer diversity of the civil service and of the tasks undertaken by those who work in it. It can hardly be over-emphasized that the civil service is an amorphous amalgam of departmental structures, within each of which we find innumerable horizontal and vertical sub-divisions and diverse organizational arrangements.

Shifting Boundaries

We must not forget that, as we discovered in chapter 1, even the definitional boundaries of our subject are indistinct. It is hazardous to try to quantify something when a penumbra of uncertainty surrounds the definition of what that something is. For this reason alone we must be circumspect in interpreting our data, and doubly so given that some of the material has been compressed to make it more digestible. Readers who aspire to jump to weightier and bolder interpretive conclusions than we have done should first read the many qualificatory footnotes to the tables, and refer back to the original sources as indicated in the tables themselves and in our bibliography.

TABLE 3.1 *Public sector and private sector employment (millions)*

	1961	*1971*	*1986*
Central government			
HM Forces	0.5	0.4	0.3
NHS	0.6	0.8	1.2
Other	0.7	0.8	0.8
Other public sector			
Local government	1.9	2.7	3.0
Public corporations[a]	2.2	2.0	1.2
Total public sector[b]	5.8	6.6	6.5
Total private sector[b]	18.6	17.8	18.1
Total public and private sectors[b]	24.5	24.4	24.6
% employed in public sector	23.7	27.1	26.4

[a] The Post Office is included in the category of public corporations for all three years (see note to table 3.2).
[b] Rounded totals.
Sources: Social Trends, 1983; Economic Trends, 1987 Annual Supplement

Table 3.1 brings us up against one aspect of the boundary problem just mentioned. The civil service, currently employing about 0.6 million people, is by no means synonymous with 'central government' (2.3 million employees), and still less synonymous with the public sector as a whole (6.5 million employees, accounting for over 26 per cent of the working population). It is not even coterminous with the 'other' category of central government employment (see table 3.1), since the latter includes such non-civil service categories as judges and MPs. Nor must we forget the fact that the boundaries between public and private sectors are much less clear cut than table 3.1 might at first sight suggest: thus a truly comprehensive analysis would have to take account (though it would be difficult to translate into quantitative terms) of such matters as private commercial firms which owe their continuing viability to state contracts (and whose employees may for example, in consequence, be liable to the constraints imposed by the Official Secrets Acts); state shareholdings in private (or semi-private) firms; and the proliferation of quasi-governmental and quasi non-governmental bodies, popularly but misleadingly lumped together under the label of 'quango'.

An analysis of civil service statistics is made harder by the ever-changing shape of the machinery of government. Part of this arises from the episodic re-alignment of 'departmental' boundaries, considered in more detail in chapter 4. Even more confusing is the habit that governments have of transferring functions from one authority to another within the public sector. Thus, in 1974, during the period covered by table 3.1, the administration of water services was transferred from local authority responsibility to the domain of the public corporation; and in the same year local authority health functions were transferred to the restructured National Health Service.

Administrative changes can radically affect the definitional boundaries of the civil service. Observing (as we ourselves have done) that 'the cold statistics of the Civil Service have to be used with care', F. M. G. Willson cites the case of the Post Office:

Until October 1969 the Post Office was an orthodox government department, headed by a Minister, the Postmaster General, whose huge staff were all civil servants. Until 1965 about three-quarters of them were classified as 'non-industrials' while the remaining quarter were 'industrials' [see below]. In 1965 all but a few hundred of those previously classified as 'industrial' became 'non-industrial'. Four years later, when the Post Office became a public corporation, all its staff from then onwards ceased to be civil servants. About 15,000 of the former establishment remained civil servants, however, some in the new and short-lived Ministry of Posts and Telecommunications (its separate identity was lost in 1974), but the majority in the new Department of National Savings which took over the banking services of the 'old' Post Office.[1]

The 1961 column of table 3.1 prematurely translates the Post Office into its public corporation form in order to facilitate comparisons, though at that time its staff were really civil servants.

Other examples noted by Willson include the Manpower Services Commission, set up by the Employment and Training Act 1973, which took over 18,000 staff from the Department of Employment in 1974. These staff thereupon lost their civil service status, but they re-acquired it at the beginning of 1976. In 1973, 5,400 staff of the non-civil service Atomic Energy Authority attached to the Atomic Weapons Research Establishment became civil servants in the Ministry of Defence. And, in the wake of the Beeching Royal Commission Report on Assizes and Quarter Sessions 1969, and the Courts Act 1971, a large number of locally employed court administrators were brought into a newly constituted Courts Service under the control of the Lord Chancellor. The ebb and flow of such changes are faithfully recorded in numerous explanatory notes in the annually published *Civil Service Statistics*.

Merely charting changes in the size and composition of the civil service, even over quite short periods of time, is fraught with difficulty, and interpreting these changes is even more hazardous. The observer has constantly to be aware of the wider political and economic context of the events with which he is concerned. To take one example: the Thatcher government, elected in 1979, presided over a period of rapidly growing unemployment, accompanied by attempts to cut back substantially on civil service numbers and restrain public sector pay. During 1985, while the Ministry of Defence suffered a net staff loss of about 4,900, the Department of Employment took on nearly 900 extra staff in response to the sustained pressure on the services it provides. Global statistics describing the growth or shrinkage of the civil service as a whole mean very little, even though politicians often try to make political capital out of them. Relating changes in the civil service to those occurring elsewhere in the public sector, it is important to bear in mind the central government's capacity to enforce public sector staff cutbacks and wage restraint in the civil service where it is the employer, whereas over other bodies, such as local authorities and public corporations, its capacity for influence is more indirect and less certain.

The figures in table 3.1 remind us, finally, that for many years (and probably since the mid-1950s) the size of the civil service has remained more or less constant, while public sector growth, encouraged by the hiving-off of functions, has occurred elsewhere, particularly in local government. As it stands, however, these figures do not indicate how far such an effect has come about through the growth of the 'hidden bureaucracy' associated with quasi-governmental bodies (see chapter 1).[2]

Industrial/Non-industrial Staff

The umbrella term, civil servant, covers 'blue-collar' as well as 'white-collar' jobs. Table 3.2 distinguishes industrial and non-industrial categories of staff (see chapter 1). It reveals that the industrial category has been shrinking steadily in both absolute and relative terms (camouflaging a broadly upward trend – reversed only recently – in the size of the non-industrial civil service), and now accounts for only about one-sixth of civil service manpower. Nearly 80 per cent of industrial staff work for the Ministry of Defence in, for example, naval dockyards (though the Thatcher government has taken steps to contract out some dockyard services to the private sector); other industrial staff are employed in, for example, the Property Services Agency, the Royal Mint and in sundry research establishments.

TABLE 3.2 *Industrial and non-industrial staff in the civil service (full-time equivalents in thousands)*

	1951	1961	1971	1981	1986
Industrial	399.6	357.8	201.7	149.7	96.2
Non-industrial	675.4	650.2	498.4	539.9	498.2
Total	1,075.0	1,008.0	700.1	689.6	594.4
Industrials as % of total	37.2	35.5	28.8	21.7	16.2

Comparisons between different years have to take account of changes in the structure of government (see text). By far the most significant change during the period covered here was the transformation of the Post Office from government department to public corporation in 1969. The Post Office employed 248.9 thousand non-industrial and 71.4 thousand industrial staff in 1951; 261.0 thousand non-industrial and 89.4 thousand industrial staff in 1961. Thus in 1969, when these staff ceased to be civil servants, the overall size of the civil service fell by about one-third.

Sources: Annual Abstracts of Statistics; 1952, 1962, 1972 and 1987

Taking a longer period than that covered by the table, the proportionate shrinkage of the industrial civil service is even more marked. At the outbreak of the First World War nearly two-thirds of civil servants belonged to the industrial category. The subsequent decline reflects the changing balance of government responsibilities (notably the growth of the vast administrative machine needed to run the welfare state) and the rise of the new-style multi-functional departments in the first half of the twentieth century. We must also take account of the tendency towards the hiving-off of manpower-intensive services, exemplified by the transformation of the Post Office (a quarter of whose massive staff establishment comprised industrials) into a public corporation (see above).

Interesting light is thrown, incidentally, upon the rapidity of change in central government (see chapter 4) if we reflect upon the list of departments named in the 1961 edition of *Annual Abstract of Statistics* as employing industrial civil servants. They were: the Admiralty, the War Office, the Air Ministry, the Ministry of Supply, the Ministry of Aviation, the Post Office, the Forestry Commission, the Home Office, the Stationery Office and the Ministry of Works. After 25 years of departmental amalgamations and the hiving-off of Whitehall functions, only the Home Office, the Forestry Commission and the Stationery Office remain, and all three have been affected in one way or another by organizational changes.

Civil Servants and Departments

The civil service is distributed unevenly among a series of semi-autonomous departmental empires. Perhaps the most obvious starting point for differentiating one government department from another is by the simple criterion of size. Figure 3.1 illustrates the disparate staff complements of the various departments. More than three-quarters of civil service staff work in one of six major departments; over a quarter of all civil servants are currently employed by the Ministry of Defence. But size alone does not determine the muscle-power of a department. The crucial departments at the nerve centre of government – the Treasury and the Cabinet Office – are too small even to be accorded separate segments on the chart.

As table 3.3 illustrates, another factor which differentiates one department from another is the location of staff. Only a few departments have their functions and staff concentrated in Inner London. Most departments are physically highly decentralized: DHSS and Employment deliver their services direct to the public via local offices; the revenue departments are mainly concerned in performing tasks of policy implementation which do not require detailed ministerial supervision and which can be discharged any-where (and preferably at a prudent distance from irate taxpayers);

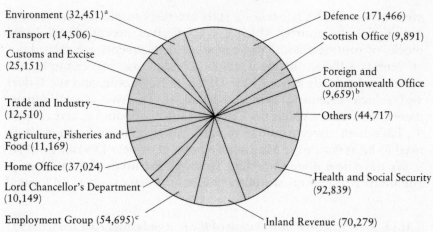

Figure 3.1   Civil service manpower by main departments, 1 January 1986 (from *Civil Service Statistics*, 1986)
[a] Includes Property Services Agency (25,821).
[b] Includes Overseas Development Administration (1,541).
[c] Includes Department of Employment (29,728); Manpower Services Commission (20,793); Health and Safety Commission/Executive (3,556); and Advisory Conciliation and Arbitration Service (618).

TABLE 3.3   *Location of non-industrial civil servants, January 1986*

	Total no. of non-industrial civil servants	% Located in Inner London[a]
Agriculture, Fisheries and Food	10,498	20.5
Cabinet Office	1,659	73.3
Customs and Excise	25,151	15.2
Defence	94,015	11.1
Education and Science	2,405	51.9
Employment Group	53,959	10.3
Energy	1,037	79.6
Environment and Transport	35,358	22.2
Health and Social Security	92,582	9.4
Home Office	33,910	18.4
Inland Revenue	70,255	10.1
Lord Chancellor's Dept	10,149	29.2
Trade and Industry	12,149	54.9
Treasury	2,521	61.9

[a]   Inner London is within five miles of Charing Cross.
Source: *Civil Service Statistics*, 1986

most of the Lord Chancellor's staff are responsible for the smooth running of the courts, which are themselves decentralized. Large blocks of routine clerical work in some departments are carried out at central offices outside Greater London as, for example, the centralized records office of the DHSS at Newcastle, and the Driver and Vehicle Licensing Centre at Swansea. The two central departments, the Treasury and the Cabinet Office (see above, and chapter 4), have high concentrations of staff based in Inner London: both need to be at the Prime Minister's elbow, in or near Downing Street.

We have now done something to dispel the myth of a civil service commuting to various structurally identical departments, all located

TABLE 3.4   *Regional distribution of the non-industrial civil service, 1971 and 1986*

	1971		1986	
Economic planning region	% of civil service	% of total population[a]	% of civil service	% of total population[b]
South East (whole) of which	45.8	30.9	38.8	30.2
Inner London	20.5	⎰ 13.4	15.0	⎰ 12.0
Outer London[c]	9.3	⎱	8.1	⎱
South West	8.1	6.8	9.5	7.8
West Midlands	4.7	9.2	5.7	9.2
North West	8.9	12.1	9.8	11.5
Northern	6.3	5.9	6.2	5.6
Yorkshire and Humberside	4.7	8.6	6.0	8.7
East Midlands	3.4	6.1	3.9	6.9
East Anglia	2.2	3.0	2.6	3.4
Wales	3.9	4.9	5.5	5.0
Scotland	8.3	9.4	9.7	9.2
Northern Ireland	0.7	2.8	0.6	2.8
N	500,100		497,900	

[a]   1971 Census.
[b]   1981 Census.
[c]   Outer London Zone divided into Intermediate Zone and new Outer Zone at 1 October 1983.

Sources: *Civil Service Statistics*, 1971 and 1986; *Annual Abstracts of Statistics*, 1986.

in Inner London. Table 3.4 underlines the extent to which civil service jobs are spread (albeit unevenly) around the country, with only about one in six being located in central London. But the prosperous South East of England still contains nearly 40 per cent of the non-industrial civil service (despite some migration to other regions during the 15-year period spanned by table 3.4), and has the highest per capita ratio of civil servants to the regional population as a whole. The next highest per capita ratio is in the South West, and the lowest in Northern Ireland, though the latter figure is misleading because administrative functions formerly entrusted to the devolved Northern Ireland government in Belfast are still carried out by the Northern Ireland Civil Service, which is not included in our statistics. A ten-year programme involving the dispersal of 31,000 civil service jobs from London to other parts of Britain, mainly areas of high unemployment, was announced by the Labour government in 1974, following consideration of the Hardman Report of 1973.[3] But five years later the newly elected Conservative government announced a drastically modified programme involving only 6,000 posts.[4] Whereas in 1974 the government was expanding the civil service, the Thatcher government was committed to reducing it. The dispersal programme was a victim of this change in policy.

Grades and Personnel

Despite some welcome rationalization following the Fulton Report of 1968 (see chapter 2), the civil service remains afflicted with numerous horizontal sub-divisions, which cut across the vertical division of central bureaucracy into departments and sub-departments. This gives rise to the difficulties of nomenclature discussed in chapter 1, and any prospect of achieving a straightforward organization chart covering a single sheet of paper, onto which all groups and grades of personnel could be fitted, remains a utopian dream. As the House of Commons Expenditure Committee observed in 1977:

When the Fulton Committee reported in 1968 there were 47 general service classes (i.e. classes used in more than one Department) and over 1,400 departmental classes each used in only one Department. There are now 38 general service and 500 departmental classes so that the unification of the grading structure has not progressed as fast as was envisaged when the Fulton Report's recommendation on unified grading was accepted. We must stress that most of these classes consist of several separate grades.[5]

TABLE 3.5   *Non-industrial home civil service: men and women in main non-specialist grades, 1 January 1986*

	Men	Women	Total	% of women
All non-industrial grades	256,914	234,617	491,531	47.7
incl. part-time staff[a]	1,141	19,203	20,344	94.4
Open structure level[b]				
Grade 1 (permanent secretary)	37	1	38	2.6
Grade 2 (deputy secretary)	132	2	134	1.5
Grade 3 (under secretary)	464	23	487	4.7
Grade 4 (executive directing bands and corresponding professional and scientific grades)	179	7	186	3.8
Grade 5 (assistant secretary and corresponding grades)	1,945	144	2,089	6.9
Grade 6 (senior prinicipal and corresponding grades)	3,203	174	3,377	5.2
Grade 7 (principal and corresponding grades)	10,844	954	11,798	8.1
Total	16,804	1,305	18,109	7.2
Administration group				
Senior executive officer	6,966	746	7,712	9.7
Higher executive officer (D)	171	64	235	27.2
Higher executive officer	18,911	5,480	24,391	22.5
Administration trainee	77	29	106	27.4
Executive officer	25,199	19,653	44,852	43.8
Clerical officer[c]	25,733	55,735	81,468	68.4
Clerical assistant[c]	15,850	45,534	61,384	74.2
Total	92,907	127,241	220,148	57.8

[a]   Most part-time staff are employed as cleaners or in clerical and secretarial posts.

[b]   Open structure: unified pay and grading structure for senior personnel introduced in 1972 and subsequently extended.

[c]   Changed to administrative officer/assistant in January 1987.

Elsewhere in the civil service: Women hold 167 posts out of 12,619 (1.3%) in the professional and technology category; but women also occupy: 4,416 out of 9,138 (48.3%) of messenger posts; 1,460 out of 1,741 (70.3%) of telephonists' posts; 1,567 out of 1,655 (94.7%) of cleaners' posts; 24,374 out of 24,525 (99.4%) of secretarial posts.

Source: Civil Service Statistics, 1986

Even if, as in table 3.5, we confine ourselves to the non-specialist part of the non-industrial civil service, the multiplicity of grades is considerable. And the reader must always remember that separate but parallel hierarchies exist for the various specialist groups (see table 3.6) and that separate departmental classes have not disappeared. Moreover, the beguilingly simple linear shape of the table disguises the fact that separate modes of recruitment are employed at different levels of the hierarchy, and that (partly in consequence of this) invisible horizontal bulkheads exist to impede passage from one level to the next, e.g. from executive officer to administration trainee. This is a matter to which we will address ourselves later.

Another complicating factor relating to table 3.5 is the existence (as a small but tangible monument to Fulton) of an 'open structure', covering the grades of principal and above. It is a complication because qualified specialists as well as non-specialists are eligible to apply for posts at this elevated level (which is why the concept of an open structure was invented). This, of course, means that not all those included in the table are strictly non-specialists, though the numbers in the open structure are small in terms of statistics which cover all grades in aggregate; only 3.7 per cent. The top policy-making grades of the civil service constitute an even smaller fraction of the service as a whole. Even if we take the 2,934 open structure posts at assistant secretary and above, we are talking about just 0.6 per cent of the non-industrial civil service. The pyramid of the civil service hierarchy has a very broad base and a very narrow apex.

The other feature of table 3.5 concerns the position of women in the civil service. Here the statistics speak for themselves with embarrassing eloquence. Women make up nearly half of the total numerical strength of the non-industrial civil service; they have the lion's share of the clerical jobs at the base of the hierarchy, and a virtual monopoly of secretarial posts. But as we ascend the ladder we find a sharp reversal in female fortunes. At the middle-ranking executive officer level only 43.8 per cent of posts are held by women. Only a quarter or so of administration trainees (aspirants for the top advisory and managerial jobs a generation hence) are women, but even this very small proportion falls dramatically away to a mere 9.7 per cent at the relatively modest level of senior executive officer, and to a derisory 7.2 per cent in the open structure. At the time of writing, there is only one woman permanent secretary, Miss Anne Mueller, Second Permanent Secretary in the Cabinet Office, who is only the fourth woman ever to reach this level in the civil service.

In 1970 the Civil Service Department (CSD) was sufficiently concerned about the position of women in the civil service to set up the Kemp-Jones Committee to look into the subject.[6] The Committee reported a year later, but its recommendations, which were essentially directed towards helping women to combine domestic responsibilities with a career, fell, in the words of one commentator, 'on stony ground'.[7] More recently, in 1984, the report of another CSD initiated study was followed by the announcement of a government programme of action, including plans for extended part-time working opportunities, discussion of job-sharing at all

TABLE 3.6 *Composition of the non-industrial civil service*

	1976	1981	1986[a]
All non-industrial grades	557,363	536,218	491,531
Open structure	775	770	18,109
Administration group	248,865	237,061	220,148
Selected professional groups			
Actuaries	32	29	27
Economists	397	370	126
Factory Inspectorate	724	953	854
Inspectors of Taxes	5,922	6,531	4,616
Information officers	1,480	1,217	859
Legal category	861	890	41
Librarians	363	386	398
Medical officers	699	650	566
Mines and Quarries Inspectorate	125	97	84
Professional and technology category[b]	44,216	41,361	13,209
Psychologists	247	257	253
Research officers	446	423	222
Science category[b]	18,624	16,879	10,828
Statisticians	516	498	116
Telecommunications technical officers	1,082	1,025	868

[a] Figures for 1986 are not readily comparable with previous years because of the incorporation of many senior staff into the open structure.
[b] Figures for these categories include some related grades.
Sources: Social Trends, 1982; Civil Service Statistics, 1986

levels of the civil service, and the provision of training in the equal opportunities aspects of staff reporting for all reporting officers.[8]

In table 3.6 we move from the 'non-specialist' component of the civil service to look at the range of specialist employment the civil service offers, comparing the figures for three recent years. It should be noted that table 3.6 is selective, and that the broad categories listed often cover a huge variety of jobs ('science category', for example, covers almost every conceivable science discipline and work on a wide range of tasks in research institutions and elsewhere). The position of specialists in the civil service has been much discussed in recent years, particularly in the wake of the Fulton Report (see chapter 7) and in the light of a widespread view that the 'generalist' tradition of the service, firmly consolidated in the nineteenth century, is no longer appropriate to the needs of a complex and technically advanced society. We will return to this issue in due course. Meanwhile, let it suffice to point out that the figures further undermine the credibility of the stereotyped popular image of civil servants as bowler-hatted Whitehall mandarins. Very few generalists conform to the stereotype. Most specialists manifestly do not.

Recruitment

Table 3.7 underlines the variety of employment offered by the civil service from the standpoint of recruitment. The table summarizes the recruitment statistics recorded in the Civil Service Commission's *Annual Report* for 1985. It must be remembered that no year's recruitment figures are entirely 'typical', and that patterns will vary according to prevailing official policies regarding the expansion or contraction of public services and in the light of extraneous factors affecting the availability of recruits, such as fluctuating bulges in the birth rate 20 years previously and the current level of unemployment. The first half of the 1980s has been characterized by sharp cutbacks in civil service recruitment generally, accompanied by a very high demand for jobs.

It can readily be seen that in almost every sector of the civil service the ratio of applications to vacancies is very high indeed; 47 people applied for every administration trainee vacancy (the ratio is appreciably higher if we exclude applicants applying from within the civil service) and nearly 100 for each vacancy at a similar level in the diplomatic service. The ratios are only slightly less discouraging in the competitions for more specialized posts (where more of the

TABLE 3.7   *Recruitment by the Civil Service Commission, 1985*

	Vacancies	Appli- cations	Appoint- ments[a]
Administration group[b]			
Higher executive officers (D)	For all who qualified	67 (nomina- tions)	17
Administration trainees/higher executive officers (D)[c]	72	3,421	63
Administration trainees/higher executive officers (D) (Accountant)	7	143	1
Diplomatic service (grades 8 and 7)	20/25	1,980	21
Inspectors of Taxes	90	6,155	107
Executive officer and equivalent	5,056	32,087	4,540
Principals (accountancy functional specialism)	23	286	14

Senior executive officers/higher executive
    officers (accountancy functional
    specialism)
	86	218	38

Science group			
Grade 6 (formerly senior principal scientific officers)	2	27	2
Principal SOs	10	98	4
Senior SOs/higher SOs/SOs	650	11,135	512
Professional and technology group			
Architects	95	588	83
Civil, structural and public health engineers	160	1,289	125

Mechanical, electrical, electronic, chemical
    and production engineers and naval
    architects
	541	1,930	198

Building, estates, valuation and quantity surveyors	437	1,558	257
Oil industry specialists	21	345	5
Marine staff and Marine Survey Service	26	165	9
Advanced level technical trainees	52	405	46
Cadet valuers and Royal Corps of Naval Constructors (trainees)	46	1,627	44
Economists and statisticians			
Economic advisers	21	55	13
Senior economic assistants, economic assistants and cadet economists	49	399	45
Statisticians	13	82	6
Senior assistant statisticians/assistant statisticians/cadet statisticians	52	274	22

Lawyers

Legal assistant/senior legal assistants (incl. Scotland)	144	651	72

Other specialists

Actuaries and actuarial officers	8	92	4
Information officer group	87	2,094	66
Museums category	85	3,822	72
Social work group	23	218	18
Research officer category (home civil service)	36	998	29
Research officer category (diplomatic service)	3	121	2
Senior pyschologists and pyschologists	31	731	22
Assistant prison governors (trainee)	31	399	27
HM inspectors of factories and assistant agricultural inspectors	45	1,271	16
Linguists	78	1,110	22
Veterinary officers	22	68	21
Senior medical officers and medical officers	101	641	60
Advisory officers etc. (agricultural services)	48	738	48
Agricultural science specialists	5	429	5
Agricultural and higher agricultural officers (Scotland)	13	182	13
Dental officers	3	77	3
Communications, science and technology officers, etc. (GCHQ)	89	287	13

Excludes clerical (now administrative) officers, clerical (now administrative) assistants and equivalent grades, most of whom are locally recruited. Similarly the table excludes such staff as telephonists, messengers and cleaners.

a   Some of the figures in this column *include* appointments carried over from previous competitions and/or *exclude* candidates recommended but not actually appointed.
b   Excludes appointments to House of Commons clerkships, and to the Northern Ireland Civil Service.
c   Figures for administration trainees include 334 internal applicants, 7 of whom were appointed.

Source: Civil Service Commission Annual Report, 1985

demand is syphoned off by the competitive attractions of suitable and perhaps better-paid jobs outside the service, e.g. lawyers and architects going into private practice); 45 people applied for each vacancy in the museums service, and 17 for each job in the scientific officer grades. It is mainly in these specialist grades that we find the greatest discrepancies between the 'appointments' and 'vacancies' returns (namely oil industry specialists, linguists and some of the categories in the professional and technology group), indicating that while the civil service seldom has difficulty in attracting impressive *numbers* of applicants for such posts it has problems in finding enough recruits of a satisfactory standard. One suspects that, in some specialized fields, people with weak qualifications look upon civil service employment as a long-stop, perhaps even as a soft option which (as our figures confirm) it certainly is not. Even in the generalist categories, difficulties in finding enough well-qualified

TABLE 3.8   *Recruitment of administration trainees*

Year	Vacancies (approx.)	External candidates		Internal candidates		Total Appointed
		Applying	Appointed	Applying	Appointed	
1971	175[a]	1,302	123[b]	908	53[b]	176[b]
1972	188	1,791	141[b]	534	19[b]	160[b]
1973	239	1,729	212	391	28	240
1974	256	1,415	209	380	53	262
1975	247	1,803	211	426	43	254
1976	190	2,636	135	527	50	185
1977	160	2,388	111	510	32	143
1978	160	2,195	97	513	52	149
1979	145	1,990	84	412	37	121
1980	100	1,926	64	355	31	95
1981	55	2,144	41	334	14	55
1982[c]	44	2,174	21	169	3	24
1983	60	2,758	45	126	2	47
1984	66	2,876	51	151	8	59
1985	72	3,087	56	334	7	63

[a] Vacancies for external candidates only. The CSC Report 1971 says of internal vacancies, 'posts available for all who qualified'.

[b] Because of slight variations in the CSC Reports' format, figures for appointments made in 1971 and 1972 have been taken from table 4 of the Administration Trainee Review Committee, 1979.

[c] Revised administration trainee competition, see text.

In some cases candidates were offered deferred appointments, and they have been included in the appointment totals for the years in which they took up the appointment.

Source: *Civil Service Commission Annual Reports*

recruits are sometimes reported by the Commissioners. In 1982 a newly revised administration trainee competition proved so tough that only 24 applicants were appointed for 44 vacancies (see chapter 5).

Table 3.8 looks in more detail at the administration trainee competition since its introduction, in the wake of the Fulton Report, in 1971. The competition was introduced to replace the programme for recruiting graduate assistant principals. Under the old scheme the number of such recruits had been small; in 1964, for example, 48 assistant principals were appointed. The new scheme was intended to increase the number of good graduates entering the service, and to single out a third of them for accelerated promotion. As we shall see (in chapter 5) this has not been achieved. As table 3.8 makes clear, the number of external recruits has steadily fallen (a trend exacerbated by the Thatcher government cuts) and now stands at a level very similar to that yielded by the old assistant principal competition. The idea of singling out an elite proportion of the entry for accelerated promotion never worked in practice, and the actual proportion proved to be much higher (sometimes as high as four-fifths). In 1982 the administration trainee scheme was changed back

TABLE 3.9   *External administration trainee candidates, 1985: by university and subject of degree*

	No. sitting qualifying test $(n=2,124)^a$	% of total sitting test (rounded)	No. passing FSB $(n=66)$	% of total passing
University				
Oxford and Cambridge	309	15	42	64
Other university/ polytechnic	1,814	85	24	36
Degree subject				
Arts	1,014	48	37	56
Social sciences	780	37	18	27
Science and technology	272	13	11	17
Other	57	3	–	–

[a]   Total includes one non-graduate, who failed the qualifying test.
Source: Civil Service Commission Annual Report, 1985

to something closer to the old assistant principal system, reverting to an exclusively fast-stream entry for a smaller number of administration trainees with at least second-class honours.

The post-Fulton scheme was also intended to improve the chances of internal applicants already serving as executive officers. In 1964 there were 31 internal promotions to the administrative class (a piece of terminology which disappeared in the wake of the post-Fulton rationalization of grading, see above). Table 3.8 suggests that internal candidates did not do significantly better under the revised scheme though their *relative* position improved significantly between 1975 and 1980 as the numbers of vacancies steadily declined. This, as we shall see, has been a real bone of contention in the middle ranks of the service, particularly as the expansion of higher education and the growing incidence of graduate unemployment has enormously increased the number of graduates entering the civil service at executive officer level, from 5 per cent in 1965 to about 49 per cent in 1985.

Finally, table 3.9 throws some light upon the educational backgrounds of external administration trainee candidates recruited in 1985. It compares the university education of those sitting the initial qualifying test (the procedures are described in chapter 5) with those passing the Civil Service Commissions's Final Selection Board (FSB). There is a dramatic contrast between Oxbridge and the rest of the university and polytechnic system. The latter contributed over four-fifths of the candidates and just over one-third of those successful; putting it another way, Oxbridge's raw success rate (calculated by expressing the third column in table 3.9 as a percentage of the first column) was 13.6 per cent, compared with the non-Oxbridge rate of 1.3 per cent. Arts graduates are both more likely to apply for this generalists' competition than are science graduates, and relatively more likely to succeed in it. The Civil Service Commission can congratulate itself on managing to recruit an almost indecently large proportion of first-class graduates – 30.2 per cent of those appointed.

These kinds of statistics have been bandied about for years, and used as the basis for various assertions about the ideological predelictions of top civil servants, the merits or otherwise of 'generalism' and the defects or otherwise of selection procedures. We will consider some of the arguments in later chapters. For the moment, we will content ourselves with the observation that it is a tough proposition to contemplate entering the higher echelons of the British civil service, and it is manifestly tougher for some candidates than for others.

4

The Universal Department

When describing the institutional environment in which civil servants work we can draw upon a rich assortment of metaphors. Thus a *mechanical* metaphor (cf. the familiar phrase 'machinery of government') may be helpful when discussing the 'efficiency' of a department in realizing its objectives without disporportionate expenditure of money and effort. A *biological* metaphor can generate colourful images of diverse species both of civil servants and of departments, of 'growth' and 'cutting back', and perhaps of the impenetrability of the 'bureaucratic jungle'. An *astronomical* metaphor may help to convey the notion of lunar civil servants following (at various speeds) diverse but concentric orbits around their respective planetary complexes of ministers and permanent secretaries, while the departmental 'planets' orbit around, at various distances from, the solar complex of Prime Minister and Cabinet.

All these metaphors stress the concept of a 'system', composed of numerous parts (or functions), continually interacting both with one another and with their environment. This chapter is concerned with a departmental system, made up of separate but inter-related units called (rather loosely, as we shall see) government departments; chapter 7 looks at the internal structure of those departments. The astronomical metaphor is particularly useful in this context, in that it describes the diversity of departments (from small fragments to massive entities), the variety of their orbits and of the gravitational pulls that they exert upon one another, and their proximity to the central 'sun'. If we extend the metaphor to express the intensity of a department's policy-making functions and its status in the hierarchy of Whitehall in terms of 'heat', then the 'hottest' departments – the Treasury and the Cabinet Office – turn out, not surprisingly, to be closest to the Prime Minister and the Cabinet. We will consider these 'high-temperature' central departments later.

What is a Government Department?

Government departments grew up in the nineteenth century along with the idea that public functions should be performed by a body headed by a minister who is responsible to Parliament. The nomenclature of such bodies still varies in a mysterious way – *Department* of Trade and Industry, *Ministry* of Defence, Foreign and Commonwealth *Office* and *Board* of Inland Revenue.

Let us take as our starting point the proposition that a department is simply a body which employs civil servants. Table 1 of the *Civil Service Statistics 1986* lists 54 such bodies. Consider just six of them:

Charity Commission (317 civil servants)
Royal Mint (993: 636 of them industrial)
Department of Education and Science (2,405)
Manpower Services Commission (20,793: 663 of them industrial)
Home Office (37,024: 3,114 of them industrial)
Inland Revenue (70,279: 24 of them industrial)

Can *all* of them be government departments? Most people would accept the Department of Education and Science and the Home Office, both headed by secretaries of state, but what of the others?

The Charity Commission was (in its original form) set up by statute in 1853, and is the custodian of a register of charities. The functions of the Royal Mint are well known: about two-thirds of its staff are industrial civil servants, and it is nominally headed by the Chancellor of the Exchequer in his little-known capacity of 'Master Worker and Warden'. The Manpower Services Commission is the interesting product of a post-Fulton 'hiving-off' exercise effected by the Employment and Training Act 1973. Headed by a chairman (who is appointed by the Secretary of State for Employment), it is separate from the mainstream of government, but is nevertheless still accountable to ministers for its work. Together with the Advisory Conciliation and Arbitration Service (ACAS) and the Health and Safety Executive, it is linked with the Department of Employment to form what is called the Employment Group. Finally, the Board of Inland Revenue is a vast organization, headed by a chairman (who ranks as a permanent secretary). It falls within the responsibility of Treasury ministers (e.g. for the purpose of determining who is to answer parliamentary questions about it). (NB: The Royal Mint became one of the new executive agencies in 1990 – on which see chapter 12. The

MSC was renamed the Training Commission in 1987, and reabsorbed into the Department of Employment in December 1988.)

Civil servants employed by the Charity Commission, some of the national museums, industrial concerns like the Royal Mint and enforcement agencies like the Inland Revenue are, for the most part, specialists (though not necessarily in Fulton's sense of that word) trained to do a particular kind of job and unlikely to move into other areas of public service employment. In that respect they differ greatly from those in the service-wide grades who are, in theory and often in practice, totally mobile across departmental boundaries.

Departments not only differ greatly in size, they also vary greatly in status and character and (perhaps most crucially) in their proximity to ministers. Some departments are more 'departmental' than others. A group of academic researchers who embarked upon a territorial survey of departments came up against a bewildering array of lists, statistics and accounts used by the government itself for various purposes and found little definitional consensus among them. They conclude that:

There are about twenty 'Departments' – the familiar 'big names' such as Environment, Employment, the Home Office and so on – which might be termed 'five-star' departments, in that they will appear on *any* list of 'Departments' . . . Outside these are about another twenty 'Departments' which might be termed 'four-star', in that they will appear on any list except a Parliamentary one. The big tax agencies [Inland Revenue and Customs and Excise] are 'Departments' of this type. The real problems appear with about forty other 'Departments' which are counted as 'Departments' for one or more purposes, but not for others.[1]

They mention the component parts of the composite Scottish Office (sometimes counted as separate departmental units, sometimes not) and the semi-autonomous Property Services Agency (cf. the Manpower Services Commission, see above) as being in the latter category.

But it does, of course, depend upon where the line is drawn. The authors of a major treatise on departmental functions, published in the mid-1960s (just in advance of the major explosion of 'giant' departments, see below) considered that, 'despite the existence of a number of marginal cases, it is possible without too much equivocation to draw a line around about thirty major departments, together with some forty or fifty minor departments, and refer to them collectively as the central administration.'[2] Such departments are staffed by a largely unified civil service and are bound by the collective responsibility of ministers to ensure that departmental policies do not conflict.

The main departmental galaxy – comprising the four-star and five-star departments, but not those more peripheral and often ephemeral satellites in which civil servants sometimes find themselves stationed – is reflected in the composition of a Cabinet of senior ministers (not all of them with departmental portfolios) who orbit around the Prime Minister. The configuration of major departmental functions, immediately after the June 1987 election, is shown in table 4.1: the sub-headings are purely arbitrary as, to a large extent, are departmental boundaries themselves.

Why *are* departmental functions distributed in this way?[3] Why, for example, does the list not include ministries of Finance, of the Interior or of Justice, familiar features of the central bureaucracies of most other European countries? Why do we not have a Ministry for Children, instead of distributing relevant functions between several departments like the DES, the Department of Employment and the Home Office; why do we not have single ministries to deal with local government affairs (shared mainly, so far as England is concerned, between the Department of the Environment, the DES, the Home Office and the Department of Transport) or with the nationalized industries (shared between the Departments of Trade and Industry, Energy and Transport)? A historical examination of how British administration came to have the list of departments given in table 4.1 yields a story of incremental change, based upon shifting administrative fashions, prime ministerial hunches and changing needs and priorities. The process has aptly been described as one of continuous 'creation, fusion, fission and transfer'.[4] One manifestation of this has been the shifting arrangements of the central departments grouped around the Treasury (see below). Another has been the rise and fall of the so-called 'giant departments'.

TABLE 4.1   *The functions of central government in Britain (showing the main government departments as at June 1987)*

Foreign affairs and external security
Foreign and Commonwealth Office
Ministry of Defence

General home affairs
Home Office (e.g. Royal prerogative; criminal law; prisons; firearms; drugs; police; broadcasting; civil defence; fire service; honours) (NB links with local government)
Cabinet Office

Social services
Department of Education and Science (NB links with local government)
Department of Health and Social Security (NB links with local government)
Department of Environment (includes planning; environmental protection; housing; local government finance)

Economic affairs
The Treasury (headed formally by Prime Minister – in practice by Chancellor of Exchequer. Functions include responsibility for civil service pay and manpower. The large tax departments of Inland Revenue and Customs and Excise are also associated with the Treasury)
Department of Employment
Department of Energy
Department of Trade and Industry
Department of Transport
Ministry of Agriculture, Fisheries and Food

Regional affairs
Scottish Office
Welsh Office
Northern Ireland Office (NB until 1972 Northern Ireland was partly self-governing)

Legal matters
Lord Chancellor's Department (including the appointment of judges)
Law Officers' Department (Attorney-General and Solicitor-General)

Cabinet
Following the June 1987 General Election the Cabinet had 21 members. Apart from the ministers in charge of the departments listed above, that total included: the Prime Minister; the Lord President of the Council and Deputy Prime Minister; the Lord Privy Seal and Leader of the House of Commons; and the Chancellor of the Duchy of Lancaster. The Treasury was unique in having two ministers of full Cabinet rank: the Chancellor of the Exchequer and the Chief Secretary to the Treasury; however, from 1987, the Department of Trade and Industry was headed by a secretary of state, sitting in the House of Lords (Lord Young of Graffham), and by a Minister of Trade and Industry, Kenneth Clarke, who also held office, and sat in Cabinet, as Chancellor of the Duchy of Lancaster.

Giant Departments

We have already noted the vast disparities in the size of government departments. Common sense suggests that if a given range of central government functions is allocated to a small number of large departments, rather than to a large number of small departments, then the number of senior departmental ministers (and hence the size of the Cabinet) can be reduced; and instead of having some departments not directly represented in Cabinet at all (and hence perhaps being regarded as 'second-class' ministries) all ministerial heads can be included. Reduction in the number of departments also cuts down the number of inter-departmental boundaries across which, in a system characterized by departmentalism (see below), friction and dispute so often arise. A policy of fusion would appear at first sight to have many attractions – a more streamlined Cabinet, less inter-departmental bickering, easier co-ordination of policy.

On the other hand, bickering across *inter*-departmental boundaries all too easily gives way to equally fierce disputes across the inevitably larger number of *intra*-departmental boundaries, marking the sub-divisions within enlarged departments; this is particularly evident if mergers are forced marriages between incompatible partners. Vast departmental empires can be difficult to manage and co-ordinate, lines of communication from the centre to the periphery become dangerously stretched.[5] And, the most serious problem of all, how can ministerial responsibility – a constitutional principle that is hard enough to realize in practice – be expected to work in a department that has a multiplicity of functions (see chapter 8)?

Recent history suggests that, in general, the practice of merging (fusion) and un-merging (fission) departments owes more to pragmatism than to principle, though the period immediately following Mr Heath's installation as Prime Minister in 1970 is probably an exception. In 1953, for instance, the Ministry of Pensions was dissolved, and its functions distributed between the Ministry of Health and the Ministry of National Insurance, the latter becoming the Ministry of Pensions and National Insurance (re-named the Ministry of Social Security in 1966 when it took over the National Assistance Board). A major reason for the change was to eliminate costly and cumbersome duplication of the elaborate decentralized administrative arrangements for making cash payments to those entitled to pensions and insurance-based welfare benefits: an enormous expansion of the welfare state had taken place immediately after the Second World War, and rationalization of the relevant departmental machinery had been contemplated from the outset. Similar thinking lay behind the eventual merger in 1968 of the Ministry of Social Security and the Ministry of Health to form the giant Department of Health and Social Security (DHSS). Similarly, in 1955, the Ministry of Food, deprived of much of its *raison d'être* by the end of post-war food rationing, was merged with the Ministry of Agriculture to form the Ministry of Agriculture, Fisheries and Food (MAFF).

Apart from the establishment of the DHSS, the 1960s saw a spate of departmental mergers, the largest of which amalgamated the separate departments responsible for the three branches of the armed forces (Admiralty, War Office and Air Ministry) into the huge Ministry of Defence. In 1968 the Foreign Office merged with the Department of Commonwealth Affairs (which had itself absorbed the old Colonial Office) to form the Foreign and Commonwealth Office.

But the heyday of the giant department began in 1967, when the Ministry of Aviation was merged with the Ministry of Technology; then, in October 1969, the latter ministry also absorbed the Ministry of Power and took over some functions of the Board of Trade (see discussion of the Vehicle and General case below) and of the Department of Economic Affairs (DEA), the latter being disbanded. The DEA's responsibilities for regional economic planning went to enlarging the Ministry of Housing and Local Government, later to be the nucleus of the giant Department of the Environment.

In 1970 the process of fusion was carried still further by the in-coming Prime Minister, Mr Heath. The rationale of giant departments was expounded in his White Paper, *The Reorganisation of Central Government,*[6] which emphasized the advantages that would accrue from a further unification of departmental functions:

(i)   A capacity within such unified departments to propose and implement a single strategy for clearly defined and accepted objectives.

(ii) A capacity to explore and resolve conflicts both in policy formulation and executive decision within the line of management rather than by inter-departmental compromise.

(iii) A capacity to manage and control larger resource-consuming programmes, in terms of both formulation and administration, within departmental boundaries, making possible in turn more effective delegation of executive tasks.

(iv) The easier application of analytic techniques within large and self-contained blocks of work and expenditure.

(v) More direct identification to the community of the Ministers and
     departments responsibile for defined functions, programmes and
     policies, more open communication between government and the
     public about these, and better opportunities to discuss and chal-
     lenge them.

(vi) A capacity to contribute more effectively to the formulation and
     development of the Government's overall strategy.

The White Paper went on to stress the need to preserve collective
ministerial responsibility and to make sure that large and complex
departments were properly managed: here there are strong echoes of
the Fulton Report which, two years earlier, had called for 'accountable management', a subject to which we will return in due course.

One major product of Mr Heath's predilection for giant departments was the merger between the Ministry of Housing and Local
Government, the Ministry of Transport and the Ministry of Public
Building and Works, to form a huge Department of the Environment
with 72,000 civil servants. The out-going Labour administration had
been planning to do much the same thing. A more contentious
change was the dispersal of the functions of the Ministry of
Technology, whose responsibilities for civil and military aerospace
matters went to a new Ministry of Aviation Supply (28,000 civil
servants), while the rest of 'Mintech's' functions were merged with
those of the Board of Trade, and the monopolies functions of the
Department of Employment, to form a new Department of Trade
and Industry (27,000 civil servants). A few months later the Ministry
of Aviation Supply was disbanded, and its functions shared out
between the departments of Defence and Trade and Industry.

But in due course the forces of fission began to assert themselves.
Mr Heath himself responded to the fuel crisis of 1973–4 by
resurrecting the old Ministry of Power in the guise of a Department
of Energy to take over the relevant functions of Trade and Industry.
When Mr Wilson's Labour government returned to office in 1974 the
separate Department of Energy was retained, and the DTI was
further dismembered into three separate departments – Industry,
Trade and Prices and Consumer Protection. In 1976, Transport was
detached from Environment (though the two departments retained,
and still retain, various shared administrative arrangements, e.g. a
common legal department), and Overseas Development, which Mr
Heath had merged with the Foreign and Commonwealth Office
(FCO) in 1970, re-emerged as a separate entity. The tide had turned
against giant departments, though in 1979 Mrs Thatcher did decide
to re-merge Prices and Consumer Protection with Trade, and to send

Overseas Development back to the FCO; after the 1983 election, Trade and Industry were again united under one secretary of state.

Mr Wilson's Cabinet in 1966 had numbered 23; two posts were lopped off this figure by the re-organization of functions in 1979. Mr Heath's in 1970 was 18; it later dwindled to 17. Five years later, Mr Wilson had a Cabinet of 23. Mrs Thatcher's in 1979 was 22; in 1987 it was 21. Apart from considerations of administrative streamlining and the need to adapt bureaucratic and ministerial arrangements to changed circumstances (e.g. the break up of an Empire or the quadrupling of oil prices following a war in the Middle East), we must remember that the construction of a Cabinet has a strong political dimension. The exercise of prime ministerial patronage at this level involves the balancing of different factions within a political party. If the Prime Minister has many shades of party opinion to satisfy then he or she may be tempted to have a large Cabinet so as to satisfy the ambitions and harness the energies of both friends and potential rivals. This is a line of argument which may help to explain the large Cabinets of Mr Wilson and Mr Callaghan, given the notorious propensity of the Labour Party for inter-factional warfare; it may even help to explain the small Cabinet of Mr Heath, given his notorious insensitivity to backbench ambitions;[7] but it is less helpful in the case of Mrs Thatcher's reversion to a large Cabinet, given her disinclination to recognize faction, let alone appease it.

The Vehicle and General Case

One episode which may have helped to discredit the fashion for giant departments was the collapse of the Vehicle and General Insurance Company in 1971, which left in its wake many disgruntled creditors and about a million vehicle owners without motor insurance cover. It was alleged that sensitive information about the company's affairs had been leaked from the Department of Trade and Industry. There were also suggestions of possible negligence on the part of civil servants, exercising responsibilities under the Insurance Companies Acts, based originally in the Board of Trade and latterly in the DTI. A judicial inquiry was set up by the Home Secretary to look into the circumstances of the collapse. It reported in February 1972.[8]

The report named and blamed three senior civil servants whose conduct in the case had to varying degrees, it said, fallen below an acceptable standard of diligence and competence. We will return in a later chapter to the implications of holding civil servants directly accountable for their actions, given the importance attached to the principle of ministerial responsibility; of more interest in the present context are the Report's comments about the structure of the giant DTI:

The Department now employs some 26,000 non-industrial staff and has about 70 Under Secretaries ... Throughout the period [1961–71] the Department has been headed by a President [of the Board of Trade] or a Secretary of State who has been assisted by a number of junior ministers ... The proportion of the work of the Department that is referred to Ministers is very small – well under one per cent. The Ministers give political direction to the Department's operations and pilot legislation through Parliament. Once the legislation has been passed and any Ministerial guidance has been given, the civil servants are expected to take entire charge of the administration unless there are problems about which they need guidance from higher up, or unless there are any matters of particular political sensitivity about which they think ministers would wish to know ... It is the normal practice in the department ... that almost all the work allocated to a Division is dealt with in full and finally at the level of Under Secretary or below.[9]

The duties of the DTI in relation to the supervision of insurance companies had in practice been delegated to its Insurance and Companies Division, a delegation considered by the Tribunal to be 'proper and inevitable'.[10] Ministers and permanent secretaries cannot possibly watch over the day-to-day work of very senior officials at the elevated rank of under secretary. But does this absolve those at the top from responsibility for things that may go wrong at divisional level? The Tribunal thought, at least in this case, that it did, holding that, on the basis of the information that had been available to ministers and permanent secretaries, the latter had had no cause to intervene in the work of the Division until the Vehicle and General was about to collapse. The blame rested, it said, with the under secretary in charge of the Division, whose conduct of the affair had amounted to 'negligence', and, to a lesser extent, with the two assistant secretaries who had headed the Insurance Branch of the Division during the period.

The case illustrates vividly the problems of establishing and managing adequate lines of vertical communication in a very large department, though it should be added that such problems, and the much more worrying issue of where ministerial responsibility begins and ends, exist in *all* departments, large and small. Size and complexity are merely factors which aggravate a chronic and endemic problem. And the process of 'fusion, fission and transfer' itself can give rise to confusion and breakdown in communication and in morale as civil servants strive to maintain an understanding of their roles and of their relationships with others in a changing institutional environment. Prime Ministers who embark upon programmes of reform in the apparatus of central government must be aware of such costs.

The DTI was disbanded in due course, though Mrs Thatcher partly revived it after the 1983 election. Giant departments remain very much an established part of the Whitehall scene, though their size is diminishing as civil service numbers are cut. The *raison d'être* of the grade of under secretary has also been called in question.[11]

Departmental Fragmentation and Machinery for Co-ordination

'Newcomers to Whitehall', Anthony Sampson observes, 'are often surprised to find civil servants in different departments viewing each other with such suspicion that they hardly seem to belong to the same nation. The Treasury talks about "those MAFF people" with disdain; Transport and Environment are constantly at loggerheads; the Foreign Office is treated like a rather hostile foreign power.'[12] He goes on to allude to the elaborate process of inter-departmental consultation, with its own 'complex diplomacy', giving unlimited scope for official battles in committee. And he points out that the compartmentalization of departmental interests is exacerbated by the fact that 'each department represents not only its own minister's policy, but the interests of its clients, whether farmers, industrialists or local councils.'

Mr Heath's preference for giant departments – to resolve conflict 'within the line of management rather than by inter-departmental compromise' – was intended to remedy what was seen as a serious problem.[13] And it is one that affects the position of ministers. The greatest danger to a Labour Cabinet, Richard Crossman told an American audience towards the end of his own term of ministerial office, a few months before Mr Heath came to power:

is that its members will be corrupted from being a team of socialists carrying out a collective Cabinet strategy into a collection of departmental Ministers. The greatest temptation is that we should be too interested in the praise of the Department and too pleased at being told how well we are doing: 'Wonderful, Minister, you're putting all this party thing behind you, and really working for the Department – that's so fine of you'. And before we know what, we are beginning to lose interest in the causes for which we were sent to fight in Parliament.

Thanks to the minister's private office, said Crossman, 'there is nothing easier than being a departmental success.'[14]

Crossman's lament is in part a variation on the familiar theme of the hapless minister being manipulated and often thwarted by the machinations of the civil servants (see chapter 8). But it also highlights the chronic problem of departmentalism that impedes the development of coherent government strategy and stands in the way of long-term policy planning. In theory (at least until the theory was shaken by the Westland affair), British Cabinet government is based upon *collective* decision-making. Ministers ultimately are *collectively* responsible for every aspect of government policy, only a small part of which will have emanated from their departments and with which they (at least in the privacy of Cabinet) may personally disagree. Ministers may also be saddled with *individual* responsibility for actions taken by officials in their own departments of which they knew nothing, but that is another story.

In real life the dream of ministers and departments all pulling at the same speed and in the same direction seldom comes true. The only situation in which the dream does approximate to reality is in the nightmare circumstances of war, when many (but by no means all) animosities are suspended in pursuit of the national interest and when the apparatus of government itself is adapted to a specially streamlined style of decision-making, e.g. by the use of a very small and multi-party 'war Cabinet'. Whitehall is a seething mass of discrete departmental interests (and the picture is further complicated by the constant intrusion into this of another mass, equally seething, of outside interests and pressures). However the map of departmental territories is drawn, functions will overlap, encouraging both confusion and friction. Departments may have (though senior civil servants may deny it) long-standing policies of their own, which can colour advice to ministers and be a further potential source of conflict with other departments.[15]

Above all, departments constantly compete for scarce resources, and the minister is expected to 'fight his corner' on his department's behalf – a role which can conflict with the task of working out an optimal order of government priorities on the basis of long-term and rational, rather than short-term and self-interested, criteria. The annual Public Expenditure Survey Committee (PESC) exercise, presided over by the Treasury, turns the Cabinet and its committees (including the official committees composed of civil servants) into arenas for hard inter-departmental bargaining for the maximum slice of the public expenditure cake.[16] When – as has frequently been the case in recent years – the Chancellor of the Exchequer demands substantial cuts in public spending, strong departments seldom if ever stand aside to see that justice is done to their weaker brethren.

Such bargaining is not confined to money. Permanent secretaries exhibit a strong territorial imperative which resists attempts to lop off a department's functions (and hence some of its staff) and transfer them elsewhere. One of Richard Crossman's earliest clashes with his formidable permanent secretary in the Ministry of Housing and Local Government, Dame Evelyn Sharp, occurred when he casually allowed the department's responsibilities for physical planning to be handed over to a new Ministry of Land and Natural Resources. Crossman recorded in his diary, 'as soon as she realised this Dame Evelyn got down to a Whitehall battle to save her Department from my stupidity and ignorance.'[17] Note the reference to *her* department, with no irony apparently intended. Another resource for which departments are in mutual competition is parliamentary time: at the beginning of every session the Cabinet's Legislation Committee has to determine which Bills, sponsored by the various departments, can be fitted into a very crowded timetable.[18]

It must be conceded that, although hard bargaining is a feature of much Whitehall and Westminster life, and departmentalism can be a very real problem, it would be a gross over-simplification to depict central government wholly as a matter of conflict. And such conflict as does occur – in particular the perennial battle for money – is justified by those engaged in it very much in terms of their own perceptions of the public interest. It would be absurd, for example, to depict the efforts of the Ministry of Defence to protect its budget as being simply a cynical game of bureaucratic power politics designed to maximize departmental self-interest: the ministers and civil servants who fight such battles have their own view of the level of funding that is *necessary* to provide the country with adequate capacity to defend itself. In so far as departments seeking more resources, or to keep what they have in the face of pressure to make cuts, have to justify their policies to other departments who must suffer in consequence, then conflict and bargaining are a healthy feature of government.

The Cabinet is in some respects the main arena for inter-departmental conflict at ministerial level; but it is also a powerful instrument of integration since it epitomizes collective decision-making at the highest level of government. Crossman claimed that the Cabinet, and more particularly Cabinet committees, are manipulated by civil servants who fight departmental battles in their own official inter-departmental committees, and then brief their unsuspecting and over-burdened ministers to go to Cabinet to ratify the bargains that have been struck. There may be some truth in this interpretation (it is corroborated by another ex-minister, Joel Barnett) and it is certainly true that a great deal of civil service and ministerial effort at the highest levels of decision-making is channelled through inter-departmental committees.[19] But the fact remains that once the Cabinet has arrived at its collective decision, recorded in its minutes and notified to senior officials, then for the time being the matter is closed and the bickering must stop.[20]

And a different interpretation to that put forward by Richard Crossman stresses the importance of inter-departmental committees as instruments of cohesion rather than arenas of conflict and conspiracy. Thus the White Paper of 1970 that heralded Mr Heath's experiment with giant departments observed that: 'The existing system of inter-departmental committees is designed to maintain the collective responsibility of ministers for the Government's policies in each of the main sectors of governmental concern, by bringing together the differing views of Ministers and ensuring that the final decisions command the agreement of the Cabinet as a whole.'[21] The White Paper went on to suggest ways of reinforcing this machinery, which we will consider below.

The working of the Cabinet, both politically and in terms of the bureaucratic apparatus that supports it, is of supreme importance in any account of the workings of central government. And it is in the role of the Prime Minister and that of the Cabinet and its associated bodies that we find the main counterweights to departmentalism.

There has long been a debate about whether Britain has moved from 'Cabinet government' to 'prime ministerial government'. Crossman was one vigorous exponent of the view that such a movement had taken place, and he found it deeply worrying that departmental ministers, vulnerable to manipulation by civil servants from below, were also dominated and played off against one another by a Prime Minister, to whose patronage they owed their jobs.[22] The finer points of this interesting, but ultimately rather sterile, debate cannot long detain us here. Suffice it to say that the office of Prime Minister is undeniably quite *different* from that of any departmental minister, one which epitomizes collective decision-making in government. The Prime Minister has no departmental responsibilities and is therefore not preoccupied with having to defend a special area of interest. He or she can remain above the battle and can usually (particularly if a powerful colleague, like the Chancellor of the

Exchequer, gives support) orchestrate matters to secure a desired outcome, which is then recorded in the Cabinet minutes as collectively binding government policy. It may be simplistic to depict the Prime Minister as an autocrat; but autocracy is at least an antidote – albeit an unpalatable one with worrying side-effects – to departmentalism in government.

Successive Prime Ministers have resisted any temptation to set up a department of their own, largely because having to run such a department would cramp their style. And they do not go short of advice. Their small but high-powered private office has a hot line to all Whitehall departments – necessarily so given that the Prime Minister, both as head of government and as policy co-ordinator, needs often to be briefed at very short notice about almost anything that crops up within the sphere of government interest (and, given the extent of the modern interventionist state, that means almost anything at all). Prime Ministers sometimes bring in their own political staff. This practice, dating back to Lloyd George's famous 'kitchen cabinet' and perpetuated in Harold Wilson's 'garden suburb', underlines the important, but difficult, distinction between a Prime Minister's role as head of government (for which he or she is entitled to civil service assistance at public expense) and his or her political role as party leader (for which he or she is not). Sometimes there can be a blurring of the two categories of staff: Mrs Thatcher, for example, caused some comment when she appointed a senior Whitehall information officer, Bernard Ingham, as her press officer, and Mr Ingham subsequently intensified such comment by seeming to interpret his role in a highly political way (see chapter 9). And the Prime Minister also has particularly close access to the Cabinet Office (though strictly speaking it exists to serve the Cabinet as a collective entity) via the Cabinet Secretary, who for many practical purposes can be regarded as the Prime Minister's permanent secretary. This is even more obviously true when (as under Mrs Thatcher) the Secretary is also designated Head of the Civil Service, a area for which the Prime Minister has explicit ministerial responsibility.

Debate about the nature and extent of the Prime Minister's functions intensified with the arrival of Mrs Thatcher, a Prime Minister with an uncompromising style and a very clear view of the role of civil servants. We will discuss in later chapters various aspects of this, notably her insistence on cuts in civil service manpower and some hints that she was less than happy with the traditional view of a wholly politically neutral civil service. Mrs Thatcher's apparent irritation with the nature of advice received from some top departmental civil servants was associated in the minds of some observers with appointments she made of special advisers, attached to her private office.

In reply to a parliamentary question, Mrs Thatcher has denied any intention of setting up a Prime Minister's department. She pointed out, quite rightly, that her predecessors had set up various advisory units: there are plenty of precedents for importing special advisers into No. 10 Downing Street, and the scale on which she and others have done this hardly amounts to a new 'department', still less to a prime ministerial counter-bureaucracy.[23] But, on an earlier occasion, when asked another parliamentary question about the staffing of her 'department', she had replied with information about the Cabinet Office.

One significant decision made by Mrs Thatcher was her announcement, in the summer of 1983, that the Central Policy Review Staff (CPRS) was to be abolished. The origins of this body – designed to combat departmentalism and to help to sharpen the definition of government strategy – can be found in Mr Heath's 1970 White Paper. Having acknowledged the importance of inter-departmental committees, the White Paper admitted that there was need for reinforcement 'by a clear and comprehensive definition of government strategy which can be systematically developed to take account of changing circumstances and can provide a framework within which the government's policies as a whole may be more effectively formulated'.[24] It announced the establishment of 'a small multi-disciplinary central policy review staff in the Cabinet Office' which will:

form an integral element of the Cabinet Office and, like the Secretariat and other staffs in the Cabinet Office, will be at the disposal of the Government as a whole. Under the supervision of the Prime Minister, it will work for Ministers collectively; and its task will be to enable them to take better policy decisions by assisting them to work out the implications of their basic strategy in terms of policies in specific areas, to establish the relative priorities to be given to the different sectors of their programme as a whole, to identify those areas of policy in which new choices can be exercised and to ensure that the underlying implications of alternative courses of action are fully analysed and considered.[25]

Or perhaps, as the first chairman of the CPRS put it, quoting a colleague, its first purpose was 'sabotaging the over-smooth functioning of the machinery of government' or, as he said in another context, 'thinking the unthinkable'.[26] The CPRS was an interesting experiment in the importation of 'outside' ideas into a traditionally closed system of government: half its membership, which fluctuated around 18, consisted of bright young civil servants seconded from their departments (it would be interesting to discover how their colleagues reacted to them when they returned), and the other half was made up of people recruited from universities, industry and commerce on temporary civil service contracts. It was linked in the 1970 White Paper to the introduction of a new technique called Programme Analysis and Review (PAR), which was, in turn, intended to reinforce the inter-departmental expenditure planning reforms (PESC) developed in the 1960s: PAR required departments to justify and defend their various policy programmes in inter-departmental discussion, albeit on a highly selective basis.

Both CPRS and PAR were deliberate attempts to break down departmentalism by strengthening the collective basis of Cabinet decision-making. The government's overall strategy was explicitly recognized as predominating over parochial interests. But they were alien to deeply rooted traditions – ministerial as well as bureaucratic ones – and for that very reason they proved vulnerable once their progenitor, Mr Heath, had left office. PAR gradually fizzled out during the 1970s, and was abolished soon after Mrs Thatcher became Prime Minister.[27] Some, however, see in Sir Derek Rayner's Efficiency Unit (see chapter 10) a variant upon what Mr Heath's reform had been intended to achieve.

The CPRS lasted a little longer, preoccupied in its later stages with major Conservative policy issues such as privatization and the curbing of trade union power. Much political capital was made in the run up to the 1983 election out of a leaked CPRS report which was represented as advocating a sharp reduction in the scope of the welfare state. It was, in the end, too small and too alien to survive without active prime ministerial support. Inevitably, it had made powerful enemies in pursuing its role of challenging established departmental positions, and it was abolished in the summer of 1983.

Mrs Thatcher's robust style of leadership, her preference for surrounding herself with like-minded ministers and personal advisers and her determination both to keep the civil service in its place and (literally) cut it down to size, add up to a powerful antidote to departmentalism. The gravitational force of a dominant Prime Minister reinforces the constitutional convention of collective responsibility, and Mrs Thatcher clearly believes that she can establish and enforce a collective strategy without artificial aids such as a CPRS. Some would certainly argue, however, that the CPRS provided a welcome breath of fresh air in the rather stultifying atmosphere of Whitehall, and that its abolition was undeserved. Others might be less than sanguine about the current health of collective Cabinet government given episodes like the Westland affair.

Mr Heath had attempted to work out coherent principles (some of them reminiscent of those set out in the Haldane Report as long ago as 1918) for reforming governmental machinery in the context of what was then a new fashion for strategic policy planning. Mrs Thatcher is more of a pragmatist. As one Whitehall journalist put it: 'She is impatient with Whitehall's cumbersome Cabinet committee structure, preferring, instead, to set up *ad hoc* committees on a particular issue, preferably with herself in the chair. In short, she is not greatly interested – to the great disappointment of academics looking for tidy solutions – in the machinery of government and constitutional theory.'[28]

'Village Life' in Whitehall

Between the villagers of Whitehall and the villagers of Tuscany, there was sometimes surprisingly little to choose.[29]

We have so far been looking at the Whitehall environment of civil service activity mainly in terms of organizational structure and political control. Such an approach requires us to consider the distribution of activity between institutions called (though we have noted some definitional problems) 'departments'. Lateral communication is effected mainly through an elaborate network of official and ministerial inter-departmental committees. There is, however, another approach, which stresses the informal bonds which play a vital part in the working of all complex organizations and which are crucial to an understanding of the civil service. The hero of John le Carré's novel, *The Honourable Schoolboy*, refers to the inhabitants of Whitehall as 'villagers', conjuring up an image of a close-knit community, suspicious of outsiders, and one in which everyone knows, through a grapevine of gossip, everyone else's business.

The same metaphor has been used by two American researchers, Hugh Heclo and Aaron Wildavsky, who set out to unravel the tangle of inter-departmental bargaining over public expenditure presided over by the Treasury and associated in particular with the annual PESC cycle.[30] A central theme of their study is the importance of an exclusive 'expenditure community', the core of which consists of senior officials in the supply divisions of the Treasury and the principal finance officers who are located in the various spending departments, but who also owe allegiance to the Treasury. The activity of this small and tightly-knit community is lubricated by close working relationships founded upon personal trust and mutual esteem. Members of this community – and, indeed, civil servants in general – judge one another in terms of criteria such as intellectual calibre, capacity for influencing colleagues and ministers and above all reliability or 'soundness'.

The 'village' metaphor can in fact be extended to the rest of the higher civil service, and to specialist groups within the service (no doubt inspectors of schools and of factories or civil service lawyers have their own informal professional networks, as well as being part of a more general network within their respective departments). Heclo and Wildavsky quote a Treasury official as saying that 'the Civil Service is run by a small group of people who grew up together.'[31] We have noted already that the higher civil service as a whole is really very small (sub-groups such as the 'expenditure community' are of course very much smaller). Senior civil servants tend to come from kindred social and educational backgrounds, and hence to see things from similar points of view and discuss them in a common language, which probably becomes more marked as an official becomes assimilated into the organization and learns (probably quite unconsciously) the accepted body language and linguistic codes:

They develop like any closed profession, a culture and a language of their own. They communicate with each other in terms that they understand; phrases like 'at the end of the day', 'ball's in your court', a 'sticky wicket' are largely used inside the civil service. And I think the sorts of argument they use are phrased in terms which they recognise and which convey their meaning to each other, but which wouldn't carry so much conviction with an outside audience . . . The thing about the language of Whitehall is that it makes it unnecessary very often to carry arguments right through to the end, because so many assumptions are shared.[32]

Career patterns constantly intersect: this is particularly true of those identified early on as 'high-fliers', whose postings are deliberately arranged to give wide-ranging experience. Even the social chatter that goes on in the London clubs is part of the network of informal inter-relations and an extension of the Whitehall grapevine. In the civil service unwritten rules and informal relationships are every bit as important as formal rules and constitutional principles.

This is something that no civil servant can afford to forget (though he might not see things in quite the terms expressed here) and neither must we.

The Central Departments

The Treasury is not just the hub of an 'expenditure community'; it is also (to revert to the astronomical metaphor) one of two 'high-temperature' departments which orbit close to the centre of govern-mental power. The other such department is the Cabinet Office, whose history is closely bound up with that of the Treasury. These small but highly prestigious departments are intimately concerned with decision-making at the most rarified heights of government and share responsibility for administering the civil service itself.

In chapter 2, we left the story of the Treasury at the point, soon after the First World War, when its pre-eminence in Whitehall was firmly established and with its permanent secretary designated Permanent Head of the Civil Service. The subsequent, inter-connected, histories of the two central departments – histories which well illustrate the phenomenon of 'creation, fusion, fission and transfer' – can readily be traced through published sources. One aspect of that history – the changing inter-relationship between the top civil service posts of Permanent Secretary to the Treasury, Cabinet Secretary and Head of the Civil Service (from 1956 to 1962, for example, the Cabinet Secretary doubled up as Head of the Civil Service and was located in the Treasury) – is outlined in table 4.2. It will be noticed that in 1968 the complex picture was complicated still further by the advent of a new Civil Service Department (CSD). We will pick up the story at that point.

The CSD was set up in response to the Fulton Committee's call for a separate department to take over the pay and management functions of the Treasury and to preside over what the Committee hoped would be a major period of civil service reform (see chapter 2). The Head of the Civil Service moved from the Treasury to take charge of the new department, and thus there was a triumvirate of 'super permanent secretaries' sharing responsibility for economic policy, the running of the Cabinet and the operation of the civil service, all with access to the Prime Minister (who is ultimately responsible for the civil service). This arrangement survived through the 1970s, though some critics had from the outset doubted the wisdom of separating Treasury responsibility for public expenditure

TABLE 4.2 *The top posts at the centre of government*

Year	Treasury	Cabinet Office	Civil Service Department
1916	Permanent Sec.	Cabinet Secretariat created out of CID Secretariat[a]	—
1919	Permanent Sec. designated Head of Civil Service	Cabinet Sec.	—
1938	Permanent Sec./ Head of Civil Service	Cabinet Sec. ceases to be Sec. of CID	—
1956	Permanent Sec. (answerable to Chancellor) + Cabinet Sec. becomes Treasury's second Perm. Sec. and is designated Head of Civil Service (In both capacities answerable to PM)	—	
1962	Separate posts of: (a) Permanent Sec. (b) Head of Civil Service	Cabinet Sec. ceases to be Head of Civil Service. Moves out of Treasury	—
1968	Permanent Sec. (Head of Civil Service moves to new CSD)	Cabinet Sec.	New Dept. headed by Head of Civil Service, moved from Treasury
1981 (Nov.)	Permanent Sec. Treasury assumes responsibility for civil service manpower and pay	Cabinet Sec. New Cabinet Office Management and Personnel Office takes over other CSD functions. Cabinet Sec. later designated Head of the Civil Service	CSD disbanded (on retirement of Sir Ian Bancroft as Head of Civil Service)
1987 (August)	Treasury regains former MPO management responsibilities for civil service pay and conditions.	MPO disbanded. Residual functions go to new Office of Minister for the Civil Service.	

[a] Committee of Imperial Defence Secretariat.

from CSD responsibility for civil service manpower, and widespread criticism about the patchy progress made in implementing the rest of the Fulton Report also raised doubts about the rationale of the new department.

Conflicting views about the way in which functions were distributed between CSD and Treasury were canvassed in evidence given to the House of Commons Expenditure Committee in connection with its enquiry into the civil service in 1976–7.[33] The then Cabinet Secretary, Sir John Hunt, advocated hiving off the public expenditure divisions of the Treasury and re-locating them in the CSD to form something resembling the Office of Manpower and Budget in the USA, and leaving the rump of the Treasury as a Ministry of Finance. Critics pointed to various weaknesses in this proposal, including the undesirability of separating the ministry responsible for running the economy from the task of controlling departmental expenditure, and some of them advocated reinforcing the Treasury by giving it the CSD's manpower functions and attaching them to Treasury expenditure divisions. This was the solution that eventually commended itself to the Committee, though had it been implemented it would have left the CSD with little to do to justify its separate existence.[34] Here, as elsewhere, eliminating one set of anomalies immediately gives rise to another set. In deciding upon the optimum way of allocating departmental functions there are seldom any 'right' answers.

When Mrs Thatcher came to office in 1979, the future role (if any) of the CSD became entangled with the wider issue of civil service manpower cuts and the quest for greater efficiency in Whitehall (see chapter 10). Sir Derek (later Lord) Rayner, then Head of the Efficiency Unit, and someone whose views were well respected by the Prime Minister, was known to favour a merger between Treasury and CSD in order to bring civil service manpower under the tough regime of Treasury control. He gave evidence to this effect to the Commons Treasury and Civil Service Committee, which chose the future of the CSD as a subject of inquiry.[35] Sir Derek was also critical of the absence of professional managerial expertise in the CSD. The Cabinet Secretary also favoured a merger, but the CSD was vigorously defended by its permanent secretary, Sir Ian Bancroft. The Committee, faced with conflicting evidence, gave the CSD the benefit of the doubt and recommended relatively minor changes in existing administrative machinery. Meanwhile, it appears that the Chancellor of the Exchequer had expressed misgivings to the Prime Minister about the desirability of Treasury ministers, already heavily burdened with responsibility for the government's economic policies, being given a heavy additional workload. In a White Paper replying to the Committee's report, the government accepted the view that the CSD would be 'an essential instrument' in achieving a smaller and more efficient civil service.[36]

In November 1981, however, Mrs Thatcher announced that the CSD was to be abolished.[37] Responsibility for civil service manpower and remuneration would go to the Treasury. Functions to do with the organization, management and efficiency of the civil service, together with personnel matters and policy on training and recruitment, would be exercised by a new Management and Personnel Office, associated with the Cabinet Office. Sir Ian Bancroft and his deputy were unceremoniously pushed into early retirement. The Cabinet Secretary, Sir Robert Armstrong, was subsequently designated Head of the Civil Service. The triumvirate was reduced to two once more, and the Treasury re-acquired much of its lost territory. The process of territorial reclamation was carried a stage further in August 1987, when the MPO itself was disbanded. Its managerial responsibilities for civil service pay and conditions of service were restored to the Treasury, while the MPO's residual functions went to a new Office of the Minister for the Civil Service (irreverently referred to by some insiders as 'Omsk'), attached to the Cabinet Office.

One factor which appears to have influenced the Prime Minister in abolishing CSD was what she considered to have been the weak handling of a major industrial dispute in the civil service in the summer of 1981 (see chapter 6). The passing of the Department was lamented by the civil service unions on the grounds that there is now no separate department to stand up to the Treasury on behalf of civil service interests when cuts are threatened – which, many would argue, is precisely why the CSD is no more.

The House of Commons Treasury and Civil Service Committee examined aspects of this subject in 1986, prompted in part by the Westland affair. It recommended, *inter alia*, a separation of the posts of Cabinet Secretary and Head of the Civil Service, on the grounds that assigning both roles to one person imposes too onerous a burden and may in some circumstances (e.g. GCHQ and Westland) give rise to a conflict of duty.[38] The proposal found little favour either with Sir Robert Armstrong,[39] or with Mrs Thatcher,[40] and the combining of these two major jobs was not affected by the changes of August 1987, noted above.

5

Recruitment and Training

How and why do people – about 45,000 of them a year according to the annual *Civil Service Statistics* – join the civil service? This question is not as straightforward as it looks. The sheer diversity both of the civil service and of the departments of central government greatly complicates any examination of recruitment and training. This chapter must, therefore, be selective (we cannot, for instance, look at *all* the many different entry procedures for the numerous specialist and semi-specialist groups) and concentrates on broad principles rather than on matters of detail. And it cannot, of course, match the recruitment and career information literature available (free of charge) from the Civil Service Commission.

Aspects of our discussion will build upon foundations laid in earlier chapters – for instance, the role both of the Treasury and of parts of the Cabinet Office in respect of civil service manpower and management, and the discussion (in chapter 2) of the nineteenth-century origins of open competition. We will also be referring back, from time to time, to the statistical tables, and the commentary upon them, in chapter 3.

Joining the Service

Table 5.1 summarizes the main routes of entry into the generalist grades of the home civil service. Two groups, both of them 'generalist' in terms of entry qualifications but 'specialist' in terms of job specification, namely tax inspectors and assistant prison governors, are included for purposes of comparison. It is worth noting here that the adjective 'generalist' can be highly misleading, and becomes less and less relevant as we move down the job hierarchy, away from the small cluster of open structure posts at the top of the service. For

TABLE 5.1 *Entry and promotion: main generalist grades*

Grade	Entrants (in 1985)	Age limits	Minimum qualifications	Normal promotion
Administrative assistant (formerly clerical assistant)	19,739	None	2 GCE O levels[a] or CS test	Administrative officer
Administrative officer (formerly clerical officer)	5,880	None	5 GCE O levels[a] or CS test	Executive officer
Executive officer	1,994	17½–49	2 GCE A levels + 3 O levels[a] or equivalent	Higher executive officer
Administration trainee	32	under 36	2nd Class honours degree or comparable postgrad. degree[b]	Grade 7
Inspector of Taxes	87	under 36	2nd Class honours degree or comparable postgrad. degree[b]	Grade 7
Assistant prison governors	27	at least 24	Degree or diploma (in an academic discipline) is 'an advantage'	Governor (Grade IV)

[a] Including English language.
[b] Civil servants with at least two years' service can be considered for the administration trainee scheme.
Sources: Civil Service Statistics, 1986; Civil Service Commission Annual Reports

many jobs, specific subject and professional requirements may not be prescribed as conditions for appointment, but post-entry training often encourages specialization. Once a department has invested time and money in training a recruit to use a computer, for instance, or taught him or her the intricacies of land registration procedure, it is loath to waste that investment by moving the recruit to other work. Some kinds of staff, e.g. tax inspectors and auditors, are not required to have studied particular subjects before entry, but must undergo intensive training and pass tough professional examinations in order to progress in their careers, or even to stay in the service at all. 'Specialists' in the full-blooded (i.e. Fulton) sense of the word are the professional lawyers, economists, accountants, engineers etc., recruited by the Civil Service Commission through special selection competitions which lay heavy stress on pre-entry qualifications in the relevant professional field. But the civil service also appoints many other kinds of staff, such as shorthand typists and linguists, who must obviously be able to demonstrate their competence before appointment. And are prison officers, factory inspectors and museum curators really 'generalists' as that word is commonly understood?

Then there is the matter of 'interchangeability'. An important feature of the development of the modern civil service was the emergence in the second half of the nineteenth century of 'Treasury classes', comprising staff who are interchangeable between one department and another. Like the concept of generalism, this is of greater relevance to jobs at the top of the hierarchy than to those nearer the bottom. A 'high-flier' in the upper ranks may indeed be moved from department to department to give him the breadth of experience needed in a future permanent secretary. But the great majority of civil servants, once recruited to a department, spend the rest of their working lives there. The disinclination to move trained staff from one job to another *within* a department is exceeded only by the unwillingness of departments to relinquish their own personnel to others. Some interchange does take place (it is for instance an almost inevitable by-product of any structural changes in the machinery of government itself) and is more likely to occur when the size of the civil service as a whole is being reduced, so that more thought has to be given to the optimum way of distributing scarce resources.

Yet another factor to be considered is mobility. About three-quarters of non-industrial civil servants work outside London, many of them in extensive networks of local and regional offices of central departments. The terms of service of many staff above the level of administrative officer (formerly clerical officer) require them to accept postings to any part of Britain, if necessary at very short notice. In practice, however, this requirement (which bears particularly heavily on a married civil servant whose spouse is also in employment) is applied flexibly, though it has been an important ingredient in the debate between government and the civil service unions about the decentralization of posts. It is acknowledged by the Civil Service Commission itself that location is the most serious impediment to recruitment at executive officer level. What mobility means in practice is that an ambitious civil servant who is willing to move around the country may be promoted more rapidly than one who is not; in this respect, a civil service career is not unlike those in many areas of the private sector, such as banking or retail management.

Administrative officers and administrative assistants (formerly known as clerical officers and clerical assistants), and office staff such as typists, are recruited directly by local offices. Job centres (which are themselves local offices of the Employment Service Agency, set up in 1990) play an important part in co-ordinating such recruitment and publicizing vacancies. As we shall see, the Civil Service Commission no longer takes responsibility for recruitment at these lower levels, but concentrates all its attention on posts at executive officer level and above (ones to which the 'mobility' requirement applies).

Table 5.1 gives the age limits and academic requirements for the posts listed. It may be noted, for instance, that the executive officer grade, designed in theory for school leavers with A level passes, is open also to graduates; able executive officers, under 32, can apply to join the administration trainee scheme, and graduate executive officers are exempted from the two-year service requirement that applies to non-graduates. The expansion in higher education that took place from the mid-1960s until the cuts of the early 1980s put more graduates onto the job market; but at the same time, that market shrank with rising unemployment. Graduates have turned to the civil service (itself afflicted with severe manpower cutbacks) for employment, and graduate recruitment to the executive officer grade has increased dramatically. In 1965, just 5 per cent of those recruited as executive officers had degrees; in 1985, about half of those appointed were graduates, many of them with second-class honours or better.

The Fulton Report envisaged enhanced promotion prospects for executive officers wishing to get onto the ladder leading to the top jobs in the civil service. In practice, however, as we saw in chapter 3 (table 3.8), the proportion of internal executive officer candidates entering the administration trainee scheme has been disappointingly small. The presence of a large body of frustrated graduate executive officers over-qualified for the work they are doing but denied any realistic prospect of promotion to the upper ranks, has been a significant ingredient in recent debate about the alleged elitism of the higher civil service, and was part of the reason behind the introduction of the HEO(D) scheme, as described below. But the problem remains.

The last column of table 5.1 gives basic information about promotion. The Northcote–Trevelyan Report of 1854 called for promotion to be on the basis of merit. This is the principle that operates today, with a civil servant's career progress depending very much on the annual reports of his or her superiors (to which the officer himself has access). However, as in all organizations, seniority ('Buggins' turn), and the sheer luck of a suitable post falling vacant at the right time, plays a major part. Moreover, the civil service hierarchy operates rather like a funnel, which narrows rapidly towards the top. The quest for promotion becomes, for many civil servants, a game of musical chairs, in which 'merit' must seem to play but a small part in the outcome of events. Reference back to table 3.5 (p. 64), showing the numbers employed at each grade of administrative post, demonstrates this funnel effect very clearly.

The Civil Service Commission: a Direct Line to the Treasury

There was no telephone system within the office; there was one telephone in the hall for the use of the whole staff including the Commissioners. That had been installed only in 1911 (although a direct line to the Treasury had been installed in 1903). In 1880 the Commissioners had asked for a private telephone to the Albert Hall and to London University (the main examination centres) but withdrew their request since they were assured 'as confirmed by our city friends, that the telephone is at present a failure'. Incoming calls were received by the messenger in the hall; if he happened to hear them he searched for the officer required, who rushed to the box in the hope of catching the call before it was cut off.[1]

The Civil Service Commission, set up in 1855, has always prided itself on its detachment from the rest of Whitehall, as befits the body that enshrines the Northcote–Trevelyan ideals of open competition and a non-partisan career civil service. The history of the Commission has reflected developments in the British educational system, such as the broadening of university and school examination syllabuses and the development of new techniques of performance evaluation. There was, for instance, in the inter-war years, a movement away from assessment based purely on academic written examinations towards an increasing emphasis on performance at interview, though there was (and perhaps still is) some resistance to this development on the grounds that reliance on interviews may give an unfair advantage to 'a "nice" boy with engaging manners and a pleasant accent'.[2]

The history of the Commission has also been entangled with that of the Treasury, inevitably so given the latter's historic role in relation to departmental budgets and staffing. But in 1981 (when the Civil Service Department was wound up, see chapter 4) the Commission was attached to the Management and Personnel Office, which was a part of the Cabinet Office. The MPO (now the OMCS) was responsible, among other things, for recruitment, though policy relating to staff numbers has reverted to the Treasury. There is still a lot of truth in the assertion of Mackenzie and Grove, 30 years ago, that despite the special constitutional position of the Civil Service Commission, 'it is perhaps most realistic now to treat it as if it were a special organ of the Treasury for a special purpose.'[3]

There are four full-time Civil Service Commissioners, plus one or two part-time Commissioners appointed from outside the civil service. They are headed by the First Commissioner, who ranks as a deputy secretary. From 1983–89, this post was held by Mr Denis Trevelyan, who happens to be a descendant of the co-author of the Northcote–Trevelyan Report. Commissioners are appointed by Order in Council, a weighty procedure that underlines their special and independent status; but the Commission's annual budget is met, as is the case with an ordinary government department, out of annual estimates approved by the Treasury and by Parliament, and its staff (351 in 1985) are ordinary civil servants. Recent editions of the Commission's *Annual Report* have stressed the increasing preoccupation with efficiency and effectiveness in the recruitment process. A by-product of civil service manpower cuts since 1979 was a streamlining of the Commission's own organizational structure. From July 1981, the number of recruitment divisions was reduced from five to four, as follows:

1 *The Administration Group Division*, responsible for recruitment to the Administration Group, including administration trainees and executive officers, and to corresponding posts in the diplomatic service and the tax inspectorate.
2 *The Science Division*, responsible for recruitment to scientific, medical, veterinary and analogous grades.

3 *The Technology Division*, concerned with recruitment of engineers, architects, valuers, surveyors, petroleum specialists and their
   support staff.
4 *The General Competitions Division*, responsible for recruitment
   to other specialisms, including lawyers, economists, statisticians,
   research officers, accountants, linguists, information officers and
   museum staff.

The historical basis of the Commission's functions, affirmed and
developed through a succession of Orders in Council and through the
Civil Service Superannuation Acts, is the principle that all established civil servants must hold the Commission's certificate of
eligibility. However, from the mid-1960s, the practice developed of
delegating the recruitment of 'non-mobile' staff, amounting to some
90 per cent of the annual intake, to the departments themselves, with
the Commission, save in rare instances where there was some room
for doubt, merely rubber-stamping a departmental nominee's eligibility for established status. In 1981 it was announced that, partly to
enable the Commission to cut its own staff, this essentially formal
requirement of certification was to be abandoned for virtually all
posts below the level of executive officer. This disengagement of the
Commission from the lower levels of recruitment gave rise to little
comment: there is little likelihood, even in an age of high unemployment, that ministers will be importuned by hordes of people eager to
procure a vacant administrative assistantship (formerly clerical
assistantship) through the exercise of political patronage.

However, the battle for a neutral civil service, appointed exclusively through open competition, is not quite over. Indeed, it is
arguable that the purist's position on political neutrality has become
out of date. For example, the position of temporary advisers
appointed by ministers became a matter of dispute during Mr
Callaghan's government in the late 1970s.[4] The Civil Service
Commission ruled, after taking legal advice, that such people were
not covered by the requirement of a certificate of eligibility applicable
to permanent appointments in the civil service, and were not
required, as had hitherto been supposed, to relinquish their appointments after a five-year period.

The issue has re-surfaced during the period of Mrs Thatcher's
administration. One aspect of the controversy relates to the appointment or secondment of staff, some of them very senior, into the civil
service from outside. This may be done where no internal candidate
is available to supply the necessary expertise felt to be required for

the post. Between 1979 and 1985, about 70 appointments were made from outside the service at the level of under secretary or above.[5] The issue came to a head with the announcement, in December 1984, that Mr Peter Levene, former Chairman of United Scientific Holdings, a defence contracting company, was to be appointed Chief of Defence Procurement in the Ministry of Defence. The outcry over possible conflicts of interest was not diminished by the revelation that Mr Levene was to be paid £95,000 a year – perhaps quite modest by the highest commercial standards, but well above the going-rate for top civil service salaries. The Prime Minister announced in February 1985 that Levene's appointment was to be on secondment; but the government's lawyers subsequently advised that this kind of secondment did not obviate the need for the Civil Service Commission's certificate of eligibility, and this meant that something had to be done to regularize the position, not just of Mr Levene but also of many others holding similar appointments. The government's handling of the Levene appointment was subsequently criticized by both the Public Accounts Committee and the Defence Committee of the House of Commons. As a result of this row, the regulations relating to secondments have been amended, and the departments must now abide by a strict set of guidelines, and seek the Commission's approval for such appointments, particularly those involving senior grades.[6]

The problem needs also to be set into the wider context of speculative debate about the possible 'politicization' of the civil service, which has intensified since Mrs Thatcher became Prime Minister (see chapter 8). In its report on *Civil Servants and Ministers*, published in 1986, the Commons Treasury and Civil Service Committee absolved the government from charges of politicization, but went on to argue the case (as others have done before) for the introduction of ministerial policy units, based in ministers' private offices, and made up of career civil servants and temporary appointees from outside the civil service.[7] If such developments do occur (and the government itself did not reject the proposal out of hand) then this might have significant implications for the role of the Civil Service Commission, having to vet the influx of a growing number of political appointees.

Meanwhile, the Commission undoubtedly does have an important part to play in resisting any attempts to weaken long-established principles of political neutrality in the civil service. However, it must be borne in mind that the Commission is not concerned with *promotions* within the service (which is what much of the recent 'politicization' debate has been about) and that it could probably do little (without itself appearing 'political') to stand in the way of an elected government that was determined to use its parliamentary majority to effect legislative changes in the rules and principles relating to civil service recruitment. But the political risks of embarking upon such a policy are high, and it is far more likely that a government would effect any such intentions by covert and gradual means, rather than by risking head-on confrontation.

Administration Trainees and HEO(D)s

The Civil Service Commission has concentrated its increasingly limited resources upon recruitment to the 10 per cent of 'mobile' posts at or near the top of the civil service. But this still amounts to a lot of work. In 1985, the Commission handled 102,716 applications, held 601 competitions and appointed 7,620 candidates.

However, over the years, public attention and debate has tended to focus on the mechanisms for recruiting the very small number of graduate generalists who are destined in due course, usually by way of a 'fast stream' of accelerated promotion, to become senior policy advisers. In 1985, there were 3,421 applications for direct entry and in-service competitions for posts of administration trainee or HEO(D), resulting in 63 appointments; in addition, 17 HEO(D)s (four of whom were recommended for appointment as principal) were recruited by way of departmental nomination. A disproportionate preoccupation with the top 1 per cent or so of the recruitment programme (though it does take up much more than 1 per cent of the Commission's own efforts) is inevitable, given the strategic importance of such positions, and the problematic nature of the relationship (clear-cut though it may appear in terms of orthodox constitutional theory) between top civil servants and their ministerial masters (see chapter 8). But we must, in the discussion that follows, bear in mind that we are talking about just one small aspect of civil service recruitment.

In the mid-1960s, when the Fulton Committee embarked upon its inquiry into the civil service, about 80 graduates were being recruited each year into the Administrative Class (as it was then called), mainly at the level of assistant principal. The competition was very tough, but once appointed a graduate entrant could expect fairly rapid promotion to the substantive grade of principal. There were two modes of competition. Method I consisted of a qualifying written test in general subjects, followed by an interview and then by written academic papers in optional subjects at honours degree level. Method II (discussed more fully below) began with the same qualifying test, followed by two days of aptitude tests and interviews at the Civil Service Selection Board (CSSB, known by the phonetical name of 'Cizbee') and then (for those who surmounted the first two hurdles) an interview before a Final Selection Board (FSB).

By Fulton's time, Method I had outlived its traditional purpose. It produced only six successful candidates in 1966, compared with the 117 who passed by Method II: 'with around 160 question papers [covering the entire range of university honours syllabuses] to be prepared for the July examination, there were over four times as many question papers as there were candidates to take them.'[8] Method II had steadily gained ground since its introduction after the Second World War. A majority of the Fulton Committee wanted to retain the option of Method I in modified form, a view that was linked to the recommendation that preference should be given to candidates offering 'relevant' degree subjects (see chapter 2); but 'preference for relevance' was rejected, and 1969 saw the last appearance of the Method I competition. The Fulton Committee also called for an investigation into Method II. A subsequent inquiry by J. G. W. Davies concluded that Method II was 'a selection system to which the Public Service can point with pride'.[9] It remains to this day the main route through which generalist graduates enter the upper reaches of the service.

The grade of assistant principal perished in the wake of Fulton, only to be resurrected in a new guise in response to the cuts imposed by the Thatcher government. Fulton proposed a new training grade for graduate entrants, as well as for 'those who have shown the highest ability among non-graduate entrants'.[10] When the new Administration Group was created in 1971, recruitment and training procedures were revised, with a view both to attracting greater numbers of able graduates from outside the service and to enhancing the promotion prospects of executive officers. The main features of the new arrangements were:

1   Replacement of the grade of assistant principal by new grades of administration trainee (AT) and higher executive officer (HEO)(A).
2   Some 250–300 ATs were to be recruited each year, given special training (including courses at the new Civil Service College) and

given the opportunity for accelerated promotion. A *maximum* of 175 were to be recruited from outside the service, with the rest of the AT positions being reserved for internal candidates.

3   The best of the ATs (about one-third of them) would be promoted to HEO(A), with the prospect of becoming principals after a further two or three years. The rest would become ordinary HEOs, with some hopes of eventually becoming principals via the intermediate grade of senior executive officer.

This was what was *meant* to happen, but the results were not quite as planned. First (see table 3.8, p. 70), only in the years 1974–5 did the number of AT recruits reach the target of 250 plus. Thereafter, there was a steady decline in numbers (though the number of applicants actually increased) to the point, in the early 1980s, when the AT competition was completely reconstructed, as described below. Secondly, the hoped-for influx of internal recruits did not materialize. Instead of 100 or so being recruited, the highest annual total was 53 (in 1971 and 1974). After 1975, as the number of AT vacancies declined, internal candidates began to do *relatively* a little better (i.e. as a percentage of all appointees) but not in terms of absolute numbers. Successive reports of the Civil Service Commission have bemoaned the shortage of candidates from the ranks of serving executive officers (many of whom are graduates) and noted the apparent over-reluctance of departments to make nominations, though part of the problem may lie (as noted elsewhere) in the unwillingness of would-be recruits to uproot themselves and move to London. Finally, the proportion of ATs selected for 'fast-streaming' proved to be far higher than one-third; in practice, only about a fifth of ATs were assigned to the ignominy of the 'slow stream'.

In 1977, the House of Commons Expenditure Committee, echoing both long-standing concern about the socio-educational elitism of graduate civil service recruitment and the growing complaints of civil service unions about the plight of able executive officers denied access to the higher grades of the service, recommended abolition of the administration trainee scheme.[11] All graduates wishing to enter the higher ranks should enter the civil service as executive officers, then compete (along with non-graduates) for entry onto a new higher-management training course 'designed to train those who will reach the highest levels of the service', i.e. at assistant secretary level and above. In December 1979, a Civil Service Commission Report (denounced by some commentators as decidedly complacent in tone), responding to the Expenditure Committee's allegations of bias in its recruitment procedures, took pains to praise the inherent fairness of those procedures, though it did recommend minor changes (see below).[12]

In 1980, the Civil Service Department proposed a new HEO(D) scheme intended both to enhance opportunities for in-service personnel and to ensure that the civil service continued to harvest the pick of each year's crop of graduates. The new procedure (the 'D' standing for 'Development') was introduced more or less in parallel with an exclusively 'fast-stream' version of the administration trainee scheme – in effect, a reversion to the old assistant principal scheme, called by a different name and rendered more palatable by the expressed intention that in-service and external graduate recruits should be recruited in equal numbers to the new HEO(D) grade. After two or three years in 'testing' jobs, they would be eligible for consideration for promotion to principal.

The first applicants for appointment under the new-style AT competition sat the qualifying test in November 1981. At the same time, new arrangements were put in hand to identify serving staff for the HEO(D) grade. The outcome of the first round of the new AT programme was described by the Commission as 'very disappointing'. Despite about the same number of applicants coming forward as in previous years (2,343), a mere 24 out of 44 vacancies were filled, just three being in-service candidates. Moreover, in this, the second year of the HEO(D) scheme, just 40 departmental nominees (a figure described by the Commission as 'surprising') were put forward, only eight of them being appointed. In 1983, however, the AT competition showed a slightly better, though still distinctly meagre, return, with 47 out of 60 vacancies being filled (though only two came from inside the service); but although the number of internal HEO(D) nominations crept to 47, only seven were deemed worthy of appointment, an outcome described, with some understatement, as 'disappointing'.

Worried by the problems of recruiting graduates of 'fast-stream' calibre, the Commission set up an inquiry, chaired by Sir Alec Atkinson. A similar inquiry into recruitment of tax inspectors, chaired by E. V. Adams, was conducted at the same time. Atkinson reported in February 1983, broadly vindicating the existing recruitment procedures, but suggesting better liaison between the Commission and schools, universities and polytechnics, the relaxation of existing age limits and modifications to the timing of the qualifying and CSSB stages of the selection process so that undergraduate applicants would know the results before the end of the Easter vacation.[13]

The Commission took steps to improve its procedures along the lines suggested, and its 1984 *Annual Report* cautiously attributed a modest improvement in the AT figures (3,027 applicants for 66 vacancies, 59 appointments) to post-Atkinson reforms. However, 1984 saw a further deterioration in internal HEO(D) recruitment, just six appointments from 49 nominees. In 1985, the AT competition filled 63 out of 72 vacancies, a result regarded by the Commission as rather disappointing in the light of its reform, e.g. raising the age limit to 32. However, the HEO(D) competition did show modest improvement, with 17 appointments from 67 nominations. We may note in passing that, in the same year (1985), the Commission managed to fill just one of seven vacancies under a variant of the AT scheme introduced the previous year to recruit specialist accountants. In the present economic climate, market forces work against civil service recruitment in sought-after and well-paid specialist fields, but potentially in its favour in respect of generalists, a fact that makes the recent figures for AT/HEO(D) recruitment particularly worrying (see discussion of pay below). But, also in 1985, the Commission was triumphantly able to proclaim that it had managed to recruit 107 tax inspectors to fill 90 declared vacancies!

While the Civil Service Commission anxiously scans the recruitment figures and tries (with an eye on the 'efficiency and effectiveness' ethic that now pervades Whitehall) to find ways of streamlining its procedures and improving its productivity, many of the relevant factors lie outside its control. It must be alert to the overall state of the job market, and the difficulties and opportunities it presents to civil service recruitment; but it has to take the market as it finds it. The Treasury, not the Commission, is responsible for pay and pensions: the non-political Commission cannot get embroiled in industrial relations matters, though its reports may provide information and ammunition to be used in that context. Part of the problem is the image that the civil service presents to would-be recruits. The Commission has worked increasingly hard to sell its products, for instance by visiting educational institutions and inviting lecturers and career officers to observe the selection process. In December 1986 there were two programmes in the BBC2 *40 Minutes* series showing the Cizbee/FSB process in action – not entirely to flattering effect. There are some things that are hard to explain away. We have already discussed, for example (see chapter 3), some features of the phenomenon of 'Oxbridge bias'. There is a risk of over-dramatizing the case or of over-simplifying the lessons to be drawn from complicated statistics, but how does one explain to an undergraduate at a redbrick university or a polytechnic why it is that in 1985 a fair and unbiased selection procedure for ATs attracted 309 Oxbridge applications, 42 of whom (14 per cent) eventually passed the Final Selection Board, compared with 24 out of 1,814 (1.32 per cent) of those from other universities and polytechnics? Readers might usefully look at the more detailed statistics for themselves (in recent *Annual Reports* of the Commission, as well as in table 3.9 on p. 71), and try to devise a plausible (and, if possible, reassuring) explanation.

The Mechanics of Method II

Clever, brilliant now and then, but touchy, aloof and angular. Doesn't think he's properly appreciated. Practically asexual. Possible homo. Make a first class civil servant.[14]

The AT/HEO(D) competition attracted 2,412 candidates in 1985, 288 of them (11 per cent) in-service candidates (mostly EOs), the rest from outside the service. Eighty-two per cent were eliminated at the first hurdle, which is a written qualifying test comprising a précis exercise, analysis of statistical tables, an exercise in drafting advice on the solution to an imaginary government problem and various intelligence, comprehension and numeracy tests. Internal applicants did slightly better than external ones at this stage, with Oxbridge candidates (55.6 per cent eliminated) doing markedly less badly than other graduates (84.6 per cent eliminated).

The next stage for 364 survivors of the 1985 batch of would-be ATs was Cizbee, a procedure introduced after the Second World War and based on the War Office selection procedures for choosing officers in the armed forces. Originally, it was run as a residential 'country house party', whose ambience can be savoured by reading the late Sir Alan Herbert's wickedly satirical novel on the subject, but nowadays the proceedings take place on a non-residential basis in rather austere offices in central London.

Kellner and Crowther-Hunt's graphic description of the proceedings at Cizbee can still be read with profit, though it pre-dates the HEO(D) era.[15] The following outline is based largely on the Civil Service Commission's own description, which summarizes the proceedings thus:

At present, candidates are seen at CSSB in groups of five by teams of three assessors [normally a retired senior civil servant, a psychologist and a younger civil servant]. Candidates and assessors work together over two days, and the assessors take a third day to review evidence, arrive at a team decision for each of their five candidates, and then write reports on each . . . The emphasis is on aptitude or potential, not on attainment . . . Assessors order their impressions in terms of a set of qualities which, between them, cover in detail the broad areas of problem-solving and decision-making ability, effectiveness with other people, and internal personal strengths.[16]

The assessors take account of four categories of evidence:

1 *Attainment information.* This is evidence of what the candidate has achieved in terms of education and/or work.
2 *Job simulation tasks.* Candidates are required to assimilate a mass of documentation on a complex administrative problem and draft a reasoned solution; to draft a firm but tactful response to 'a sensitive personal relations issue'; to contribute effectively to a meeting, and to take a turn as its chairman.
3 *Cognitive tests.* To assess verbal and non-verbal intellectual abilities.
4 *Interviews.* There are one-to-one interviews, each lasting 40 minutes, with each of the three assessors.

Candidates are given a composite mark made up of an array of marks by each assessor. In 1985, Cizbee recommended 111 candidates (30.5 per cent) to a Final Selection Board (FSB), which consists usually of one of the Civil Service Commissioners, two other senior civil servants, an academic and a trade union officer or an industrial manager. Of 108 candidates who attended the Board in 1985, 75 were deemed to have passed (the highest casualty rate being among the 23 remaining internal candidates, only nine of whom passed). The FSB is by no means a formality, but it seldom overturns a firm recommendation from Cizbee.

Training in the Civil Service

Perhaps the most prominent feature of the British tradition of civil service training is that there is not very much of it, at least in any formal sense. The generalists of the old Administrative Class (unlike lawyers, accountants, engineers and other specialists, who are required to have the appropriate professional qualifications before entering the service) were always intelligent all-rounders, expected to learn the job mainly through experience and by emulating their colleagues rather than by way of formal instruction. It may indeed be true that in 1985 'the total number of staff devoted to full-time training duties within the Service now stands at 3,200' and that, following various recent management initiatives, 'within Departments many line managers are much more interested in training issues',[17] but the traditional view of civil service training as being the icing on the cake of experience remains the dominant one.

This view, epitomizing the 'amateurism' denigrated by the Fulton Committee, has often been contrasted unfavourably with the more rigorous training arrangements to be found abroad, notably in France. Several members of the Fulton Committee paid a short visit to France, on the basis of which they recorded their favourable impressions of the role of the École Polytechnique (providing rigorous training for the technical *corps* of the civil service and for the technical staffs of other bodies, including the armed forces) and for the École Nationale d'Administration (ENA), which carries out both recruitment and training for the prestigious *grand corps* of the French higher civil service.[18] Other observers have similarly noted, often with a note of envy, the unashamedly elitist arrangements (though the Mitterand government has recently sought to make them less exclusive) that characterize civil service training in France.[19]

The ENA was created in 1945 to provide high-calibre civil servants to take charge of France's post-war reconstruction. Britain has nothing remotely resembling it, but there has been long-running debate about the need for some kind of service college, a debate which was also set in motion by the exigencies of the Second World War.[20] The Assheton Report on the training of civil servants, published in 1944, did not take on board the notion of a fully fledged civil service staff college, and the idea of a British ENA has never (notwithstanding the favourable impression formed by Fulton) been a serious item on the policy agenda.[21] But Assheton did recommend centralized arrangements on a small scale (watered down still further when it came to implementation) for training entrants to the Administrative Class. A year or so later a Training and Education Division was set up in the Treasury and a modest two-week course on the machinery of government was provided for assistant principals.

The next significant step was the setting up of a Centre for Administrative Studies in London in December 1963. Then came the Fulton inquiry, which received a large body of evidence (from, among others, the civil service unions) advocating the expansion of the Centre into a new staff college. The Fulton Report recommended the establishment of a Civil Service College to discharge three main functions:

1　Provide major training courses (some on a residential basis) in administration and management (including provision of some of the training for graduate administration trainees); courses in management and administration for specialists; additional courses in management for those in their 30s and 40s moving into top management.
2　Provide a wide range of shorter training courses in management and vocational subjects, especially for more junior staff.
3　Conduct research into problems of administration and machinery of government.[22]

The Wilson government accepted the recommendation, and the Civil Service College – based in central London, Sunningdale and Edinburgh – began work in 1970.

The fortunes of the College have been mixed. Its research function never got off the ground and the early practice of staffing it partly with academics on fixed-term contracts was soon discontinued. In 1976 it became part of the new Training Group of the Civil Service Department and the post of Principal of the College was effectively downgraded from deputy secretary to under secretary. In 1977 the Edinburgh centre was closed on the grounds of economy. The courses for administration trainees and HEO(D)s (a small fraction of the College's total activity, but an important one in the light of our earlier discussion of 'fast-streaming'), originally based on two 15-week multi-disciplinary blocks, has been cut and restructured on a modular basis, now comprising 12 distinct modules offering a total of 22 weeks of training.[23] Since the early 1980s the policy of providing courses free to government departments on an 'allied service' basis has been abandoned. Departments now have to pay to have their staff trained at the College, and the College has to sell its wares to customers whose budgets are (like the budget of the College itself) subject to tight constraints.

But the College has survived and claims, with some justification, to provide an impressive programme. According to its Annual Report, in 1985–6 it attracted about 26,000 students to its 1,300 courses, amounting to a total of 89,000 student days. Of the courses provided, 530 covered 'systems' (information technology and management services), 230 were in the field of 'management studies', 140 were on 'statistics and operational research' and 120 on 'accountancy and internal audit', these four categories accounting for 78.5 per cent of the courses on offer. About one-third of the civil servants attending came from HEO/HEO(D) level. Sixty-two per cent of those attending were in the lower and middle ranks of the administration group; 17.8 per cent were in the top seven grades that now comprise the open structure.

Two further points should be made. The first is to emphasize that the Civil Service College has never been a staff college. In the words of a former principal:

The expression 'staff college' suggests an organisation (like the Army Staff College) which members of a specific profession who show high promise attend at a certain stage in their careers and where they are expected to 'pass' a long course before qualifying for promotion. The suggestion has sometimes been made that the College should be a staff college in this sense but the decision has always gone the other way. The College is not and never has been an 'elitist' organisation dealing with only a small group of high fliers. (Even the AT/HEO(D) 'fast-stream' training accounted for only 3,300 student days in 1982–83 out of a total of 72,000 student days). Nor does the College in general issue certificates or award 'passes'. Naturally we attract people who are expected to go further in their careers but very little of the training is mandatory.[24]

The second point is that although the College performs an important role and may be regarded as one of the few visibly enduring monuments to the Fulton Report, it is in fact responsible for only a small fraction of all civil service training. Its importance is probably as much symbolic as real. In 1983–4, for instance, 73.8 per cent of training (as measured by trainee-days) was provided by departments themselves, 21.2 per cent came from institutions external to the service and a mere 5 per cent was provided centrally via the College.[25] Although in the early 1980s there was a slight increase in the tendency for departments to use both the College and external institutions, while at the same time the development of new procedures (like the Financial Management Initiative) and new technologies (information systems and computers) may have helped to focus the minds of civil service managers on the importance of training, it is evident that the departments themselves have been slow to relinquish their traditional predominance in this field.

Postscript

From April 1991, departments and the new executive agencies (see chapter 12) will be free to carry out their own recruitment of staff below Principal, except for fast-stream candidates. From the same date, much of the work of the Civil Service Commission (together with that of Cizbee) will become part of the new Recruitment Agency.

6

Conditions of Service

For many historical reasons civil servants are subject to peculiar
conditions of service that reflect their unique constitutional relationship with the Crown. However, in recent years, important
changes have taken place, many of which have brought civil service
employment more closely into line with conditions of service that
prevail elsewhere. Civil service unions, formerly subdued by ministerial prerogative, have become increasingly assertive. Some of the
more archaic and anomalous features of civil service employment
law have been eliminated. The GCHQ case in 1985 proved to be a
major landmark in redefining and clarifying the legal basis of civil
service employment and in making clear that disputes in this context
are, in principle, susceptible to review by the courts. Civil servants, in
most contexts, can also have recourse to industrial tribunals when
they believe themselves to have been wrongfully dismissed or to have
been victims of racial or sexual discrimination.

We begin, however, with an issue that is particularly close to the
hearts of all employees – pay, and the basis on which it is negotiated,
and entitlement to retirement pensions.

Pay and Pensions

Following the 1986 round of pay increases, a clerical/administrative
assistant aged 16 received an annual salary of £3,055; moving from
the bottom of the hierarchy to the top, we find that the salary of the
Head of the Civil Service was £77,400. As is common in other
occupations, most civil servants, at all levels below the very top, are
on incremental scales: thus the main scale for clerical/administrative
officers has six points, from £4,800 to £6,293; executive officers start
(aged 18) at £5,250, and can expect, two years later, to be earning

£9,452; the principal scale has eight points, from £14,318 to £19,465. Specialists (outside the open structure) have different salary scales, but for the most part their pay is broadly similar to that of generalists of comparable seniority. Civil service jobs are scattered across the whole country, but although economic conditions (e.g. local levels of unemployment) vary greatly from one area to another, pay scales are negotiated nationally; however, civil servants working in London do receive a London allowance on top of their basic salaries. Performance-related bonuses have been introduced, experimentally, in the higher grades (see below). Established civil servants, in common with many other public sector employees, enjoy pensions which are index-linked to the cost of living and which are, in theory, non-contributory (though the Treasury calculates a notional contribution when it considers pay claims).

The machinery for determining civil service pay has a long and chequered history. The subject is technically complex and politically sensitive. Governments have to balance their need for staff of adequate calibre at all levels against their responsibility to Parliament and, ultimately, the taxpayer for public expenditure. Civil servants have been both the architects and (particularly for the past few years) the front-line casualties of government attempts to minimize pay increases on economic grounds, especially in the public sector. Ministers expect their officials to give loyal service to the government of the day; the civil service unions (see next section) retort that loyalty cuts both ways and that the government owes its employees a fair wage and decent conditions of employment.

But what is a fair wage in the civil service? The key word (albeit, as we shall see, one with an elastic meaning) is 'comparability'. But comparability with what and with whom? Should specialists, who have historically been accorded a somewhat inferior status in the civil service, be paid what they would earn outside? If so, accountants, petroleum engineers and lawyers would be earning a lot more than they do now, and more than their generalist counterparts. Many civil service jobs defy exact comparison with employment in the private sector. Productivity can be measured quite easily in the commercial world but is much harder to quantify in the case of, say, an assistant secretary in the Prison Department of the Home Office. Should the Head of the Civil Service be paid more, or less, than the Managing Director of Marks and Spencer? What about fringe benefits, like company cars and free medical insurance? Can the absence of such tangible benefits be offset by reference to intangible benefits, like job security and the patriotic satisfaction of serving one's country? The answers to such questions cannot be found scientifically, but attempts have been made to minimize the amount of guesswork and to take civil service pay, as far as possible, out of the political arena. Recent events, however, have exposed the ultimate impossibility of achieving objectivity in circumstances where the policies of government and the self-perceived interests of its civil service have increasingly diverged.

In 1955 the Priestley Commission on the Civil Service enunciated two main principles for determining the level of civil service pay.[1] The primary principle, it said, 'is fair comparison with the current remuneration of outside staffs employed on broadly comparable work, taking account of differences in other conditions of service'. Secondly, 'internal relativities' (particularly 'vertical relativities' between a given grade and the one above or below it) should be used as a supplement to the primary principle of fair comparison in settling the details of rates of pay. As Geoffrey Fry points out, the Priestley Report was published at a time of economic optimism and high employment; its principles, though widely accepted at the time, were not destined to survive the advent of a harsher economic and political climate.[2]

From 1957, pay scales in the higher civil service were reviewed by a small Standing Advisory Committee, reporting directly to the Prime Minister: in 1971 its functions passed to a new, more wide-ranging Top Salaries Review Body (TSRB), responsible not only for reviewing salaries at the top (under secretary grade and above) of the civil service but also for making recommendations in respect of senior judicial, ministerial and armed forces salaries. Since 1981 its chairman has been Lord Plowden. The TSRB's findings have not always been welcome to governments preaching pay restraint and pressing Members of Parliament to set a good example to others in respect of their own salaries (though the latter are now index-linked to civil service pay). The Thatcher government was almost defeated in the Commons in July 1985 over its acceptance of the TSRB proposal to raise salaries for top civil servants, judges and military personnel by an average of 46 per cent.

Soon after publication of the Priestley Report, a Pay Research Unit (PRU) was set up to apply the principle of 'fair comparison' to the bulk of the non-industrial civil service from the grade of assistant secretary downwards. Pay negotiations based on the PRU research cycles have one major drawback. As Geoffrey Fry points out, despite the massive public expenditure implications of civil service pay, 'ministers were excluded from the post-PRU negotiating process until near its end'.[3] The civil service unions regularly grumbled about government 'interference' with PRU-based settlements. But it is ministers who have to account, constitutionally and politically, for the allocation of taxpayers' money. As the economy went deeper into depression in the mid-1970s, and pay restraint became the order of the day, politicians and trade unionists became increasingly indignant at the apparent generosity of pay settlements to civil servants, perceived by many as advocates of tighter belts for everyone but themselves. Thus the independent machinery designed to take civil service pay out of the political arena came under increasing strain in an era of economic decline. Civil servants themselves were predictably dismissive of the view that they had had it too good for too long and were not slow to point out the constitutional implications of expecting a politically neutral civil service, loyally serving the government of the day, to be put in the front line of a government's attempts to impose economic discipline.

Pay research was suspended in 1976, the same year that saw the introduction of cash limits which have, since then, effectively dominated pay bargaining throughout the public sector. Although the PRU was later restored by the Callaghan government, with new safeguards intended to enhance its perceived impartiality and independence, Mrs Thatcher announced in October 1980 that its most recent findings were to be set aside. The government had already rejected the substantial pay rises for top civil servants, recommended by the TSRB, and was dismayed by the prospect of having to implement the substantial 'catching-up' public sector pay increases agreed, under pressure from militant unions, by the Callaghan administration. The civil service unions were denied access to the PRU's data (and failed later to persuade the courts that the information should be divulged). A cash limit of 6 per cent was set for the coming pay round. The civil service unions, having decided to ask for 15 per cent, began to talk about further industrial action if, as seemed certain, they did not get it.

At this point they did gain one crumb of comfort at the government's expense when a committee of inquiry into pensions, chaired by the Deputy Chairman of Lloyds Bank, Sir Bernard Scott, reported in February 1981.[4] This exercise had clearly been intended to deal with one of the most sensitive issues concerning civil service terms of service, namely the provision of (in theory) non-contributory indexed-linked pensions, a subject about which Mrs Thatcher is known to feel strongly.[5] However, to the government's dismay, the Scott Report not only endorsed the principle of inflation-proofing for public service pensions (subject to possible upward adjustment of the notional contribution element) but also concluded that private sector pension funds needed greater protection by way of new inflation-proof gilt-edged bonds. There was eventually an inconclusive Commons debate on the Scott Report on 22 October 1982, but little has since been heard on the subject. Some impetus has now gone out of the issue as the rate of inflation has diminished.

The civil service unions' campaign of industrial action in support of its pay claim began in March 1981 and ended 21 weeks later. The different unions, representing diverse vertical and horizontal groupings in the service (see next section), were for almost the first time united against what was widely seen as the last straw in the government's high-handed attitude towards the civil service. Even the First Division Association, representing the top advisory and managerial grades, narrowly voted to support the campaign (its first involvement in industrial action had been in 1979, in support of a 'day of action' which may, perhaps, have first encouraged the Thatcher government's antipathy towards civil service unions). Peter Hennessy noted at the time the irony of senior civil servants helping to plan industrial action while at the same time servicing the official Cabinet committee set up to devise counter-measures on behalf of the government.[6] Action mainly took the form of selective strikes by a small number of key personnel, particularly by staff operating the complex computer systems at the heart of the government's revenue-raising machinery. This had the advantage of hurting the government at small cost to union strike funds, and of not directly affecting the immediate comfort of the general public. The campaign also touched upon the operation of defence and security installations, precipitating the GCHQ crisis, discussed below. Eventually, the strike came to an end, having apparently achieved very little. The cost to the public sector borrowing requirement resulting from lost tax revenues was enormous; the unions won a settlement of just 7.5 per cent (the government having originally agreed 7 per cent), and promises of arbitration (whose findings would be subject to a veto by the House of Commons in the over-riding national interest) to resolve any differences in the next pay round. The strike hardened the government's attitude towards the unions, and was probably a major factor in Mrs Thatcher's decision to dismantle the Civil Service Department and transfer its responsibility for pay to the Treasury (see chapter 4). However, the government did decide to set up a major official inquiry into civil service pay to be chaired by Sir

John Megaw, a retired Lord Justice of Appeal and former President of the Restrictive Practices Court.

The government's own views were made clear in its submission to the arbitration tribunal set up to resolve the deadlock that arose in the next pay round. Having offered increases of between nothing at all and 5.5 per cent, depending on the market forces applicable to the recruitment of different categories of staff, the Treasury rejected the unions' argument that special help should be given to the low paid (a subject particularly close to the heart of the CPSA, the union which represents nearly 150,000 officials in the lower grades). The Treasury told the tribunal, in April 1982, that 'pay is a matter for the market place and social needs are the province of the social security system.'[7] The tribunal awarded an average increase of 5.9 per cent, with something for everyone, but no special treatment for low-paid staff. However, the Treasury awarded pay increases of up to 18 per cent to computer staff (who had spearheaded the 1981 dispute) to encourage recruitment in a fiercely competitive market.

The Megaw Report was published in July 1982 (with a dissenting report from the Committee's trade union member).[8] It recommended that pay comparisons should be used as a basis for 'informed collective bargaining' but that they should have 'much less decisive influence than in the past'. They should be more broadly based and take more account, for example, of rates paid by smaller firms: there should be annual reviews of pay trends, with a fuller review of total remuneration (providing an opportunity for 'catching-up' exercises) every fourth year. Data collection and analysis should be carried out by management consultants working under the auspices of an independent Pay Information Board (PIB) appointed by the Prime Minister. Market forces affecting recruitment should be taken into account in negotiations, though the Committee rejected proposals for significant decentralization of pay bargaining to departments. The Committee rejected the unions' contention that cash limits should not be fixed until after the completion of pay negotiations, but said that 'realistic' pay assumptions should, as far as possible, be built into cash limits. The Report recommended the introduction of performance-related pay (a proposal endorsed 14 years earlier by the Fulton Committee, but also very much in the fashionable spirit of 'Raynerism' etc., see chapter 10) at all but the most senior levels of the service, and the abolition of incremental scales for grades from principal to under secretary in favour of merit scales based on annual reports. The Civil Service Arbitration Agreement should be renegotiated to give both employers and unions the right to refuse to go to arbitration.

The 1983 pay round, against the backcloth of a 3.5 per cent cash limit for public sector pay, began with much sabre-rattling from the unions. There was a strike by DHSS staff in Birmingham and Oxford in protest against staff cuts which, as the unions forcefully pointed out, made it increasingly difficult to cope with a rising tide of demand for social security payments at a time of high unemployment. This strike eventually collapsed, but industrial unrest has flared up intermittently since then, and the problem of chronic undermanning of social security offices in deprived inner cities (some offices have closed down altogether) remains unresolved. In May 1984, about 380 computer staff at the DHSS offices in Newcastle went on strike over proposed cuts in pay for shift working: changes intended to cut public spending by £50,000 eventually cost the taxpayer some £200 million, mostly in payments to the Post Office to whom the essential work of processing pensions had to be sub-contracted. The Treasury was prompted to consider the desirability of decentralizing the civil service's computer network to make it less vulnerable to industrial action.[9]

Meanwhile, so far as the 1983 pay dispute was concerned, it was apparent both that most rank and file civil servants, remembering the negligible returns that had accrued from the 1981 dispute, had little stomach for the prospect of another major confrontation, and that the unions themselves were seriously divided. Eventually, a settlement of around 4.9 per cent was agreed.

In their 1983 election manifesto, the Conservatives proclaimed themselves 'committed to fair and reasonable levels of pay for those who work in the public services', and promised to seek 'sensible arrangements' for determining civil service pay following the Megaw Report. The unions were by no means united in their response to Megaw: some categories of civil servant, like the scientists represented by the IPCS (see next section), stood to do better out of the proposals than others. Most union leaders feared that the new PIB would undermine their negotiating role; but most of them also tacitly accepted that something along the lines proposed would be introduced eventually, the main question being when? In December 1984, a three-year experiment with merit bonuses, open to selected staff above the grade of principal, was announced – and denounced by the First Division Association as being arbitrary and divisive. The Association complained that the criteria of merit were too vague and that the scheme was being interpreted differently in different departments.

In October 1985, the Treasury unveiled its package of proposals based on the Megaw Report but without the PIB. Rather than entrusting comparability research to a new quango, the task would be carried out by the Office of Manpower Economics. There was renewed talk of introducing regional variations into civil service pay structures to reflect geographical differences in 'market forces' (the IPCS has since agreed to proposals that may open the door to local bargaining). Protracted negotiations ensued, with the unions (again divided on the issue) particularly concerned about the absence of any provision for binding arbitration. At the time of writing, the issue of pay comparability remains unresolved (the unions accepted a one-off 6 per cent pay offer in 1986), but it is difficult to envisage the Thatcher government (or indeed any other government) offering much more than the half-loaf baked by Megaw.

The Civil Service Unions

The civil service in the 1980s is intensively unionized at all levels. At least 80 per cent of non-industrial civil servants belong to a union.[10] The main civil service unions, federated under the umbrella of the Council of Civil Service Unions (CCSU, see below) are listed in table 6.1. But this state of affairs has not come about without a struggle. Historically, civil servants were employed, and could in theory (though not in practice) be summarily dismissed, according to 'Her Majesty's pleasure'; civil servants could not directly negotiate with the state about their terms of service; they could not sue in the Queen's courts for arrears of pay owed to them by the Crown. Only quite recently (see below) has most of the law relating to civil service employment been brought more or less into line with employment law elsewhere. Nineteenth-century permanent secretaries exercised autocratic control over their subordinates and negotiated personally with the Treasury about matters to do with pay, pensions and staff numbers.

Effective unions in the civil service were first founded in the Post Office in the 1880s and 1890s, and had spread slowly and haltingly to other areas of the public service by the beginning of the First World War.[11] The process continued under the umbrella of Whitleyism (see below) in the inter-war years, though the General Strike prompted the enactment of the Trade Disputes Act 1927, which made it illegal for any established civil servant to join a union unless its membership was confined to civil servants, was not associated with any organization outside the civil service, had no political objectives and was not affiliated to a political party. This Act was repealed by the Attlee government in 1946. Now even the

TABLE 6.1   *Unions affiliated to the Council of Civil Service Unions (1985)*

Union	Civil service membership[a]	Seats on CCSU	Main categories of staff represented
Civil and Public Services Association (CPSA)	147,189	19	Clerical and secretarial staff
Society of Civil and Public Servants (SCPS)	90,397	12	Lower and middle managment grades
Institution of Professional Civil Servants (IPCS)	85,689	11	Professional, scientific and other specialist staff
Inland Revenue Staff Federation (IRSF)	54,057	7	Clerical, secretarial and middle management grades in Inland Revenue
Civil Service Union (CSU)	36,135	5	Support staff such as cleaners, telephonists and messengers
Prison Officers' Association/ Scottish Prison Officers' Association (POA/SPOA)	25,575	4	Prison officers
Northern Ireland Public Service Alliance (NIPSA)	19,483	3	Staff employed by the Northern Ireland Civil Service[b]
First Division Association and Association of HM Inspectors of Taxes (FDA/AIT)	7,609	2	Higher management and equivalent specialist grades, and tax inspectors
Total	466,134	63	

[a]   Some unions include non-civil service members.
[b]   The Northern Ireland Civil Service is constitutionally separate from the British Civil Service, and is not generally included in other statistics in this book.
Source: Council of Civil Service Unions, Constitution, October 1985

First Division Association, representing higher management grades, is affiliated to the TUC (since 1977). Some civil service unions, increasingly at odds with the Thatcher government's tough stance towards trade unions and towards the public sector (attitudes having been hardened by the GCHQ dispute), have recently conducted ballots about the desirability of establishing 'political funds' to campaign against aspects of their employers' policies, and the CPSA has in fact done so. Industrial action has been a regular feature of civil service industrial relations, at least since 1973 when there was the first of an intermittent series of strikes about pay (including those discussed above). The extent to which the landscape has changed in this context is underlined by the GCHQ case, considered below.

One name at least has achieved immortality in the modern history of labour relations in the civil service, that of J. H. Whitley, the Liberal MP for Halifax, later to became Speaker of the House of Commons, who chaired a sub-committee of the wartime Reconstruction Committee, set up in 1916 to consider ways of improving relations between employers and employed. The first Whitley Report, published the following year, proposed a series of standing negotiating councils, organized on an industry-by-industry basis and operating at national, district and works levels to bring together both sides of industry.[12] Although these proposals were intended to apply to commercial organizations rather than to local and central government, pressure from public service staff leaders, who were not slow to highlight the government's reluctance to abide by recommendations that it was urging upon other employers, eventually forced the government to agree to the establishment of joint Whitley Councils throughout the civil service. The first meeting of the new National Whitley Council took place in July 1919.

Others have written histories of Whitleyism, and the story need not be retold here.[13] Suffice it to say that the introduction of Whitley Councils encouraged the growth of civil service unions simply because the whole system was predicated upon the existence and the co-operation of representative staff bodies. Whitleyism has been the basis of national, local and departmental machinery in central and local government ever since, and the Treasury itself, at least until very recently, has long encouraged civil servants to join their staff unions.[14] Nevertheless, it became abundantly clear from the outset that this negotiating machinery was not going to be allowed to compromise the government's sovereignty over its civil service: it was formally agreed in 1921 that 'the government has not surrendered, and cannot surrender, its liberty of action in the exercise of its authority and discharge of its responsibilities in the public interest.'[15]

And herein lies the rub. The polite conventions of Whitley negotiation, if they are to work, require almost superhuman self-restraint from unions who are constantly being asked to accept the government's ultimate responsibility to the taxpayer and the fact that their ministerial employers are answerable to Parliament and to the electorate for the conduct of public policy. Once civil service unions start behaving like other unions – affiliating to the TUC, threatening industrial action, criticizing the government's policy towards public sector pay (and how can civil servants fight for more pay in an era of cash limits without doing precisely that?), talking about setting up political funds – then Whitleyism is dead, in spirit if not in body. And, for one reason or another, the civil service unions have been moving, not all of them at the same speed, in this direction, at least since the late 1960s, though the Whitley machinery still flourishes at a local/departmental level.

In 1980, following a vigorous and successful bout of industrial action against the previous Callaghan government, the National Staff Side of the Whitley Council was replaced by the CCSU, and the Staff Side became the Trade Union Side at all levels of the Whitley system. The change was in part symbolic, but it also relected, as Fry observes, an overtly confrontational attitude on the part of the unions towards the new Thatcher government.[16]

The GCHQ Case

The constitutional relationship between ministers and civil servants has altered in many important respects, and the changing character of trade unionism in the civil service is both a cause and a consequence of the constitutional shift that has occurred. The extent of that shift is well illustrated by the GCHQ case, which unfolded in 1984.[17]

The Government Communications Headquarters (GCHQ) is an important part of the security system, whose main function is to provide signals intelligence for the government. Since its formation in 1947, the civil servants who staffed it had been allowed to join national civil service unions, and there were long-established practices of consultation between management and staff. However, between 1979 and 1981 there were seven instances of industrial action at GCHQ; most of these were minor incidents, but during the major dispute of 1981 the civil service unions decided, unwisely as many of them would probably admit with hindsight, to hurt the Thatcher government by directing part of their action at security and defence installations, and GCHQ was closed down for a short period. The Government was angry and embarrassed (particularly, it appears, in the eyes of its NATO allies) by what it saw as a grave and irresponsible threat to national security and took steps to negotiate an agreement that would prevent any recurrence. However, in December 1983, without warning, and with meetings between unions and management imminent, Mrs Thatcher privately issued an oral instruction in her capacity as Minister for the Civil Service, banning trade union membership among GCHQ staff.

The ban, together with a decision to deprive GCHQ staff of the statutory right of recourse to industrial tribunals, was announced to the House of Commons a month later. It was announced that staff would be offered £1,000 taxable compensation for the loss of their statutory rights. There was a storm of protest from many quarters, and the unions tried to persuade the government to accept a draft agreement to limit future industrial action at GCHQ. These representations made no headway, and the CCSU decided to seek a legal remedy against the government in the courts. In July 1984, Mr Justice Glidewell gave a judgement which, although it rejected several of the points advanced on behalf of the unions, ruled that the staff at GCHQ had a 'legitimate expectation' that they or their unions would be consulted before withdrawal of their rights and that the applicants were entitled to a legal declaration that the Prime Minister's instruction was invalid.

The unions' euphoria was short-lived. Three weeks later, the Court of Appeal upheld the government's appeal, accepting its contention (not raised in the court below) that the decision to ban the unions, and the procedures by which this had been achieved, were governed by over-riding considerations of national security, which the courts were not competent to question. In November, this ruling was finally upheld in the House of Lords, though there were crumbs of comfort for the unions, particularly in so far as the law lords repudiated the government's contention that action taken under the royal prerogative (which is the main basis of the legal relationship between the Crown and its employees) cannot in principle be reviewed in the courts. The door is now opened to litigation by civil servants and their unions to resolve many kinds of dispute about matters to do with employment and terms of service – so long as 'national security' is not invoked by ministers to forestall judicial intervention.

The government got its way, but at considerable cost. Whether right or wrong in principle, it was widely regarded as having handled the matter with astonishing heavy-handedness and unnecessary inflexibility. Industrial relations in the civil service, already in a fragile state, were further damaged, perhaps permanently. The case served to unite unions whose interests, in other contexts, were often divided. The issue has been kept alive by some of the staff at GCHQ, who have continued to defy the ban on union membership. In seeking to defend national security the government gave enormous publicity to the hitherto low-profile activities of GCHQ. (The mishandled Wright case in Australia in 1986–7 similarly raised the public profile of MI5 and MI6.)

The case went to the European Commission of Human Rights in Strasbourg early in 1987, and the unions failed to win a hearing before the Court of Human Rights. But despite this anti-climactic outcome, and whatever the *legal* implications of the GCHQ case (which will doubtless be debated by constitutional lawyers for many years to come), the crucial point is that it happened at all. When unions representing civil servants feel obliged to take the government – to whom their members owe their principal professional loyalty – to court, then we must surely begin to re-examine some of our fundamental assumptions about the present-day relationship between ministers and civil servants – a subject we shall return to in chapter 8.

The Legal Basis of Civil Service Employment

The law relating to civil service employment – an amorphous mixture of statute, Order in Council, formal Treasury regulations and less formal Treasury minutes – has evolved slowly and untidily. The ancient prerogatives of the Crown have had to adapt to the modern realities of, on the one hand, Cabinet government and parliamentary democracy and, on the other, the vastly complex bureaucracy required by a modern interventionist state. The law governing Crown Service has justly been described by one commentator as 'much criticised, confused and based upon unconvincing reasoning'.[18] This is an area of law into which the courts have seldom ventured, though there are a few scattered cases dealing, for instance, with the rather obscure, and surprisingly troublesome, question of whether civil servants have a legal right to sue for arrears of pay.[19]

The GCHQ case has almost certainly widened the potential scope for judicial resolution of industrial disputes between government and the civil service. It also introduced a much needed breath of fresh air into a very musty and hitherto obscure area of jurisprudence. Lord Roskill, for instance, was dismissive of the antique doctrine that civil servants are dismissable at will. In reality, he said, 'the management–staff relationship is governed by an elaborate code . . . [and] I have little doubt that, were management to seek to alter without prior consultation the terms and conditions of civil servants in a field which had no connection with national security or perhaps . . . with urgent fiscal emergency, such action would in principle be amenable to judicial review.'[20]

However, even after the GCHQ case, it is to be hoped that litigation over industrial disputes will be the exception rather than the rule so far as the day-to-day work of civil servants is concerned. It is unlikely that the courts, as such, will ever become a regular forum for resolving industrial disputes in such contexts. One reason for this is that, in the field of employment law generally, much of the responsibility for conflict resolution is assigned to specialist industrial tribunals. Legislation on such matters as sexual and racial discrimination applies explicitly to civil servants (as well it might, given that these are areas where the government should surely be setting a good example). Cases of wrongful dismissal, and discriminatory refusals to appoint or promote, are regularly resolved via the relatively informal procedures of tribunals, where aggrieved civil servants are usually represented by their trade unions: the civil service also has its own *internal* machinery for dealing with disputes. To cite just one notable illustrative example of this, in November 1986 Mrs Susan Rogerson, assistant head of the United Nations Department of the Foreign and Commonwealth Office, went to an industrial tribunal claiming that the Department had denied her appointment as Deputy High Commissioner in Zambia on sexually discriminatory grounds. The Department conceded that the allegation was true, and the case was withdrawn on the understanding that Mrs Rogerson would be given another posting of equivalent seniority.

Restrictions on Political Activity

Until the eighteenth century, it was not uncommon for civil servants to combine their official tasks with those of ministerial office. In most other EEC countries today, civil servants may become members of the legislature without resigning from their official posts, being given leave of absence for the discharge of their parliamentary duties. In Britain, however, civil servants are disqualified absolutely from election to either the House of Commons or the European Assembly, though the rules relating to local politics are less restrictive.[21] Civil servants are also subject to additional restrictions on political activity liable to give public expression to political views, rather than privately held beliefs and opinions.

Restrictions on political activity, which were formulated in 1953 in the wake of the Masterman Report of 1949, and subsequently refined in 1984 following the proposals of the Armitage Report in 1978, are a logical corollary of the convention of civil service neutrality which goes back to the mid-nineteenth century (see chapter 2).[22] The restrictions are based on the argument that a minister must be able to rely upon the loyalty of all the civil servants in his department, especially those with whom he has close contact. Civil service advice must be given as frankly and objectively as possible, and ministerial policies fully implemented, whatever the personal views of the officials concerned. In short, 'civil servants must not be so politically committed that they cannot easily comply with these basic constitutional requirements'.[23] Not only must civil servants carry out their duties with complete impartiality, but anyone who comes into contact with civil servants must also be confident that they do so. In the words of the Armitage Report, 'a democratic system of government requires that its citizens be satisfied that those they elect are enabled to govern without hindrance.'[24]

The degree of restriction will obviously vary according to the circumstances. The civil service is not a monolithic organization in which a single rule can be applied. There is no need for all civil servants to be subject to the same rules. Doubts about the political impartiality of a permanent secretary, the minister's principal policy adviser, would obviously arise if he openly supported one political party. But this would not be likely with, say, a van driver with the Property Services Agency or a typist in the Establishments Branch of the DES.

The rules relate to both national and local political activities. National political activities are defined as including adoption as a candidate for Parliament or the European Assembly, holding office in party organizations if the office impinges wholly or mainly on party politics in the field of Parliament or the European Assembly, speaking in public or expressing views in writing on matters of national political controversy, and canvassing on behalf of candidates for Parliament or the European Assembly, or on behalf of a political party. Local political activities are defined as including the same types of political activity in connection with local affairs.

For purposes of deciding the extent to which civil servants may take part in political activity, the civil service is divided into three main groups:

1 those in the 'politically free' group, consisting of industrial staff and non-office grades, who are completely free to engage in national and local political activities;
2 those in the 'politically restricted' group, comprising principals (and equivalent grades) and above, together with ATs and HEO(D)s. Civil servants in this group are debarred from engaging in national political activities, but may be given permission to participate in local political activities; and
3 those in an 'intermediate' group, comprising all civil servants not in either of the other two groups. Civil servants in this group are eligible for permission to participate in national and local politics, except candidature for Parliament or the European Assembly. However, certain staff are excluded, including those working in the private offices of ministers, and those whose work involves a significant amount of face-to-face contact with individual members of the public.[25]

How serious a restriction are these rules on the private lives and civil liberties of civil servants? As far as the politically restricted group of senior civil servants is concerned, probably not very much. As Richard Chapman puts it: 'they tend not to have burning desires to write to newspapers or become political leaders either nationally or locally. If they had wanted to do such things they would not have remained in established, senior posts in the Service.'[26] There is some evidence to support this view in the research sponsored by the Fulton Committee. One official interviewed in the survey on *Profile of a Profession* observed that because a senior civil servant works chiefly with politicians 'he soon becomes aware of the ineptitudes of any party.'[27] Or as a former official put it:

I learnt that peculiar neutrality as regards political issues which is the hall-mark of a Service which has to serve all parties alike. I learnt that the whole nation might be rent with political controversy and the papers full of scare-heads blaring forth Party slogans, yet, when one entered one's Ministry, one found the whole business hardly mentioned; that civil servants are so much concerned with the practical problems involved in implementing the policy of *any* Party, that, if they discuss politics at all, it tends to be in terms of the practical and unpractical, a subject about which cool argument is possible, rather than of right and wrong . . .[28]

Rules of Conduct

The conduct of all public servants is subject to the law of the land.
Civil servants must abide by the ordinary civil and criminal laws that
apply to all citizens. There are, in addition, particular statutes like the
Official Secrets Acts, which restrict the disclosure of official information (see chapter 9). It is an offence under the Prevention of
Corruption Act 1906 for a civil servant corruptly to accept any gift
or consideration as an inducement or reward, and there have been
several prosecutions under this Act, notably that of George Pottinger,
an under secretary at the Scottish Office who was imprisoned in
1974 for receiving money and other gifts from the architect, John
Poulson, for influencing the granting of a contract. There are, in
addition to laws as such, various written rules regarding such matters
as the acceptance of outside business appointments by senior civil
servants, and 'guidelines' for officials giving evidence before select
committees (the Osmotherly Rules, see chapter 9).

And, in a much more general sense, the legal position of Crown
servants is rather special. Thus Halsbury's encyclopaedic *Laws of
England* affirms the importance of 'the principle of legality' which
means that: 'The exercise of governmental authority directly affecting
individual interests must rest on legitimate foundations. For example,
powers exercised by the Crown, its ministers and central government
departments must be derived, directly or indirectly, from statute,
common law or the royal prerogative.'[29] We will discuss in the next
chapter how this legal principle applies in practice and the extent to
which the conduct of civil servants is susceptible to the scrutiny of the
courts by way of judicial review. Meanwhile, we shall address
ourselves to a subject which, although it may form part of the legal
framework of civil service conduct, has more to do with the somewhat
nebulous concept of 'professional duty' than with formal rules of law.

On the one hand, the civil servant owes obedience to the law. On
the other, he owes obedience to his minister (who is, of course, also
bound by law). However, there may be occasions on which the
precise nature and scope of a civil servant's legitimate obligations
may be unclear. For instance, a minister may, on political or other
grounds, give instructions to a civil servant which the latter may
consider illegal or improper. What should the civil servant do in such
circumstances? This has become a matter of considerable interest and
controversy in the past few years (e.g. in the context of the Ponting
and Westland affairs).

Experienced civil servants are familiar with the theoretical ground rules of the constitution – in particular, the conventions of individual and collective ministerial responsibility that underpin their relationships with ministers. But the practical scope and meaning of such conventions are not as clear as they may appear at first sight. This has given rise to difficulties. However, it has never been thought necessary to formulate a precise code of conduct for civil servants: 'because civil servants jealously maintain their professional standards. In practice the distinctive character of the British civil service depends largely on the existence and maintenance of a general code of conduct which, although to some extent intangible and unwritten, is of very real importance.'[30]

There are, however, a number of matters on which general instructions have been issued, and these can be found in the *Civil Service Pay and Conditions of Service Code* (CSPCSC) and the *Establishment Officers' Guide* (EOG). Thus the CSPCSC sets out a number of general principles which apply to all members of the service. They are:

1 undivided allegiance to the State at all times;
2 the avoidance of conflict between official duty and private interests;
3 refraining from private activities that might bring discredit on the Service;
4 honesty not only in fact, but also conduct that does not lay one open to suspicion of dishonesty; and
5 maintaining a proper reticence on matters of public and political controversy, so that one's impartiality is beyond suspicion.[31]

The EOG includes a number of 'specific points' which 'should be brought to the attention of new entrants'.[32] These range from instructions about the need to refrain from betting on official premises to guidelines about the purchase of articles of government property. Individual departments also have their own staff rules; for example, the Department of the Environment has its own rules about relations with contractors.

In addition to the general principles laid down in CSPCSC, and the specific points in the EOG, there is also what the First Division Association has described as a 'network of understandings and practices' among civil servants.[33] Maurice Wright distinguishes between those understandings and practices that guide a civil servant in his work, and which vary from post to post and among departments, and those professional values or basic work assumptions that seem to be common to all civil servants. These values, or basic work assumptions, include:

1 Wide acceptance of the principle of reciprocity in everyday relations with fellow civil servants;
2 disposition to reach agreement with colleagues;
3 avoidance of political embarrassment to ministers;
4 'fairness and honesty';
5 mutual trust and confidence;
6 formal and informal rules governing accessibility;
7 the importance of precedent; and
8 the ethic of secrecy and confidentiality.[34]

As Wright observes, these and other professional values give rise directly to some of the 'understandings and practices' which guide and influence the civil servant in the actual performance of his job.[35] For example, there are 'rules' which guide a civil servant in deciding whom to contact, both within and outside the service.

But does this combination of formal and informal rules of conduct provide sufficient guidelines for the civil service? The First Division Association for one, does not think so. It pointed out nearly 20 years ago that there were many situations which civil servants face in their daily work to which the general principles, now enshrined in the CSPCSC, do not provide adequate guidance.[36] More recently, in response to increasing tension between ministers and senior civil servants, it has argued for a professional code of ethics (see chapter 9).

Particular concern has been expressed about the definition of the civil servant's duty to his minister. Where do a civil servant's duties really lie – towards his minister, towards the government of the day, towards Parliament or towards the community as a whole? There are, of course, already exceptions to the presumption that the civil servant has a paramount duty to his minister. A civil servant is entitled to refuse a request from a minister to see the papers of a preceding government. A civil servant can also refuse to accept ministerial instructions to prepare a bank of parliamentary questions to farm out to friendly MPs. A permanent secretary (in his capacity as an accounting officer) can also place on record his disagreement with any expenditure decision which he considers he would have difficulty in defending before the Public Accounts Committee, carrying out the minister's decision only on a written instruction from the minister.[37] Such exceptions notwithstanding, there is a penumbra of genuine uncertainty about the parameters of civil service conduct, an issue which has come to the forefront of minister – civil service relations dramatically in the 1980s in the wake of the Ponting and Westland affairs. We shall return to this important issue in chapter 9.

Postscript

In 1988, the CSU amalgamated with the SCPS to form the National Union of Civil and Public Servants, which, with a membership of about 120,000, became the second-largest civil service union. There have also been important developments on the civil service pay front. Between 1987 and 1989 the five main unions all agreed long-term flexible pay deals with the Treasury. All five agreements were based on a single pay scale, which incorporated performance pay and arrangements for advancing pay for posts in areas where there are problems of recruitment and retention. The arrangements also included a form of pay comparability with the private sector.[38]

Important developments concerning the rules governing the conduct of civil servants took place in 1990. The CSPCSC was revised in March in order to bring it into line with the law, following the passage of the Official Secrets Act 1989 (on which, see the postscript to chapter 9). Concern about the changes to the Code were expressed by the civil service unions, particularly the FDA, who asserted that the wording of the code made the civil servant's duties too 'absolute'. The Treasury and Civil Service Committee launched an inquiry and recommended clarification of the Code to ensure that civil servants are not under an absolute duty of loyalty to ministers. It said that a reference to the duty of loyalty to the Crown being 'for all practical purposes owed to the Government of the day' should be clarified by a cross-reference to the Armstrong Memorandum (revised in 1987),[39] which qualified the duty of loyalty in several important respects. It also recommended that civil servants should have a clear right to appeal to the Head of the Home Civil Service where they believed that there was a case of illegality, impropriety or maladministration.[40] The government agreed to amend the Code to cover both these points.[41]

7

The Working Context

Civil Servants and their Departments

Government departments are a pervasive feature of civil service life, and we must give due consideration to their nature and their internal structure. Whitehall is, of course, not a monolithic bureaucracy: the size and functions of departments vary enormously, as do their internal arrangements. In evidence to the Fulton Committee an academic observer, Trevor Smith, argued that Whitehall can be viewed as a complex of departments which can be differentiated according to their organizational structures and the nature of decision-making processes within those structures.[1] At one end of what Smith calls the continuum of 'bureaucratic modernity' are departments, such as the Home Office, whose functions are mainly traditional and which fit the classic description of the conduct of government business, with generalist civil servants pre-eminent. Further along the continuum are more 'advanced' departments like the Department of Education and Science, which have, *inter alia*, greater internal functional division. At the other end of the continuum are departments like the Treasury and the Ministry of Defence which represent 'the high-water mark of departmental development', where decision-making is highly complex and technical and where specialists make a major, often predominant, contribution.

There is no such organization as a 'typical' government department. Departments differ greatly in size, ranging from the tiny Department of Energy, with just over 1,000 staff, to the giant Ministry of Defence (MOD), with over 170,000. Larger departments are more complex organizations than their smaller counterparts. As Pitt and Smith point out: 'The larger departments present different problems of specialization, line management, co-ordination and planning from the small departments . . . larger departments will probably have a more decentralized system of financial control [and] may require collegiate arrangements for personnel management and budgeting.'[2] Giant departments may also include departmental agencies – identifiable units within a department under the direction of a minister accountable to Parliament, but with an executive head, and with a degree of financial and managerial autonomy. Thus the organization chart of the MOD includes the Defence Procurement Executive, while that of the Department of the Environment (DOE) includes the Property Services Agency (see chapter 10).

Departments also differ greatly in the complexity of their functions. The DES, for example, is what Dunleavy calls a 'control' agency, supervising the activities of other public sector agencies, while having no major responsibilities for service delivery of its own. (The 'delivery' agencies which directly undertake the provision of educational services to individuals are the local education authorities and the universities.) By contrast, the Department of Health and Social Security has three agency roles: as a control agency for the National Health Service, where the delivery agencies are health authorities; as a control agency for the personal social services, which are delivered by local authorities; and as a 'transfer' agency directly administering the delivery of social security benefits to individuals.[3]

The organization charts of some departments are also complicated by the fact that certain functions are decentralized to local and regional offices. As we saw in our discussion of the statistical profile of the civil service in chapter 3, about three-quarters of the non-industrial civil service work outside London. One of the major developments in British central government since the Second World War has been the extent to which government departments have delegated authority to regional offices, partly to enable central government policy to be modified in the light of local conditions, and partly to promote speed of action. Most 'home' departments have a regional organization, although there is no uniformity about the boundaries or areas of the various regions. While, for example, the DOE (which shares it regional organization with the Department of Transport (DOT) which, as we saw in chapter 4, was part of the DOE until it regained separate status in 1976) divides England into eight regions, the DHSS has only six regions.

Regional offices perform a variety of tasks.[4] Some directly provide a service (e.g. the Department of Trade and Industry's regional offices provide financial assistance to firms). Some regional offices are concerned with the supervision of offices within the organization (e.g. the DHSS regional offices supervise a network of over 800 local social security offices). Other regional offices have 'oversight' functions concerning smaller areas (e.g. the regional offices of the DOE/DOT act as intermediaries between departmental headquarters and local authorities). The variety of regional boundaries and tasks is paralleled by different ways of organizing regional administration. The chief regional officers of the Ministry of Agriculture, Fisheries and Food are responsible for the general co-ordination of the work of the Ministry in the region. The Home Office, on the other hand, has no single co-ordinated regional structure, with regional officials directly responsible to the appropriate division at headquarters: for example, the Prison Service has four regions, each under a regional director.[5]

Several departments also have an extensive network of local offices which represent departments at the local level in the administration of national policy. Dealing directly with members of the public, such offices are the 'public face' of the department (see chapter 9). We have already referred to the extensive local office network of the DHSS. Other local offices include the local unemployment offices of the Department of Employment and the job centres of the same department.

In addition to the decentralization of authority to local and regional offices, some departments have moved headquarters units away from the London area. The dispersal of operations involving the processing of large volumes of routine clerical work from London to the provinces has the advantages of moving posts from an area where overheads are expensive to cheaper areas where, as a bonus, the availability of civil service jobs can make at least a symbolic contribution to the alleviation of high rates of unemployment. The centralized records offices of the DHSS at Newcastle and North Fylde near Blackpool, the Pensions Branch of the Department of Education and Science at Darlington, and the Driver and Vehicle Licensing Centre at Swansea are some examples. The MSC moved to Sheffield in the early 1980s, as part of the response to the Hardman proposals on the dispersal of government work from London (see chapter 3). Another type of departmental office often located in the provinces is the specialist establishment, normally engaged in performing a special function not associated with the nationwide administration of policy. Examples include research and development establishments, and the Government Communications Headquarters at Cheltenham.

In addition to the various offices located outside the London area, there are three departments specifically organized on a geographical, as opposed to functional, basis: the Scottish, Welsh and Northern Ireland Offices, each with their own secretary of state in the Cabinet. Northern Ireland, of course, has its own civil service and Civil Service Commission responsible for recruitment. There is a certain amount of intercharge of staff between it and the home civil service (in January 1986, 175 staff of the home civil service worked in the Northern Ireland Office) but this only occurs to a limited extent.[6]

The Scottish and Welsh Offices both include small ministerial offices in London which deal with other Whitehall departments and with the conduct of parliamentary business. The operational units, however, are based in Edinburgh and Cardiff. The Scottish Office comprises five departments - Agriculture and Fisheries, Development, Home and Health, Education and Industry – each under the charge of a secretary (of deputy secretary rank) who reports directly to the secretary of state. The permanent under secretary is senior adviser to the secretary of state and directly supervises the work of the Central Services Division.[7] Apart from law and order, the Welsh Office has almost the same executive responsibilities as its Scottish counterpart, and is divided into 15 major groups of services, some of which are further sub-divided into divisions.[8]

The Internal Structure of Government Departments

Although there is a variety of different departmental structures, they are all put together out of what Mackenzie and Grove call the same 'box of components', rather like a giant Lego set.[9] The fact that the number of components is limited, and the methods of fitting them together fairly simple, means that it is possible to outline the 'components' which are common to all departments. We will illustrate this discussion by reference to the internal structure of the DES (figure 7.1).

Government departments are directly under the control of a minister responsible to Parliament for the conduct of his department. Ministers are assisted by a team of junior ministers, each of whom has duties delegated to him (see chapter 8). In the case of the DES, the secretary of state is supported by a minister of state and three parliamentary under secretaries. Ministerial heads also have a private office (not shown in figure 7.1), which is the minister's own personal secretariat, and generally headed by a principal (see chapter 8).

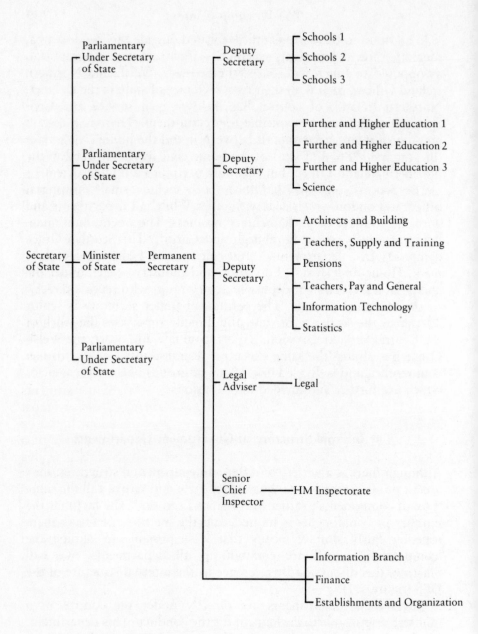

Figure 7.1   Organization of the Department of Education and Science, September 1987 (*Source:* the Department of Education and Science)

Below the ministerial team, the hierarchy of the department is, in the words of a former minister, 'all neatly plotted out like a family tree of some royal dynasty or the pedigree of an expensive dog'.[10] The most senior civil servant in the departmental hierarchy is the permanent secretary (officially titled the permanent under secretary of state in departments, like the DES, with secretaries of state as ministerial heads). The permanent secretary has four main functions.[11] He is the minister's most immediate adviser on policy; he is the 'managing director' of the day-to-day business of the department; and he has ultimate responsibility for the staffing and organization of the department. He is also the department's accounting officer, and as such has direct responsibility to Parliament for both the legality and efficiency of departmental expenditure. As we shall see in chapter 10, it is the permanent secretary, and not the minister, who appears before the House of Commons Public Accounts Committee to answer points raised in the Comptroller and Auditor-General's reports.

These functions add up to a heavy burden, and in giant departments like the MOD and the DHSS the permanent secretary is assisted by a second permanent secretary. The Treasury, the 'department of departments', has two second permanent secretaries. The Fulton Committee believed that the highest level of departments needed reinforcing even more, and recommended that in most departments responsibility for long-term policy planning should be given to a specially appointed senior policy adviser in charge of a planning unit, with direct access to the minister. This particular idea was dismissed by the Civil Service Department on the grounds that it was difficult to reconcile with the requirements of accountability and organizational effectiveness.[12]

The permanent secretary is assisted by one or more deputy secretaries. In the DES, three deputy secretaries each direct broad areas of the department's work: schools; further and higher education and science; and various subjects, including the supply of teachers and their pension arrangements. The senior chief inspector, who heads Her Majesty's Inspectorate, and the legal adviser (both of whom are specialists) are also of deputy secretary rank.

The basic operating units of a department are the branches (sometimes, confusingly, called divisions or departments) which deal with a major section of the department's functions. Branches are headed by under secretaries, described (along with the more senior and experienced assistant secretaries) by Dorothy Johnstone as 'the hinge of the Service, meaning that they have a hinge's responsibility for the firm or wobbly functioning of the whole apparatus'.[13] The vital role of under secretaries was emphasized by the report of the Wardale inquiry into the staffing of the open structure level, which described them as 'closely identified with a coherent and discrete area . . . They did the sort of job where the holder could be thought of as, say, "Mr Coal" and brought together a number of sub-elements relating to such an entity.'[14] The under secretary has been described by one permanent secretary as 'the critical level for decisions. He is the key man: he should be able to see the problem in the round, yet know enough about the small print to dip into it.'[15]

Under secretaries are key figures in the DES: according to a former Minister of Education, the under secretary 'will be well known to the university world, or the local authority world, or the teachers' organizations'.[16] Such was the influence of the under secretary in charge of the branch concerned with higher education in the local authority sector in the mid-1970s that he was described by one polytechnic director as 'the Czar of the Colleges of Education'.[17]

In 1987 the DES had 17 main branches. Five of them – statistics; information technology; legal; establishments and organisation; and finance – are all common service branches. Every major department has a finance branch and an establishment branch, although the Department of Transport has its establishment services provided for it by the DOE. In the case of the DES, the heads of both these branches (along with the head of the legal branch) report direct to the permanent secretary. A department's finance branch is headed by a principal finance officer (of deputy or under secretary rank) called the Accountant General in the DES, and responsible for the department's financial and accounting policies and procedures. The finance branch deals with forward estimating, including the costing of functions and policy for the Public Expenditure Survey; the preparation of parliamentary estimates and cash limits; and the regularity and propriety of expenditure. The principal finance officer acts as 'a bridge' between the department and the Treasury.[18] The other major common services branch, establishments, is concerned with the organization, staffing and accommodation of a department.

Branches are sub-divided into a number of divisions, each headed by an assistant secretary, and may be further sub-divided into a number of sections, each controlled by a principal. Whereas under secretaries supervise wide areas of policy, like the DES's FHE1 Branch, which is essentially concerned with higher education, assistant secretaries handle the detail of policies. Thus, FHE1 Branch in the DES has four divisions dealing with academic and institutional development in the local authority sector of higher education; higher education in the university sector; the voluntary and direct grant colleges, the Royal College of Art and Cranfield Institute of Technology; and the Secretariat to the Computer Board for Universities and Research Councils. The assistant secretary is the senior civil servant directly concerned with preparing policy advice, and 'for practical purposes many government decisions depend crucially on the work done and conclusions reached' by them.[19]

As Pitt and Smith show in their book *Government Departments*, the division of departments often reflects the distinction between administrative, managerial and professional work.[20] Some branches or divisions are concerned with 'administrative' work within a particular policy area, including policy development and the preparation of legislation; case work generated by individual decisions, which may involve ministerial correspondence and parliamentary questions (see chapter 9); financial planning and control; and the supervision of large blocks of staff. Some branches and divisions provide managerial and professional services rather than being concerned with substantive areas of a department's work. Thus some divisions are concerned with 'management' work of a routine kind, including record keeping, purchasing of equipment etc., whilst specialist branches provide technical services requiring vocationally trained personnel, such as architects, engineers and other specialists (e.g. the legal branch of a department such as the DES).

The Subordination of the Specialist

The role of specialists in the departmental structure has been the subject of debate for many years. As we saw in chapter 2, unlike the civil services of other countries where the specialist occupies a relatively dominant position, the British civil service is essentially a generalist elite, and access of specialists to higher management and policy-making posts within departments has been restricted.

Specialists have been traditionally organized into parallel and joint hierarchies. In parallel hierarchies, responsibility is bisected: finance and overall policy control are reserved for administrators, organized in one hierarchy, while technical advice is provided by specialists, organized in a separate, but parallel, hierarchy. In joint hierarchies, an administrator and a specialist are joint heads of a block of work, but at lower levels the separation of functions between the two groups still occurs.

The argument for generalist administrators has been put cogently by a former permanent secretary, who said that it is the job of the administrator 'to take and understand the advice of experts in the different disciplines on any particular problem, to analyse and assess that advice, and to reach a balanced view on the pros and cons of different possible courses of action'.[21] The danger of specialists filling such a role is that their specialism may prevent them from taking a sufficiently detached view. It is also argued that ministers need administrators who have the skills in operating the Whitehall machine, and who can take an overall view of issues which may have wider political implications. As C. H. Sisson observed in his elegant defence of the generalist administrator:

The Minister has to make sure that he is in possession of all the information that he needs about the results and risks of the course of action he is advised to take, whether or not they are relevant to the objective the specialist has in mind, and he has to place that information in a context which is not less wide than the political complex of aims and pressure in which the cabinet acts. It is because the decision to be taken is so much wider than the speciality that senior administrative officials have to learn to extract from the specialist flowers around them the honey their Minister needs, explaining as they do so that the Minister does not live on honey.[22]

Others, however, reject the myth that only generalists can understand the Whitehall machine and advise on policy. For them, the work of policy formulation and management in government departments depends on the successful integration of specialists and generalists.[23] Gunn, for example, has argued that the subordination of the specialist has serious implications for the quality of governmental decision-making. Ministers may be isolated from specialist knowledge, and kept in ignorance of the range of options available, while the transmission of expert advice through a generalist hierarchy may result in that advice being distorted.[24]

The subordinate position of the specialist in the departmental structure was a major theme of the critique of the civil service in the 1960s, and many of the Fulton recommendations stemmed from the conclusion that specialists should be accorded a more prominent role. Fulton argued that the organization of officials into parallel and joint hierarchies produced delay and inefficiency, prevented specialists exercising the full range of responsibilities usually associated with their profession, and obscured responsibility and accountability. In Fulton's view, administrators and specialists should be integrated in teams of unified hierarchies under single heads. The Committee also argued that the introduction of a unified grading structure would facilitate the introduction of such arrangements.[25]

Some integration of hierarchies did take place in the wake of Fulton, notably in the Ministry of Public Building and Works (which was to form the basis of the Property Services Agency created in 1972), the then Ministry of Housing and Local Government, and the Prison Department of the Home Office. But a Civil Service Department survey which reported in 1970 found that most departments questioned the benefits of unified hierarchies, and departments were not really encouraged to make major changes in their hierarchical organization.[26] Most departments have retained parallel hierarchies, the Fulton proposals having, in the words of John Garrett, a member of the management consultancy group employed by the Committee, been 'buried by the Civil Service'.[27]

As for the Fulton proposals on unified grading, as we saw in chapter 2 the rationalization of grading which followed Fulton included the creation of an open structure at the top of the civil service, to be filled in theory by the most suitable persons available, whether generalist or specialist. But although a substantial proportion of posts in the open structure is filled by officials whose previous service has been wholly or mainly in specialist grades – CSD evidence to the Expenditure Committee in 1976 put the figure at nearly 40 per cent[28] – most of them are working in positions in their own professional areas, e.g. a planner as Chief Planner at the DOE, and an architect as Director General of Design Services in the same department. Despite the Fulton proposals, the dominance of the generalist in the departmental hierarchy has not really changed. Policy-making is almost exclusively the preserve of the generalist administrator.

The External Environment of Departments

Any discussion of the work of civil servants must take account of the environment in which departments operate. A useful framework is that employed by Pitt and Smith, who discuss the characteristics of the environment of departments in terms of a system of values associated with institutions.[29] The values they identify are accountability, efficiency, legality, fairness, reasonableness and consultation. These values interact with departments through the medium of the institutions representing those values: Parliament, the courts, administrative tribunals, the Parliamentary Commissioner for Administration, pressure groups and so on. The values, and the institutional arrangements associated with them, 'represent constraints imposed on departments from the outside. These constraints are the expectations which the community has about the way in which departments should operate.'[30]

The values and institutions identified by Pitt and Smith are those of a liberal democratic system of government, a key component of which is the idea of 'responsible government'. As Birch demonstrates, 'responsible government' is a term which is used in a number of ways, one of which is that individual ministers are accountable to Parliament for the work of their departments through the doctrine of ministerial responsibility.[31] Accountability to Parliament is institutionalized in various ways, including ministerial correspondence, question time and select committees, all of which will be discussed in more detail in our later discussion of the civil service and Parliament in chapter 9. As we shall see in chapter 8, although the validity of the doctrine of ministerial responsibility in its classic sense of requiring a minister to resign for departmental failures has been the subject of much debate, the doctrine is still an important factor in the everyday procedures of departments. As Birch notes: 'there is no doubt that the behaviour of civil servants is affected by the knowledge that, if they make a mistake or offend a member of the public, the matter may be raised in Parliament a few days later.'[32]

The doctrine is reflected in, and reinforces, the hierarchical structure of departments, a characteristic of all bureaucratic organizations (see chapter 1). In the words of the Fulton Committee: 'Decisions often have to be referred to a higher level than their intrinsic difficulty or apparent importance merits . . . because they involve the responsibility of the Minister to Parliament and may be questioned there.'[33] The point was well put by the Director General of the Prison Service in evidence to the House of Commons Home Affairs Committee:

The bureaucracy, the headquarters organisation, is necessary because of the need for accountable government. The Home Secretary is immediately accountable to Parliament for the running of the Prison Service and it is necessary for him to have a machine which enables him to answer questions and give full account of what is going on.[34]

For this reason, the delegation of authority is particularly difficult in the civil service, an issue to which we will return in our later discussion of attempts to import private sector management techniques into government departments (see chapter 10).

Another constraint generated by the environment of departments is that of efficiency, described by Pitt and Smith as 'a public expectation, channelled again through parliamentary procedure, that government departments will be efficient'.[35] As mentioned above, permanent secretaries (in their capacity as accounting officers) have a direct relationship with Parliament, having to appear before the Public Accounts Committee to answer questions arising out of the reports of the Comptroller and Auditor-General, who is charged with the auditing of departmental accounts. Our later discussion of developments in efficiency audit (see chapter 10) will show that the PAC's role has developed far beyond the traditional concern with the legality and regularity of departmental expenditure to a wider concern with issues of administrative efficiency, effectiveness and value for money. As Mackenzie and Grove observe, the existence of the Committee affects the whole atmosphere of a department because in 'making day-to-day decisions about action and about procedure [the permanent secretary] is constantly aware that he may be called upon to answer in detail some two years later'.[36] The importance of efficiency as a constraint on the work of departments has been emphasized even more since the election of the Conservative government in 1979, and its attempts to create a 'slimmer and fitter' civil service. As we will see in chapter 10, recent developments have profound implications for the culture and working methods of departments.

As well as the constraints imposed by accountability and efficiency, civil servants are also expected to act within the law. Government departments, like other public bodies, must act legally and not do anything outside the powers conferred on the minister (*ultra vires*). The *ultra vires* rule is enforced by the courts, and there are a number of judicial remedies by which government departments can be compelled to fulfill their statutory obligations, and by which unlawful action can be quashed. Recent procedural reforms – notably the rationalization of administrative law remedies and the grouping together of judicial review cases in a special list in the Divisional Court – have facilitated and systematized the processes by which citizens can seek redress from the courts against administrative action or inaction.[37]

The willingness of the courts to review the procedural correctness of administrative action has increased markedly since the mid-1960s. One spectacular example was the 'TV licences' case in 1975, where the Home Office had threatened to revoke certain television licences purchased in advance of an announced increase in the fee. The Court of Appeal held that the Home Secretary had acted *ultra vires*, his action being an improper use of the powers given to him for other purposes.[38] More recently, regulations made by the Secretary of State for Social Services, concerning board and lodging allowances payable to unemployed people, were successfully challenged in the courts, as was the decision by the Secretary of State for Transport to raise the level of the tolls on vehicles crossing the Severn Bridge.

Civil servants also have a personal responsibility for criminal action. Ministerial responsibility to Parliament for the actions of their officials does not absolve the individual civil servant from his obligation to act within the law in carrying out his duties. For example, if a civil servant is knowingly a party to a decision to conceal or misrepresent the legal entitlement of an individual, he is open to a charge of conspiracy to defraud. The kind of problems involved were raised in a report by the Parliamentary Commissioner for Administration in 1978, involving a case where the DHSS, and its forerunner departments, had deliberately withheld arrears of payment of war pensions because checking all the cases would have been too great an exercise. Officials deliberately chose not to correct administrative procedures for existing pensioners except when they had to, and even then disguised what they were doing by a misleading explanation. Following the publication of the Commissioner's report, the matter was referred to the Director of Public Prosecutions to consider whether a charge of conspiracy to defraud should be brought against the officials concerned.[39] No charge was made, but the episode gave rise to concern that civil servants, in carrying out their duties in administering the legal entitlement of members of the public, and in taking decisions that they believed to be justified on administrative and economic grounds, might run the risk of acting illegally. Thus the requirement to act lawfully casts a long shadow over the civil servant's desk. As a former senior civil servant has pointed out, legal concepts 'must always be in the forefront of the minds of those working in administrative systems'.[40]

Individual grievances against departments may, of course, arise from actions which, while legal, are seen to be unfair. Thus another constraint within which civil servants have to operate is the expectation that they act fairly in their dealings with members of the public. One consequence of the growth of government activity discussed in chapter 2 is that government departments are responsible for administering a variety of benefits and exemptions for which individuals are eligible, provided that they meet certain criteria. DHSS officials, for example, take millions of decisions each year concerning the entitlement of claimants to social security benefits.

Inland Revenue staff take similar decisions on the entitlement of taxpayers to exemptions. There is often disagreement between individuals and departments over the assumptions made by civil servants on the application of general policy rules to specific cases. Is Mrs Brown entitled to social security benefit? Has Mr Green been correctly assessed for income tax by his tax inspector?

As Pitt and Smith point out: 'Such conflicts between the department and the citizen must be resolved in a way which is accepted as fair by both sides.'[41] Hence the provision of administrative tribunals to adjudicate in such cases. Thus if Mrs Brown is dissatisfied with the decision by her local DHSS office about her claim for social security benefit, she may appeal to a local social security appeal tribunal. If Mr Green does not accept that he has been correctly assessed for income tax, he has a right of appeal to the General Commissioners of Income Tax.

The existence of such adjudicating machinery has a profound effect on the working arrangements of the departments concerned. As Pitt and Smith note: 'They place a special responsibility on departmental officials to take reasoned decisions which will stand up under scrutiny of a tribunal. Codes, departmental rules, guidelines and instructions have to be formulated to control the discretion of officials when working within broad and perhaps vague statutory prescriptions.'[42]

Not only are civil servants expected to behave fairly in their dealings with members of the public, but they are also expected to conform to acceptable standards of administration: what Pitt and Smith refer to as 'reasonableness'.[43] Although there is no formal code of 'good administration' in the British civil service, the value of reasonableness is institutionalized in the office of the Parliamentary Commissioner for Administration, commonly known as the Ombudsman, although he is a pale shadow of his Scandinavian namesakes.[44] Established in 1967, the office deals with complaints of injustice arising from maladministration by government departments, a concept not defined in the relevant legislation, but generally agreed to include such lapses as bias, delay, incompetence and arbitrariness. Examples of cases where injustice caused by maladministration has been found include mishandling of tax affairs by the Inland Revenue and numerous instances of discourtesy or failure to answer letters. Predictably, it is the two departments with the largest number of dealings with members of the public, the DHSS and the Inland Revenue, which are at the top of the league table when it comes to complaints received and upheld.

It is often argued that one of the benefits of the Commissioner is the additional care that civil servants take in the way they carry out their duties. According to the first holder of the office, Sir Edmund Compton, the presence of the Commissioner has a 'tonic effect' upon departments in improving the quality of administration, a view which has been reiterated by another former Commissioner, Sir Cecil Clothier: 'I have no doubt that in a number of cases potential complaints have never reached me simply because an administrator, aware that some day his actions might be investigated by me, has taken a little more time and trouble in dealing with someone's affairs.'[45]

It has sometimes been argued that the presence of the Commissioner is liable to lead to 'defensive' administrative techniques and encourage the bureaucratic traits of rigidity and working 'according to the book' referred to in chapter 1. Clothier, however, 'saw no sign of such an effect'. On the other hand, 'there was ample evidence of a healthy regard for the need to avoid the attentions of the PCA.'[46]

Despite such benefits, however, there are inevitably costs. The Commissioner's investigations generate increased workloads for the departments concerned – what Compton refers to as the 'coefficient of friction' – calculated at about one and a half man-days per case, although one department has suggested that the figure is at least five man-days.[47] It is also possible that the presence of the Commissioner may work against delegation, with civil servants referring decisions upwards to their superiors in the departmental hierarchy.

The work of government departments is also influenced by the political culture, that sum of attitudes and beliefs which, in the words of Dennis Kavanagh, 'create predispositions for people to behave in a particular way or which provide justifications for behaviour', and which results in certain forms of political behaviour and institutions being regarded as 'normal' and others as 'abnormal'.[48] One type of political behaviour which is regarded as 'normal', and is, as we shall see in chapter 9, actively encouraged, is the convention that government departments consult with certain groups in the process of policy formulation and administration. As Kavanagh observes, the practice of consultation with affected and recognized interests is a 'cultural norm' in British government. Pressure groups 'expect' to be consulted about the detail of forthcoming legislation and adminstrative change likely to affect them. Consultation is a 'rule' of policy-making and political etiquette.[49]

Consultation as a cultural norm is, of course, reinforced by functional necessity. In the age of the modern collectivist state, departments are increasingly dependent on certain pressure groups for advice, information and co-operation, and consultation is institutionalized in a variety of formal (and informal) working arrangements. Indeed, it has been suggested that such arrangements are a major feature of the British policy style, with policy the outcome of a process of adjustment between pressure groups and government departments.[50] We will discuss this further in chapter 9.

Postscript

The hiving off of civil servants from many government departments to executive agencies as a result of the Next Steps programme introduced in 1988 (see chapter 12) has important implications for the status of departments which have acted as transfer and delivery organizations. Thus the hiving off of large sections of the Department of Social Security to agencies like the Social Security Benefits Agency means that the department will be transformed from a transfer to a control organization.[51]

8

Ministers and Civil Servants

The relationship between ministers and permanent secretaries has been described as 'the vital joint in Whitehall – the elbow of government, between decision and execution'.[1] It is a relationship which has been compared by Lord Beveridge with that of husband and wife in a Victorian household. The minister is the head of the household, formally taking all important decisions, but doing all this on advice, which he usually finds 'very uncomfortable to disregard'. Though head of the household, he is not really in charge of it. The household is minded by the permanent secretary, who sees 'that the Minister, before he goes out to his daily toil in Cabinet or Parliament, is properly equipped with all necessary information'. Like the Victorian wife, the permanent secretary 'has no public life; is quite unknown outside the house; wields power by influence rather than directly'.[2]

Underpinning the traditional relationship between minister and civil servant is what Gunn refers to as a 'chain of inter-locking conventions', which maintains that ministers are responsible for the actions of their departments, and that civil servants are anonymous, permanent and politically neutral.[3] Let us look briefly at the links in this constitutional chain before turning to discuss their status in today's civil service.

The heart of the relationship between ministers and civil servants is the convention that ministers are individually responsible to Parliament for the conduct of their civil servants, a doctrine regarded by Sir Ivor Jennings as 'the overriding constitutional convention which regulates the whole service'.[4] The idea of 'responsibility' is an elusive and slippery one resembling, in Geoffrey Marshall's words, 'the procreation of eels'.[5] It has two main strands: the first is that a minister has an obligation to answer for, and explain to Parliament, the work of his department: what has been referred to as 'explanatory accountability'.[6] The second strand is that the minister, in addition to being responsible for his own conduct, is also responsible for every failure of departmental policy and administration, and should resign if the failure is a serious one. Although, as we shall see later, ministers rarely feel obliged to resign for departmental failures, the answerability strand of the doctrine is still important. As we saw in chapter 7, the obligation on the minister to defend and explain departmental actions to Parliament through such procedures as question time, adjournment debates and select committees has profound implications for departmental organization and the work of civil servants.

Individual ministerial responsibility is complemented by the tradition of civil service anonymity. All decisions are taken in the minister's name, and civil servants are neither publicly identified with the decisions and policies of the government of the day, nor directly accountable to Parliament for their actions. The shield of anonymity is necessary, it is said, partly to maintain the fiction, enshrined in the doctrine of individual ministerial responsibility, that all departmental decisions are taken by the minister, and partly because public identification of officials with particular government policies could lead to a situation in which a future government of a different political party might find it difficult to work with them. Thus the doctrine leaves civil servants free of any repercussions arising from their advice. Mackintosh cites the case of senior officials in the Department of Employment and Productivity in 1969 who advised the Secretary of State, Mrs Barbara Castle, to press for sanctions against official strikes. As Mackintosh observes, if the names of the officials had been known, large sections of the Labour Party might have been 'baying for their blood' but, protected by the shield of anonymity, the officials could tell Mrs Castle what they believed to be proper, and 'still meet the TUC on good terms then and later on'.[7]

As Gunn reminds us, the anonymity of civil servants is 'the price that they, and we, have been prepared to pay for the benefits of a "permanent" civil service'.[8] These benefits include continuity and the development of administrative expertise. British civil servants are permanent career officials who serve successive governments of different political persuasions, a concept which is in sharp contrast to the situation in other Western countries, where the government of the day fills top policy-making positions with officials who share its politics. Thus, in the USA, although a career civil service provides continuity, the top posts in the federal bureaucracy are occupied by political appointees: what is commonly known as the 'spoils system'.

Partisan loyalty to the President's party, and commitment to his policies, are taken directly into consideration as part of the appointment process. Roughly 3,000 positions, out of about three million, are filled on this basis, and there is virtually a complete turnover of such posts when a new President is elected.[9]

Posts at the top two levels of the West German federal bureaucracy are classed as 'political', with the governing party appointing officials of their choice, mainly from within the career civil service, on the grounds of political allegiance.[10] In France, each minister has a small private staff of between ten and 30 personally appointed officials called a *cabinet*, whose role is to advise the minister; act as a filter for political pressures; and help follow up policy initiatives, including the co-ordination of policy.[11] The majority of members are high-ranking civil servants on temporary loan, many of whom are chosen because they share the same political views as the minister.

This brings us to the fourth link in the constitutional chain of conventions. Because civil servants must serve successive governments of different political parties, they must observe strict political neutrality. As Ridley notes, the principle of political neutrality in the British civil service is an ambiguous one, and has two aspects.[12] The first of these is the principle of professional neutrality, whereby officials are viewed in the classic Weberian sense as non-political experts. Civil servants are expected to provide impartial advice to a minister, presenting him with alternative solutions to policy problems, but leaving the final decision to the minister. The British concept of political neutrality also means that civil servants are expected to identify with and promote the minister's policies. They are expected to behave like chameleons: 'changing colour as governments change'. As Ridley observes, this is not neutrality in the sense of impartial advice on policy, but 'the "neutrality" of the barrister who pleads in court for a criminal one day and the police another'.[13]

These four conventions form part of a collection of long-standing assumptions about the relationship between minister and civil servant, which were restated by Sir Robert Armstrong, Head of the Home Civil Service and Secretary to the Cabinet, in a *Note of Guidance on the Duties and Responsibilities of Civil Servants in Relation to Ministers* in February 1985 (now known as the Armstrong Memorandum).[14] But events since 1979 have rendered traditional assumptions significantly out of date. The relationship between minister and civil servant is an area of the constitution which has changed dramatically, and is likely to change further. The Armstrong Memorandum was seen by many as an unhelpful restatement of outdated platitudes, inappropriate to present-day circumstances, one critic commenting that it read like 'a plea for the retention of the amateur captain in county cricket. It is romantic and unrealistic. It deals with a situation which no longer exists.'[15] The extent to which these traditional assumptions have changed will be considered in the rest of this chapter.

Ministerial Responsibility: Myth and Reality

Ministerial responsibility to Parliament in its classic sense of requiring a minister to resign if a significant mistake is made in his department has long been a myth. However, ministers do frequently resign over personal indiscretion: Hugh Dalton resigned as Chancellor of the Exchequer in 1947 for inadvertently disclosing budget details to a journalist in the lobby of the House of Commons before his Budget Speech; John Profumo resigned as Minister of Defence in 1963 after lying to the House of Commons about his relationship with Christine Keeler; and, more recently, Cecil Parkinson resigned as Secretary of State for Trade and Industry in 1983 following revelations about his relationship with his former secretary. But few ministers have resigned over departmental failures. A famous analysis by S. E. Finer has revealed that few of the ministerial resignations during the period 1855–1955 could be attributed to dogmatic adherence to a rule demanding the minister's scalp for the transgressions of his officials. Resignations were decided neither by the circumstances of the affair nor its gravity, but were the 'haphazard consequence of a fortuitous concomitance of personal, party and political temper'.[16]

The minister whose stock is high can push aside pressures for his resignation, even when manifest shortcomings are revealed in his department: while a trivial incident may prove to be the last straw for a minister whose position is already threatened. Sir Thomas Dugdale chose to resign over the Crichel Down affair in 1954, but John Strachey did not resign over the groundnuts fiasco in 1949, nor did Alan Lennox-Boyd over the Hola Camp deaths in 1959, nor did George Brown over the Sachsenhausen case in 1968, nor did John Davies in the Vehicle and General case in 1972 (see p. 81). Indeed, in the last case the buck stopped well short of the minister, and a tribunal of inquiry concluded that the ultimate failure of the department to take action lay with a named under secretary.

Ministerial responsibility is, at best, a matter of line-drawing, and the precise location of the line at any time owes much more to political pragmatism than to constitutional dogma. As Bromhead observes, the Prime Minister accepted Dugdale's resignation because there was no reason why the government should let itself be undermined by identification with the affair: it was convenient to the government as a whole that Dugdale should be sacrificed.[17] Political considerations also appear to have played a crucial part in the resignation of Lord Carrington and two other Foreign Office ministers over the Falklands campaign in 1982. Pyper has argued that far from representing a reassertion of individual ministerial responsibility, the Foreign Office resignations were an exercise in minimizing the damage to the Thatcher government's credibility, as 'true responsibility for the failures in policy, misinterpretation of intelligence reports, and the lack of military preparedness, was widespread, and would seem to have engulfed the Prime Minister.'[18] Leon Brittan's resignation over the Westland affair can be seen in a similar light.

Conversely, it was not politically convenient to assert the classic version of the convention two years later in 1984 over the highly critical Hennessy Report on the security arrangements at the Maze prison in Belfast, from which there had been a mass escape of Republican prisoners. Neither James Prior, the Secretary of State for Northern Ireland, nor Nicholas Scott, the parliamentary under secretary responsible for the Northern Ireland prison service, resigned, the Prime Minister preferring to have them both remain in the government.[19]

The growth of 'big government' has also forced changes in the traditional convention of ministerial responsibility. Gone are the days (in the mid-nineteenth century) when Viscount Palmerston could personally write every Foreign Office despatch. The vast scope of government activity and the complexity of bureaucratic organization severely limit a minister's capacity to know about, let alone control, the full range of departmental activity for which he is in theory responsible, especially in today's giant departments. The problem is highlighted by the Vehicle and General case, in which it was abundantly clear that ministerial control over such a vast empire as the Department of Trade and Industry was pure fiction. As the Home Secretary, Reginald Maudling, commented in the Vehicle and General debate: 'One must look at this classic doctrine in the light of modern developments. In my own department we get one and a half million letters a year, any one of which may lead to disaster. No Home Secretary could be expected to supervise all those one and a half million letters.'[20]

Another factor which has made the classic doctrine impracticable is the long time-span over which government decisions are made. It is difficult to pin blame on one minister in cases involving decisions made over a number of years and under a succession of different ministers. During the period with which the Vehicle and General Tribunal was concerned, there were no fewer than six senior ministers at the Board of Trade and DTI.[21]

Ministerial responsibility is not a complete myth: ministers are still required to accept responsibility for the actions of their departments in the sense of explaining and accounting to Parliament. But they rarely accept responsibility in the classic sense of accepting personal blame for departmental failure. This erosion of the doctrine, coupled with the fact that civil servants are not directly accountable to Parliament, has led one observer to talk of a 'constitutional gap'.[22] The minister acts as a buffer between Parliament and his officials, who are protected by the convention of civil service anonymity, although they are not, of course, immune from internal disciplinary procedures or from the more subtle sanctions, such as diminished promotion prospects, which accompany failure (as judged by their superiors) to do their job properly. In reality, developments such as the growth of the new investigative select committees to which civil servants can give evidence, and the advent of the Parliamentary Commissioner for Administration, mean that there has been a movement towards a degree of 'explanatory accountability' by officials but, with the exception of permanent secretaries acting in their role as accounting officers who are directly answerable to the Public Accounts Committee, civil servants are not directly accountable to Parliament.

The constitutional barriers to direct accountability are a constant source of frustration to those who are concerned about the occasional departmental scandals and the more mundane inefficiencies of central bureaucracy. There have been a few spectacular cases where civil servants have been named and blamed. Thus blame was attached to named officials in the Ministry of Aviation over the excessive profits made by Ferranti Ltd on the Bloodhound Missiles contract in the early 1960s.[23] The former under secretary in charge of the Insurance and Companies Division of the DTI bore the brunt of the Tribunal of Inquiry's censure in the Vehicle and General affair, although misgivings were expressed about the injustice of subjecting officials to this sort of *ad hoc* public denunciation in circumstances where competence of judgement, rather than legality or integrity, was at issue, and where the official concerned was denied proper opportunity to rebut the charge.

More recently, in 1986, individual civil servants in the Prime Minister's office and the DTI involved in the leaking of the Solicitor-General's letter in the Westland affair were publicly identified by the press and in Parliament. Despite the fact that the officials concerned might well have welcomed an opportunity to defend themselves in public, the Defence Select Committee was denied the opportunity to cross-examine any of the five officials involved in the leak. The government's defence of this refusal restated the traditional convention that officials are accountable only to ministers, and ministers to Parliament, a constitutional platitude which reiterated the government's earlier dismissal of a Treasury and Civil Service Committee recommendation that 'a mechanism must be provided to make officials in cases in which Ministers deny responsibility for their actions, accountable to Parliament.'[24] The Westland affair made it clear that the convention of civil service anonymity does not always work satisfactorily, and placed civil servants in what two commentators have described as 'an uncomfortable and rather badly exposed no-man's-land'.[25] It is further evidence of the need for a fundamental reappraisal of a subject upon which successive governments have been reluctant to engage in or to encourage clear thinking.

Yes, Minister – or Minister as Master?

My only great qualification for being put at the head of the Navy is that I am very much at sea.

(Sir Edward Carson, on being appointed First Lord
of the Admiralty in 1916)[26]

There has been much discussion as to whether it is ministers or civil servants who control policy-making. According to constitutional convention, there is no question: ministers decide and take responsibility for policies; civil servants advise their ministers and execute their decisions. But the fiction that ministers can personally take all decisions of any significance in a department has probably not been taken seriously since the late nineteenth century, when Lord Salisbury never consulted his permanent under secretary at the Foreign Office on any matter of importance and did much of his work at home.[27] The transition from the nineteenth century regulatory state to a modern collectivist state has been accompanied by a dramatic transformation in the scale and volume of departmental activities, and hence in the size of government departments and the number of civil servants staffing them. In 1901, there were only about 116,000 civil servants to 60 ministers; today the number of civil servants has increased five-fold, but the number of ministers is only about 100.

Ministers cannot possibly watch over the day-to-day work of a whole department: they have no choice but to delegate the bulk of departmental decision-making to civil servants. As we have seen, the duties of the giant DTI in relation to the supervision of insurance companies were in practice delegated to the Insurance and Companies Division. Indeed, the Vehicle and General Tribunal concluded that the proportion of work of the department that was referred to ministers was well under 1 per cent. A former President of the Board of Trade (which formed the core of the DTI set up in 1970) admitted that 'even after two years at the Board of Trade I had had no contact at all with the Patent Office and practically none with Weights and Measures.'[28] Thus a large part of the activities of a department are never seen at all by the minister. It is what one observer has termed 'government by exception'.[29] Of course, many decisions which are delegated to civil servants are ones which merely involve the detailed application of rules and regulations, but many are more technical policy decisions which may well have political implications. The test that a civil servant should apply in these cases is 'that each decision should, as far as humanly possible, be the one that the Minister himself would have taken if he had been able to take it personally'.[30] Hence the importance of 'knowing the minister's mind'.

The ability of ministers to cope with the demands of 'big government' is constrained by lack of time and lack of specialist knowledge. Ministers operate in a political system in which they are frequently reshuffled from ministerial post to ministerial post in a game of political musical chairs. Consequently, the minister is what one ex-Cabinet minister has called 'a bird of passage, here today and gone tomorrow. His tenure of office is a sort of short-term lease revocable by one side only, the other side, without notice.'[31] Most ministers are in a particular post for only two or three years. Consider the Department of Education and Science: from April 1944 to the appointment of Kenneth Clarke in 1990 there have been 23 ministerial heads, an average tenure of about two years. Frequent reshuffling militates against ministers acquiring any detailed understanding of the work of the department. In the words of one ministerial victim:

Too many job changes . . . means a tremendous decline in the power of the politician over the Civil Service machine and a tremendous growth in the power of the Whitehall Departments . . . a Minister needs eighteen months to get real control of his department. I had just about got it when I was moved from Housing and therefore I was deprived of the third and fourth year when I could really have achieved something.[32]

The time that ministers can devote to departmental work is also limited. At least two-thirds of a minister's working week is taken up with extra-departmental activities: Cabinet, Cabinet committees, Parliament, party meetings, official visits, constituency responsibilities and so on.[33] In the words of a former Treasury minister, 'Ministers have to be early birds and late owls as well.'[34] Little wonder that Ernest Marples described his time as a minister as 'a dog's life'.[35]

In contrast to the temporary and hard-pressed minister, permanent senior civil servants can devote the whole of their working week to the affairs of the department. Most civil servants also spend their whole careers in the same department, which reinforces the tendency for each department to develop its own individual philosophy and ethos, with the danger that the 'departmental view' may be given disproportionate weight in the presentation of departmental advice. Permanence also means that senior civil servants tend to have a near monopoly of expertise about the subject matter of the department in which they work. Few ministers have specialized knowledge of the departments they head, let alone previous experience of executive decision-making in a large organization. As Brian Smith observes, ministers are essentially 'intelligent laymen', whose parliamentary background, whilst equipping them with a training in verbal, negotiating and debating skills, does not lead naturally to departmental work.[36]

The minister's lack of specialized knowledge of the department for which he or she is responsible is compounded by the fact that few ministers seem to come to office with well-defined policy objectives and priorities.[37] Thus they often have little choice but to rely on civil servants to define objectives and subsequent policy proposals. A major reason for this is the absence of resources for policy formulation in opposition. Opposition parties have no provision for policy-making from public funds, and depend upon party funds and interest groups for resources. It is difficult in these circumstances to formulate detailed proposals. As Fry comments, British political parties are only properly organized to compete for office: they 'are organised for slogan making but not for policy preparation'.[38] One is reminded of Kogan's pertinent observation that ministers bring in with them 'high-frequency activity' which can initiate policy, while the making of policy is continuously in the hands of civil servants who create 'low-frequency policy waves'.[39] As a result 'Ministers bring with them broad ideas of how future policy should develop. But in the transformation of policy goals into realistic plans, in the execution of those plans, and, still more, in policy responses to new and unexpected developments, Ministers are largely, if not wholly, dependent on their official advisers.'[40] Given these factors, the position of civil servants in policy-making is inevitably strengthened. But there are those who argue that civil servants can actually obstruct policies of which they disapprove and push ministers into adopting policies that the department wishes them to adopt, with the relationship between minister and civil service mirroring that between the hapless Minister for Administrative Affairs, Jim Hacker, and his Permanent Secretary, the urbane and outwardly deferential Sir Humphrey Appleby, in the popular television series *Yes, Minister.*[41]

An eloquent exponent of the 'conspiracy theory' of Whitehall's relations with ministers is Tony Benn, Secretary of State for Industry, and for Energy, in the 1974–9 Labour government. According to Benn, 'the civil service sees itself as being above the party battle, with a political position of its own to defend against all-comers, including in-coming governments armed with their philosophy and programme.' What Benn describes as 'civil service policy' is an amalgam of views developed over a long period of time and drawing some of its force from a deep commitment to 'the benefits of continuity'.[42] Permanent secretaries prefer 'consensus politics' and are 'always trying to steer in-coming governments back to the policy of the out-going government, minus the mistakes that the civil service thought the out-going government made'.[43] Consequently, ministers are manipulated and thwarted by the civil service's use of various techniques: biased initial briefing; controlling information; mobilizing other departments against the minister's policy; leaking to the press in order to undermine public credibility in the minister's policy; and so on.

Although the 'conspiracy theory' is shared by other former Labour ministers, notably Richard Crossman and Michael Meacher,[44] it is a view that is questioned by other former colleagues of Mr Benn. Shirley Williams, although sharing Benn's view that Whitehall can be mobilized against what an individual minister may want to do by manipulating the inter-departmental machine, argues that the minister would overcome any such obstruction if he had the backing and confidence of the Prime Minister, a view supported by William

Rodgers.[45] The importance of prime ministerial support is emphasized by Michael Heseltine, who see Benn's thesis as 'one of the classic rationalisations of personal failure':

The reason why Benn achieved nothing is because Wilson was determined he was going to achieve nothing. He put him in a ministry, surrounded him with people who didn't agree with him, and made absolutely sure that the hare-brained policies which he alone – or not he alone, but he very substantially in a minority – believed in were not pursued.[46]

Other ex-ministers also reject the 'conspiracy theory' and echo the constitutional theory that ministers are the masters, and that it is only weak and incompetent ministers who complain that their civil servants are too powerful.[47] There is also evidence that civil servants actually prefer a decisive minister. As Heclo and Wildavsky observe: 'Given a choice between someone who passively accepts their advice and someone who can effectively protect and advance the departmental interests, officials in Treasury and spending departments would unanimously choose the stronger character.'[48] As one ex-minister puts it, civil servants want a minister 'with "bottom", and with clout'.[49]

The arguments in the 'conspiracy theory' are also open to other interpretations.[50] Civil servants do filter information, but unless information is reduced to a manageable form the already heavy burden on ministers would become totally overwhelming. Civil servants do operate an inter-departmental machine, but the overlapping of functions between departments, and the way in which policy issues increasingly converge, means that decisions in any one department usually have implications for other departments and government policy as a whole. Civil servants do point out the obstacles and problems concerning proposed policies, but they would be failing in their duty if they did not do so. As the General Secretary of the First Division Association, the top officials' trade union, has pointed out, it is the duty of the civil servant to ask three questions when a minister presents a new proposal: will it work? is it fair? will it lead to extra work or cost? A good civil servant will go further and also make positive recommendations, even if these are contrary to the views of the minister.[51]

It is obviously impossible to prove one way or the other whether civil servants do manipulate ministers in the way that Sir Humphrey often does with the unfortunate Jim Hacker. What is certain, however, is that, as Greenwood and Wilson conclude, 'civil servants have more influence, and ministers less, than constitutional theory suggests.'[52] What is also certain is that it is not desirable to have a civil service made up of officials who will always say, and mean, 'Yes, Minister'.

But even if it is difficult to draw a precise boundary between ministerial and civil service power, it is clear that the situational factors discussed earlier mean that there is an imbalance of resources between the two sides. The volume of departmental business, the technical nature of many policy issues and the conflicting demands on ministerial time, all lead to a situation in which ministers rely heavily on their civil servants for the transformation of policy goals into realistic plans. In such circumstances, if the minister and official hold differing views, 'the dice', as Ward puts it, 'is heavily loaded in favour of the civil servant.'[53] As Ward observes, the question to be asked is what can be done to tilt the balance towards the minister?

'The Loneliness of the Short-distance Runner'

One of the features of the Whitehall system which has often been said to contribute to the problems (real or imagined) faced by ministers in overcoming bureaucratic inertia and imposing their will in the face of an entrenched 'departmental view' is ministerial isolation. Unlike the USA, British ministers cannot replace the top flight of policy-making posts in their departments with politically committed outsiders. Unlike their counterparts in West Germany, British ministers cannot appoint senior civil servants who share their politics. Unlike the French system, British ministers are not permitted to form a large personal staff of political sympathizers in the form of a ministerial *cabinet*. Instead, as Gunn reminds us, ministers 'must deal with a permanent hierarchy, having, at its narrow apex, a handful of powerful ... officials'.[54] The reality of ministerial life has been described by Barbara Castle: 'The Minister is alone; the loneliness of the short-distance runner.'[55]

Traditionally, the greatest single personal resource available to a minister in his department is his private office: 'a private world little understood by the press, pressure groups or political scientists'.[56] All ministerial heads have a private office consisting of a private secretary, who is usually a principal, and up to three assistant private secretaries who are usually higher executive officers. The private office also includes a number of administrative officers and administrative assistants who deal with the minister's diary, correspondence etc.

The private office has been described by Sir Nicholas Henderson as 'fundamental to the conduct of government'.[57] It acts as the link between the minister and his department: 'the instrument, the radio-receiver for "getting the Minister's mind" and transmitting it to the department'.[58] At the heart of the private office is the minister's private secretary. Invariably a high-flying official, marked out for rapid promotion, it is in the private office that he or she develops the skills necessary for high office. It is the private secretary who acts as 'counsellor, aide, adviser, travelling companion and nurse maid'.[59] But the private secretary has a divided loyalty. In addition to being the official in permanent contact with the minister, he is also the member of the department who is in regular contact with the permanent secretary, who controls promotion within the department, and thus has the private secretary's future in his hands. As Richard Crossman, talking about his private secretary, observed:

I have got to face it that his main job is to get across to me what the Department wants. The Private Office is the Department's way of keeping a watch on me, of making sure that I run along the lines they want me to run on, of dividing my time and getting the Department's policies and attitudes brought to my notice.[60]

Another resource available to ministers is junior ministers, who share the burden of departmental and parliamentary work. Until the late 1950s, most government departments had only a minister at their head and one junior minister with the rank of parliamentary secretary. Today, nearly all departments have at least four ministers, and in some cases as many as six or seven.[61] Within such ministerial teams, the head of the department (usually a secretary of state) retains overall supervision, but the work of the department is usually divided between the junior ministers, especially in the large depart-ments which have emerged as the result of the amalgamations of the late 1960s and early 1970s. In 1987, the DHSS had a ministerial team consisting of six ministers: a secretary of state, a minister of state for health, a minister of state for social security, and three parliamentary under secretaries.

It is claimed that ministerial teams strengthen heads of depart-ments in their dealings with senior officials. Thus Barbara Castle, Minister of Transport in the 1964–70 Labour government, is on record as saying that she did not believe that she could have got the 1967 Transport Bill through the Ministry of Transport if she had not had a political team (of two junior ministers) with the same interventionist approach prepared 'to do battle' with the department's philosophy.[62]

Several commentators have argued that junior ministers should play a much stronger role in government departments.[63] But, as Theakston observes, there are very real obstacles to the greater use of this resource, one of which is the convention of individual ministerial responsibility.[64] Junior ministers do not exercise any independent statutory authority, but exercise power by delegation as the agents of the minister who heads the department. Consequently, their decisions can be (and often are) challenged by civil servants appealing to the head of the department. Greater use of, and delegation to, junior ministers is also dependent on their relationship with their ministerial superiors. There have been secretaries of state like Peter Walker who, when at the DOE in the early 1970s, made active use of junior ministers as a 'management team', but many ministerial heads are reluctant to delegate authority. Harmonious relationships are also often undermined by the fact that junior ministers are usually selected by the Prime Minister (on the advice of the Chief Whip) as part of the recurring cycle of ministerial musical chairs, and such appointments may be more part of an attempt to create a balanced government than to create powerful ministerial teams in government departments.

One recent attempt to increase the power and resources available to hard-pressed ministers has been the appointment of special advisers to provide political assistance and/or expert advice. The concept of the special adviser is not a new one. Arthur Henderson, Foreign Secretary in the 1929–31 Labour government, anxious to give more emphasis to supporting the League of Nations, brought in Lord Robert Cecil to advise him on League affairs. But the practice of ministers appointing special advisers only really took off in the mid-1960s with the Labour government's appointment of the so-called 'irregulars', such as Robert Neild and Nicholas Kaldor at the Treasury, and Christopher Foster at the Ministry of Transport.[65] Although the practice was used much less during the Heath administration, the idea was institutionalized by the Labour government of 1974–9, and at one time there were 38 such appointments. Although the Conservative Party in opposition attacked the number of special advisers appointed by the Callaghan government, the system was continued by the Thatcher government, and special advisers are now an accepted part of the Whitehall system, with 18 such appointments in 1985.

Special advisers perform a variety of roles. They act as the personal confidants of ministers; they brief the minister on non-departmental Cabinet matters; they assist in the political presentation of policies and act as a channel of communication between the minister and his party; and they play a role in departmental policy-making by commenting on civil service recommendations and extending the range of options and ideas available to the minister.[66]

There are conflicting views about the impact of special advisers. The Treasury and Civil Service Committee, in its 1986 Report on civil servants and ministers, formed the impression that in general special advisers and civil servants have been able to work creatively and harmoniously together.[67] On the other hand, there have been suggestions that they have been absorbed into the civil service system and 'house-trained'.[68] What does seem certain is that such a small group of people deployed in such an unsystematic way can do no more than nibble at the edges of an intractable problem. More fundamental proposals for change are discussed in the concluding section of this chapter.

The Thatcher Era

The traditional relationship between ministers and civil servants has been put under severe stress since the election of the Conservative government in 1979. Indeed, various commentators have argued that the advent of the Thatcher government formed a turning-point in the position of the civil service. Greenaway, for example, refers to it as comparable with the developments that occurred in the era following the Northcote–Trevelyan Report in the 1850s, while Young and Sloman argue that the higher civil service has been 'toppled from its pedestal', and sometimes identified as 'the enemy not the ally' of the government. 'Of all British institutions, not even the trade unions have suffered more than Whitehall from her [Mrs Thatcher's] capacity for unflinching scorn.'[69]

Why has the Thatcher government been so concerned with the civil service? Several factors help to explain this concern. First, Mrs Thatcher is an outsider in Whitehall: the first Prime Minister since Sir Alec Douglas Home in 1964 not previously to have been a civil servant. As Greenaway observes, she is not attracted to the qualities of detachment, versatility, caution, the ability to 'see things in the round', which are traditionally prized among British senior civil servants.[70] Mrs Thatcher's view is that radical policies require 'commitment' in pushing things through the Whitehall machine: hence, as we shall see later, her close interest in Whitehall promotions.

A second factor, closely related to the first, is that Mrs Thatcher, and other Conservatives, see the civil service as an 'adversary'.[71] As a government committed to policies which break away from the conventional wisdoms of post-war Britain, the Thatcher government is concerned that a civil service with the self-appointed role of defender of consensus and continuity, and having a duty towards what one ex-permanent secretary has referred to as 'the common ground',[72] should not attempt to water down the government's radical policies of reducing public expenditure and rolling back the frontiers of the state.

A third factor in Mrs Thatcher's attitude to the civil service is her dislike of what were seen as the 'privileges' which the civil service enjoyed, and which had accrued since the war. As we saw in chapter 6, the civil service had done well out of the pay formula set up following the Priestley Royal Commission in 1955, and Treasury evidence to the Megaw Committee of 1981–2 indicated that civil service pay was 5 per cent ahead of the pay of the private sector compared with the relative position in 1970.[73] The service also enjoyed index-linked pensions, a privilege introduced by the Heath government in 1971.

Finally, Mrs Thatcher appears to be critical of the management skills of the higher civil service, who are seen as giving too much time to policy-making and not enough time to management, especially the pursuit of efficiency and the reduction of waste. This can be seen as part of a wider concern about the efficiency of the public sector and the Conservative government's commitment to cutting back the scale of state intervention (see chapter 10).

The civil service has, of course, been fair game for ministerial attack at least since the Wilson–Fulton era, through the Crossman *Diaries* and the flak of frustrated ministers like Tony Benn. But Mrs Thatcher has removed the safety catch from the blunderbuss and blazed away with live ammunition. Some of the targets have already been discussed in earlier chapters: the abolition of the Civil Service Department and the early retirement of the Head of the Home Civil Service and his second permanent secretary; a consistently uncompromising line on pay, with the tearing up unilaterally of a pay formula based on the findings of the Pay Research Unit (PRU); the attempt (in the event unsuccessful) to withdraw entitlement to index-linked pensions.

There has also been the bitter saga of GCHQ which, although concerning only a small institution in relation to the size of the civil service as a whole, is seen by many civil servants as symbolic of a changing relationship between government and civil servants (see chapter 5). There have been severe staff cuts, with the civil service smaller than at any time since the end of the Second World War. There has, in addition, been increasing ministerial preoccupation, under the watchful eye of Mrs Thatcher, with management techniques and cost-effectiveness – as evidenced by the Rayner scrutinies, MINIS and FMI (discussed in chapter 10) – at the expense of policy-making and public service roles.

Such developments are part of what one senior civil servant has graphically described as 'a reign of terror' in Whitehall.[74] All this has generated a great deal of debate, both in Whitehall and among academics and other commentators. In the words of one commentator, there is a feeling that there has been a 'vendetta' against the service, resulting in 'an enmity between the public service and the country's political rulers unknown in Britain since the war'.[75] The election of the Thatcher government has introduced an era in which civil servants have been forcibly reorientated and, as we shall see in later chapters, this has inevitably resulted in some disorientation.

Should the Civil Service be Politicized?

The election of a Conservative government suspicious of a higher civil service with an alleged preference for consensus and continuity has added fuel to the debate on the relationship between minister and civil service, with suggestions that top policy-making posts in Whitehall should be politicized, as in other Western countries. Thus the former head of Mrs Thatcher's Policy Unit, Sir John Hoskyns, has argued for the partial politicization of the higher civil service. Hoskyns argues that senior civil servants are incapable of serving a radically minded government because they are put in an impossible position by the concept of political neutrality which, as we have seen, expects civil servants to work wholeheartedly for governments of all political persuasions. Senior civil servants can only do this, Hoskyns suggests, by 'cultivating a passionless detachment, as if the process they were engaged in were happening in a faraway country which they service only on a retainer basis'. In the words of one senior official, civil servants feel it necessary 'to withhold the last five per cent of commitment' in order to preserve their political neutrality.[76] Sir John's solution is that up to 20 senior posts in each department should be political appointees, who would come from private industry and commerce. Such outsiders might initially serve with a political party in opposition, which could, with taxpayers' money, maintain a shadow team of officials who would move into departments if and when the party won office.

Hoskyns's diagnosis (which is similar to parts of the Benn critique outlined earlier in the chapter) sparked off a lively debate on the role of the higher civil service, with an eloquent insider defence of the career civil service being provided by an ex-head of the Home Civil Service (Sir Douglas Wass), described by *The Times* as 'Mandarins' Empire Strikes Back'.[77] Sir Douglas's reply to suggestions that senior civil servants have an essentially negative attitude to ministerial initiatives was that such charges overlooked the fact that it was the duty of senior officials to ensure that ministers were fully aware of the difficulties and dangers of their initiatives. 'Ministerial enthusiasm' had to be brought face to face with the limits on public expenditure. In the view of Sir Douglas, political detachment has its value, and it is the strength of the politically uncommitted civil service that it can 'evaluate all these factors with the objectivity that sometimes escapes the political enthusiast'.[78]

Major objections have also been made to Hoskyns's prescription, it being claimed that if senior posts were no longer filled by career civil servants, ministers would lose much of the benefit of a department's 'collective and historical knowledge'.[79] Furthermore, the time horizon over which policy is formulated would become biased towards the short term: senior civil servants traditionally see themselves as the custodians of the long term and the rational, as against the short term and the politically expedient.[80] Another objection to politicization concerns its effects on civil service morale, with the fear that able young candidates would no longer apply for entry into the administration trainee grades if senior posts were likely to be denied them.[81]

Another frequently expressed objection to the Hoskyns proposals concerns the advisability of importing businessmen into the Whitehall system. It is argued that the procedures and methods of government are different from business administration: 'businessmen . . . cannot be expected to know how to run a government department any more than a civil servant can be expected to manage an industrial concern without a lot of training and experience.'[82] There would also be a major problem of ethics over business appointments when displaced officials left to take outside positions.[83] Hoskyns's proposals for outsiders from business also raises practical problems: does British business possess the talented personnel to provide up to 400 politically committed outsiders, and would such individuals be prepared to interrupt their business careers for a lengthy spell, first as part of a shadow team in opposition and then for up to five years in government, especially on present civil service salaries?[84]

Defenders of the career civil service thus deploy several arguments against Sir John's proposals, but the Hoskyns scheme is not, of course, the only possible model for politicizing senior posts. Another option would be to follow the example of West Germany and class certain senior posts as 'political' appointments, where in-coming ministers could appoint career officials who share their policies and views. A major problem raised by this particular option is the need to safeguard the career interests of the civil servants involved. In West Germany, with its federal system, displaced officials usually have no difficulty in finding an equivalent position with a *land* government of the same political party. British government, however, does not have an intermediate level of government to provide jobs for officials displaced from political posts.

Other blueprints for reform include suggestions for introducing a British version of a continental *cabinet* system which would complement, rather than replace, the higher levels of the career civil service. The *cabinet* is an option which has long been supported by the Labour Party, which argued for the introduction of the system in its evidence to Fulton two decades ago, and intends to introduce the system in each of the major departments when the party gains office.[85]

There are mixed views on the appropriateness of this particular device to the British system. One view sees *cabinets* as quite alien to the British system of government, while others regard *cabinets* as a means of strengthening the ability of over-worked ministers to chase progress on current policies and give time to long-term planning. One supporter of the concept has argued that 'if Mr Hacker had had a good *cabinet* it would cut Sir Humphrey down to size.'[86]

This more positive view is shared by the Treasury and Civil Service Committee, who proposed in 1986 that the British civil service should 'edge closer' to the European *cabinet* model, but who rejected the word 'cabinet' as being potentially confusing.[87] In a variant of an idea suggested by the Expenditure Committee in 1977, the TCSC proposed an expanded private office, in which the traditional functions of the private office would be preserved.[88] Called a minister's policy unit, it would typically consist of a number of special advisers, to keep the minister in touch with his party and to give policy advice; a number of career civil servants to keep the minister in touch with the department and to give policy advice; and the minister's parliamentary private secretary to keep the minister in touch with his backbenchers. The civil service members of the unit would be volunteers who would expect to return to ordinary departmental activities in due course, though this might turn out in practice to be easier said than done. The principle of such units was rather cautiously endorsed by the Thatcher government, but they did not propose to take a central initiative on the lines suggested.[89]

Despite her deep suspicion of the higher civil service, Mrs Thatcher has introduced neither of the two approaches discussed. But a wind of change is blowing through the corridors of Whitehall in another direction. The early 1980s coincided with the retirement of a large number of permanent secretaries – the Class of '45 – who had all entered the civil service at the end of the Second World War. Mrs Thatcher has been able to influence the appointment of more permanent secretaries than any other Prime Minister. Appointments at permanent secretary and deputy secretary level are made by the Prime Minister on the advice of the Head of the Home Civil Service, who is supported by a body called the Senior Appointments Selection Committee (SASC) which sifts proposals from departments – procedures which have been criticized for the secrecy which surrounds them and the absence of any external monitoring capacity.[90] In the past, Prime Ministers have invariably rubber-stamped SASC proposals: Mrs Thatcher's immediate predecessor, James Callaghan, is on record as not recalling ever having over-ruled its recommendations.[91] Mrs Thatcher, however, has shown a close personal interest in such appointments, and it is said that not only does her choice prevail, but that the Head of the Home Civil Service takes account of her preferences in preparing shortlists.[92] The high point of this interventionist approach towards civil service appointments took place in 1983 when eight new permanent secretaries took over the reins of departments ranging from the Treasury to the Department of Education and Science. Particularly controversial were the appointments of Peter Middleton, aged 48, only a third-ranking deputy secretary, to Permanent Secretary to the Treasury, and Clive Whitmore, Mrs Thatcher's former Principal Private Secretary, as Permanent Secretary to the Ministry of Defence, at the relatively early age of 47.

There is no evidence that this is politicization in the overt sense of senior appointments being made on the basis of a civil servant's political affiliation. Instead, Mrs Thatcher has displayed a strong preference for what has been called the civil servant who embodies the 'can do' approach and is willing enthusiastically to implement the minister's policies.[93] What has caused concern is that this emphasis on commitment to government policies conflicts with traditional notions of neutrality and impartiality, and that the traditional objectivity of the civil service will be eroded by a process of 'creeping politicization'. One result is that there is a danger that civil service advice will be tailored to what ministers want to hear, with civil servants used to offering 'honest and unpalatable advice' being either tight-lipped or offering ministers only the advice they wish to hear.[94] As Hugo Young observes: 'An important role of the traditional civil servant is to dissuade politicians from believing their own propaganda. If the machine is peopled by laundered prophets, who will play the devil's advocate?'[95]

Postscript

Although, as we concluded, there is no evidence of politicization in the overt sense of senior appointments being made on the basis of a civil servant's political affiliation, there continues to be concern about the alleged 'politicization' of the higher civil service by the Thatcher government. A leading Labour Party spokesman, John Cunningham, has argued that there must be a number of senior civil servants who are 'compromised' by the 'one of us' syndrome, and who would have to go in the event of a Labour government being elected.[96]

As one observer has pointed out, however, it is more likely that the most a Labour government would do would be to 'reshuffle the civil service top brass, not massacre it'.[97] It is interesting to note that the most important civil service appointment of the late 1980s, that of Sir Robin Butler to replace Sir Robert Armstrong as Secretary to the Cabinet and Head of the Home Civil Service in 1988, hardly accords with the 'politicization' thesis. Sir Robin has been described as a 'classic Northcote–Trevelyan high-flier' – educated at Harrow and Oxford University, with a Treasury background, and with spells on secondment at the Central Policy Review Staff and at No 10 Downing Street as Private Secretary to three prime ministers.[98]

9

The Public Face of Private Government

When discussing the civil service, it is necessary to distinguish between the so-called higher civil service – the 3,000 or so senior officials who operate in the higher reaches of policy-making and ministerial briefings (see chapter 2) – and the huge labour force which makes up the rank and file. As Kellner and Crowther-Hunt remind us, there are in fact two civil services: 'One is small, and helps make Government policy. The other is large and helps to carry Government policy out.'[1] It is the lower-ranking members of the latter group who for most people constitute the public face of government: the counter clerk at the local Department of Health and Social Security office, the official at the local job centre, the customs officer at the airport, the driving test examiner, and so on.

The day-to-day activities of the higher civil service, however, are less familiar to the public. This is partly a consequence of the fact that, in order to protect their anonymity and political neutrality, civil servants have traditionally hidden behind the constitutional doctrine of ministerial responsibility (see chapter 8). But there is more to it than this. The higher civil service is separated from the outside world by a common kinship and culture: they are a group of people whose coherence is expressed through 'exclusiveness'. As Heclo and Wildavsky observe: 'Apart from the final decisions reached, their behaviour is neither known nor intended to be known beyond government circles.'[2]

As we saw in chapter 4, the higher civil service resembles a 'village' community, in which the inhabitants have grown up together and know each other. The villagers tend to come from the same very narrow (in statistical terms) social and educational background: they are an 'unrepresentative bureaucracy'. The 'Whitehall village' is a private and tightly knit community in which the inhabitants tend to have shared assumptions and to communicate with each other in similar language, e.g. cricketing phrases such as 'a sticky wicket' and 'straight bat', and where candidates for promotion are described as 'not Test standard, but a good county player'.[3] The 'Whitehall village' is inhabited by officials who use private codes and unwritten rules although, as we shall see later, it is also a world in which the parameters of working life are set by official rules and constitutional principles. It is a world in which government is treated as a private affair, and in which official information is regarded as 'the private property of government'.[4]

This chapter examines the role of secrecy in the essentially private world of senior civil servants, and the implications this has for the workings of the Whitehall machine. It then considers some of the aspects of the public face of private government – the civil service's relations with Parliament, pressure groups and the private sector – and discusses the increasing tendency for retired senior officials to 'go public'.

Official Secrets and Open Government

> Open Government is a contradiction in terms. You can be open – or you can have government.
>
> (Sir Arnold Robinson, the fictional Cabinet Secretary
> in the television series *Yes, Minister*).[5]

Secrecy is one of the sociological characteristics of bureaucracy. 'Every bureaucracy', Max Weber tells us, 'seeks to increase the superiority of the professionally informed by keeping their knowledge and intentions secret.'[6] The British civil service is no exception. Indeed, James Michael goes so far as to suggest that 'Britain is about as secretive as a state can be and still qualify as a democracy. The working assumption at all levels is that secret government is good government.'[7] The Australian judge in the Peter Wright case expressed incredulity at what the British government assumed should be kept secret.

Why is British central government so secretive? Secrecy is partly the consequence of legislation. There are over 100 statutes making it a criminal offence for civil servants and others to disclose various kinds of information without authorization. The jewel in the crown of these legislative constraints is the Official Secrets Act 1911, which was amended in 1920 and again in 1939. Everyone who joins the civil service is required to sign the Act. Section 1 of the 1911 Act is concerned with espionage and the communication of information to the enemy, and although at least two prosecutions under Section 1 have been the subject of controversy, it need not concern us here.[8] The significant section is Section 2, which covers a number of offences under the general heading of 'wrongful communication etc. of information'. This section makes it an offence to communicate official information to an unauthorized person, or to retain any official document without authority, or to fail to take care of any official document. It is also an offence to receive any official document knowing, or having reasonable cause to believe, that it was communicated in contravention of the Act.

The main characteristic of Section 2 is that it is a 'catch-all' in two senses. All Crown servants, from permanent secretaries to police officers, are potentially covered by it. All categories of official information, however trivial, fall within its scope: in theory it is an offence to report the number of cups of tea consumed per week in a government department.

The actual number of prosecutions under Section 2 have been relatively small, an average of less than one a year since the First World War, although there has been a marked increase in the number of prosecutions since the election of the Conservative government in 1979.[9] But the inhibiting effect on civil service behaviour is what really matters. As Sir Burke Trend, the then Cabinet Secretary, said in evidence to the Franks Committee: 'I am not saying that you say to yourself "If I say something to X will I be breaching the Official Secrets Act?" But you are conscious that at the back of everything you say and do all day long there is this tremendous sanction.'[10]

Section 2 has been the subject of much discussion in the past 20 years. The Fulton Report complained that the administrative process was surrounded by too much secrecy and called for a review of the Official Secrets Act. A government inquiry into the working of Section 2, under the chairmanship of Lord Franks, was subsequently set up by the Conservative government in 1971, and its report a year later called the section 'a mess'. Franks condemned Section 2's catch-all nature and stated that 'people are not sure what it means, or how it operates in practice, or what kinds of action involve real risk of prosecution under it.'[11] Its main recommendation was that Section 2 should be replaced by a new Official Information Act, covering specified categories of information: defence and internal security; foreign affairs; law and order; the affairs of private citizens and private organizations; Cabinet papers; and currency and the reserves. The test of criminality would be whether unauthorized disclosure would cause at least serious injury to the interests of the State.

Much has been said, but little has been done in the aftermath of Franks to reform the law and practice relating to official secrecy. Both Labour and Conservative parties have acknowledged the shortcomings of Section 2 when in opposition, but have failed to repeal it when in government, although the Conservative government came near with the introduction of the Protection of Official Information Bill in 1979, only to withdraw it following the recognition that the revelation in Andrew Boyle's *Climate of Treason* that Sir Anthony Blunt had been the 'Fourth Man' in the Burgess/Maclean/Philby affair could not have been published if the Bill had been in force.[12] Clive Ponting's acquittal in 1985 of the charge of breaking Section 2 by leaking two documents about the sinking of the *General Belgrano* to a Labour MP offered another reminder of the deficiencies of Section 2, and also provided a considerable boost to the wider issue of 'open government'. 'Open government' now encompasses not only the demand for the replacement of the essentially negative Section 2, but also the establishment of a statutory right of access to official information, as in Sweden and the USA, a cause spear-headed by the 1984 Campaign for Freedom of Information. Such legislation, it is argued, would lead, *inter alia*, to increased government accountability, the encouragement of public participation and better decision-making. This had been rejected by the Franks Committee as raising important constitutional questions beyond its terms of reference.

Official resistance to a freedom of information bill has always rested on the argument that such legislation would mean that government would have to be conducted in 'a goldfish bowl', and that it would be incompatible with the constitutional conventions which govern the traditional relationships between ministers and civil servants.[13] Advocates of freedom of information maintain that both fears are unfounded. Public access legislation would be limited by exemptions protecting information concerning defence, national security, foreign relations, law enforcement and personal privacy. Provision could also be made to exempt certain Cabinet documents and policy advice. Supporters of reform also argue that the second objection is difficult to sustain now that Australia, Canada and New Zealand – all Commonwealth countries with constitutions based on the Westminster model – have adopted freedom of information legislation.[14]

But would legislative change necessarily lead to greater openness? It is important to remember that legislation tells only part of the story of government secrecy in Britain. The rest is embedded in British political culture, constitutional conventions and in the understandings and habits of civil service behaviour. We are back in the 'Whitehall village', with its private codes of language and conduct, and where (as we saw in chapter 6) the ethic of secrecy and confidentiality is one of the basic working assumptions. This is a world where, as Heclo and Wildavsky observe, esteem, and the rewards which accompany it, is measured in terms of trust and reliability.[15] In the more down-to-earth language of the Franks Report:

a civil servant who is regarded as unreliable, or who tends to overstep the mark and to talk too freely, will not enjoy such a satisfactory career as colleagues with better judgement and greater discretion. He may fail to win promotion, or he may be given less important and attractive jobs. The great majority of civil servants wish to perform their duties conscientiously and to enjoy successful careers. These are powerful natural incentives to proper behaviour.[16]

It is these private codes, and the overlapping legislation and constitutional conventions, which reinforce the idea that good government is closed government. As Kellner and Crowther-Hunt put it, the unspoken heart of the argument for closed government is that 'private debate among civil servants and ministers produces more *rational* policies, freed from public pressure, which is assumed to be irrational'.[17]

'Leaking' in the Public Interest

The unauthorized disclosure of official information, or 'leaking' as it is more commonly known, has always been regarded by constitutional purists as undermining the trust and confidence that ought to exist between civil servants and their political masters. As long ago as 1873, the Permanent Secretary to the Treasury described leaking as 'the worst fault a civil servant can commit. It is on the same footing as cowardice by a soldier.'[18] Similar sentiments were expressed over a century later by the Cabinet Secretary, Sir Robert Armstrong, who described leaks as 'unacceptable and unthinkable at any time' and something which threatened the position of the civil service as a non-political service.[19]

Nevertheless, the leaking of official information by disaffected civil servants has been a feature of most administrations. A spectacular example was provided in the 1930s by Desmond Morton, head of the government's Industrial Intelligence Centre who, with other officials, provided Winston Churchill with information about Britain's military unpreparedness.[20] More recently, the Thatcher government has been the victim of a deluge of leaks by civil servants who disagree with the government's policies, several of which have led to prosecutions.

Three of these cases raised important questions about the dilemma facing civil servants with crises of conscience involving more than mere doubts about government policy. In December 1983, Ian Willmore, an administration trainee in the Department of Employment, admitted leaking a note of what he regarded as an irregular discussion about possible reforms in industrial relations law between a senior official and the Master of the Rolls, Sir John Donaldson, to the magazine *Time Out*. Willmore was not prosecuted by the government, although he was obliged to resign. However, a few months later in March 1984, Sarah Tisdall, a junior clerk in the Foreign Office, was successfully prosecuted under Section 2 of the Official Secrets Act 1911 for leaking a document to the *Guardian* containing details of the arrival of cruise missiles. She was sentenced to six months' imprisonment. As Pyper notes, both Willmore and Tisdall leaked politically sensitive documents because they 'saw themselves having a duty to the public interest which overrode their duty to the government of the day'.[21]

A similar duty to the public interest featured in the case of Clive Ponting, an assistant secretary at the Ministry of Defence who, in August 1984, was charged under Section 2 with communicating information to Tam Dalyell MP concerning proposed ministerial responses to parliamentary inquiries relating to the sinking of the Argentinian cruiser, the *General Belgrano*, during the Falklands campaign. Ponting claimed that his motives for leaking the documents stemmed from his view that he was being required to assist ministers to evade, through deliberate deceit, legitimate parliamentary scrutiny. His defence rested on the provision in Section 2 of the 1911 Official Secrets Act that the information had been communicated 'to a person to whom it is in the interests of the State his duty to communicate it'. Ponting's defence counsel defined the 'state' to mean 'the organized community', and thereby conceived 'interests of the State' to be synonymous with 'the public interest'. Mr Justice McCowan, however, directed the jury that duty meant official duty, meaning the duty imposed upon Ponting by his position, and equated the 'interests of the State' with the policies of the government of the day. Despite this direction, Ponting was acquitted.

Any employee who betrays his employer's confidence must expect disciplinary consequences, although common sense suggests that such leaking may be justified in exceptional circumstances, such as the exposure of crime. But what, if anything, should a civil servant do if ministers require him to go further than he considers proper in obstructing parliamentary scrutiny? In the USA, a Code of Ethics asks civil servants 'to put loyalty to the highest moral principles and to country above loyalty to persons, party or government department'. In addition, the 1978 Civil Service Reform Act protects officials who leak information which they believe reveals 'mismanagement, a gross waste of public funds, an abuse of authority, or a substantial and specific danger to public health or safety'. But the British civil service has no such codes. Internal documents, such as the *Establishment Officers' Guide*, the *Civil Service Pay and Conditions of Service Code* (see chapter 6) and the *Memorandum of Guidance for Officials* appearing before select committees (which is discussed later in the chapter) are an unhelpful mixture of categorical restatements of constitutional convention and earnest, but vague, affirmations of the need to promote public understanding and to co-operate with Parliament.

In the wake of the Ponting case, the Cabinet Secretary circulated a code in the form of a *Note of Guidance*, which reasserted the principle that 'the civil service as such has no constitutional personality or responsibility separate from the duly elected Government of the day'.[22] The memorandum suggested that officials having 'a fundamental issue of conscience' should go, in the last resort, to the permanent secretary, who could take the matter up with the Head of the Home Civil Service. But established procedures would probably not have helped to resolve Ponting's dilemma. Nor were they of much help to Colette Bowe, Director of Information at the Department of Trade and Industry, who had doubts about the propriety of ministerial instructions to disclose to the press selected extracts from the letter written by the Solicitor-General to the then Secretary of State for Defence, Michael Heseltine, at the height of the Westland crisis. Miss Bowe sought to consult her permanent secretary, but he was out of London at the time.

One possible solution to the gaps in the procedures is the creation of some sort of independent appeals mechanism. The First Division

Association has drawn up a code of ethics under which civil servants who believe ministers are misleading, or lying to, Parliament and the public would have a right of appeal to the chairman of the appropriate Commons select committee or to the Parliamentary Commissioner for Administration.[23] An alternative is Sir Douglas Wass's proposal for an independent, quasi-judicial 'Inspector-General' for the civil service, to hear complaints from civil servants who feel that ministers are acting improperly, and armed perhaps with the power, in the last resort, to report *in camera* to the relevant select committee.[24]

In the absence of such procedures (and the government has made it clear that it rejects the concept of an external appeals mechanism), there will always be the danger that civil servants faced with a 'crisis of conscience' will seek to resolve them through covert channels. Ultimately, the only credible remedy against illicit leaking may be to extend the openness of government and the legitimate outflow of information from departments.

The Government Information Machine

> You know the difference between leaking and briefing. Briefing is what I do and leaking is what you do.
>
> (James Callaghan, in evidence to the Franks Committee).[25]

Section 2 of the Official Secrets Act is only concerned with the *unauthorized* disclosure of official information. Governments regularly reveal a great deal of official information through the doctrine of implied authorization. Thus senior civil servants can exercise a considerable degree of personal judgement in deciding what disclosures of official information they may properly make and to whom. Ministers are, in effect, self-authorizing and decide for themselves what to reveal. The briefing of journalists on a non-attributable basis is an accepted part of the Whitehall system.

At the heart of this system is the Parliamentary Lobby, the 150 or so accredited political or 'lobby' correspondents who, unlike their colleagues in the Press Gallery (who report on proceedings on the floor of the House of Commons), are allowed to mix freely with ministers and MPs in the Members' Lobby and other parts of the Palace of Westminster.[26] In the words of one journalist, they are allowed 'to reach the parts of parliamentary buildings that other journalists cannot reach'.[27]

Members of the Lobby are briefed at frequent unattributable meetings given by the Prime Minister's press staff (notably the press secretary), government ministers and other official spokesmen. Specialist correspondents covering particular Whitehall departments – education, labour, defence and others – also have their own specialist groups which are given regular briefings by departments on 'lobby terms'. The main rule underlying the system is that, although the information conveyed may be published, lobby correspondents should not reveal anything that would disclose the source of their information. Indeed, an inquiry by the lobby in 1986 into the practice of mass non-attributable meetings recommended tighter self-discipline of political reporters over not identifying sources.[28] Thus we are able to read in our newspapers quite detailed accounts of Cabinet deliberations, official versions of which will not normally (under the rules imposed by the Public Records Act) see the light of day for 30 years, and perhaps not even then. Such accounts appear under such headings as 'well-informed sources', 'according to government sources' and 'sources close to the Prime Minister' to disguise the origin of the information.

The lobby has been the subject of much debate. It is defended on the grounds that it facilitates the flow of information, and that ministers and other official spokesmen might be inhibited from talking frankly to journalists if they were not accorded confidentiality. But there is much criticism of what many see as a cosy and incestuous relationship, in which lobby correspondents are seen as 'the messenger boys of British democracy'.[29] The case against the lobby system has been cogently argued by Kellner:

Lobby journalists get sucked into the system so that in the end they are not so much representing the interests and questions of their audience, their public, but they are representing the interests of an institution of government, the lobby itself, of which they have become part. At the more practical level, the form of relationship that lobby journalists build up with politicians is that they do not subject what they are told in lobby briefings to the kind of detailed analytical scrutiny to which ... governments ought constantly to be subjected ...[30]

Thus the system enables government 'to control systematically the nature, content and timing of a great deal of political information and the way it reaches the public'.[31]

Even the Cabinet Secretary, Sir Robert Armstrong, has admitted that one of the objectives of the lobby system is 'to seek to influence opinion without accepting responsibility', and to place in the public domain 'ideas which the government did not wish to be seen placing there'.[32] The playing down of the official announcement of the Attlee government's decision to build nuclear weapons in 1948, and its devaluation of the pound a year later, are just two examples of the success of post-war governments in political news management. More recently, the way in which the Ministry of Defence manipulated the media during the Falklands War has been described as 'a campaign of news management that had not been equalled since the Second World War'.[33]

The middlemen (and women) in the government's dealings with the media are press and information officers, usually ex-journalists, although the Foreign Office and the Treasury employ career civil servants. The task of such officials, according to a former Director-General of the Central Office of Information, is to give 'objective statements of the truth'.[34] However, there are those who argue that the successful press officer is one who can manage the news. As Richard Crossman observed in his account of his time at the Ministry of Housing and Local Government, 'a department can, with a good press officer, make the news it wants.'[35]

The position of such officials has been the subject of increasing concern, however, with suggestions that they are being required to do more than simply present and describe ministerial policies, but are being asked to defend such policies in party political terms or to act in a political manner. There has been much criticism that Mrs Thatcher's press secretary, Bernard Ingham, has too close a relationship with the Prime Minister. Indeed, the former leader of the Social Democratic Party, Dr David Owen, has accused Mrs Thatcher of using her press secretary to convey her views on an unattributable basis to the press, thereby eroding the independence of the civil service.[36] Dr Owen has also alleged that civil servants – principally in the Central Office of Information – have been used in 'information' campaigns which are party political.[37]

The dilemma in which individual press officers may find themselves was highlighted by the Westland affair, when Colette Bowe, Director of Information at the DTI, was instructed by her minister to disclose to the press selected extracts from a letter written by the Solicitor-General to another minister. As the Treasury and Civil Service Committee observed in its 1986 report, the instruction 'was clearly politically motivated' and it was unsatisfactory to require career civil servants to break established conventions for the political purposes of the minister. The Committee recommended that ministers who require their press officers to do more than present and describe their policies should make political appointments.[38]

The Civil Service and Parliament

One point of contact between civil servants and what Mackenzie and Grove refer to as the other worlds of 'the universe of British government' is Parliament.[39] Although civil servants are not directly accountable to Parliament – the minister (as we saw in chapter 8) acting as a buffer between Parliament and his officials – the worlds of the civil service and Parliament do meet through question time, select committees and other parliamentary channels. Indeed, during debates involving their department, senior civil servants sit in the Chamber of the House of Commons in a 'box' behind the Speaker's chair, with the parliamentary private secretary acting as a messenger between them and the minister involved in the debate. At the committee stage of legislation, officials may be consulted by the minister personally on details under discussion.

Writing in the late 1950s, before the growth of select committees, Mackenzie and Grove observed that in the daily life of a government department there were two kinds of business 'which continually bear witness to the importance of Parliamentary politics': ministerial correspondence and question time.[40] Civil servants spend much of their time on ministerial correspondence with MPs: the five ministers in the DHSS alone received over 2,000 letters a month from MPs in the 1979–80 Parliament.[41] Such correspondence, which usually involves constituents' problems, will reach the level of an assistant secretary before being submitted to a minister for approval and signature.

Parliamentary questions also put a substantial workload on civil servants. The traditional method of trying to elicit information about the workings of government, questions may be either written or oral. Answers to written questions are printed in *Hansard*, while oral questions are answered on the floor of the House of Commons by ministers on a rota basis. The advantage of an oral question is that it may be followed by supplementary questions, of which the minister has no warning. As questions will usually have been tabled at least a fortnight before they have to be answered, civil servants have sufficient time to prepare answers for the minister. Many departments have a parliamentary branch, under a principal, responsible for the minister's dealings with Parliament, which gathers material for the answers from particular divisions of the department. Although the questions will usually be dealt with initially by an executive officer, who will try to establish the facts, the draft answer will be prepared by a principal, who will also prepare notes on possible supplementaries. The draft answer, which is usually considered by an assistant secretary, and might even be considered as high in the hierarchy as the permanent secretary, is 'polished till it shines'.[42]

Producing answers to a parliamentary question is an art. H. E. Dale, in his book on civil service life in the inter-war years, defined the perfect answer to a parliamentary question as: 'one that is brief, appears to answer the question completely, if challenged can be proved to be accurate in every word, gives no opening for awkward "supplementaries", and discloses really nothing'.[43] Or as Clive Ponting put it in his book on civil service life nearly half a centry later: 'answers are designed to give away as little information as possible.'[44]

The care and attention that goes into the drafting of replies to parliamentary questions reflects the civil servant's traditional role of protecting ministers from political attack or embarrassment. In the words of Kellner and Crowther-Hunt: 'The central point is that the MP is often seen as an actual or potential adversary, to be helped as *little* as possible – whereas departmental ministers need to be buttressed with as *much* help as possible.'[45] The possibility of MPs unearthing anything really embarrassing about what goes on behind the closed doors of a government department is made even less likely by the fact that there are a number of subjects on which departments simply refuse to answer parliamentary questions. These range from obvious security matters to such apparently harmless subjects as the day-to-day affairs of the White Fish Authority, agriculture workers' wages and official forecasts of future levels of unemployment. Ministers may also refuse to answer questions on the grounds that the information can only be collected at a disproportionate cost or is not available.

Question time does not, of course, involve civil servants in direct contact with MPs. There is, however, direct contact on a number of other fronts. The Parliamentary Commissioner for Administration, operating as an extension of parliamentary scrutiny of the administrative process, examines departmental files and takes evidence from civil servants. Permanent secretaries, in their capacity as accounting officers, appear before the Public Accounts Committee to answer points raised in the reports of the Comptroller and Auditor-General (see chapter 10).

The growth of select committees in the past two decades has established another link between Whitehall and Parliament. The system of select committees underwent a substantial overhaul in 1979, with the setting up of 14 new select committees on a departmentally related basis, and the maintenance of a working relationship between a department and a select committee charged with monitoring its work is now part of many civil servants' day-to-day lives. Many civil servants regularly give evidence to committees in what has been seen as a movement towards a degree of 'explanatory accountability' (see chapter 8). A total of 652 civil servants gave evidence to the 'new' select committees in an 18-month period in 1980–1, making 1,049 appearances between them.[46]

There are, however, limitations on the ability of the new select committees to call for information. The *Memorandum of Guidance for Officials* appearing before committees begins by exhorting civil servants to 'be as helpful as possible to committees', and by suggesting that information should be withheld only in the interests of 'good government' or to safeguard national security.[47] But it then sets out a catalogue of limitations on the provision of information, notably the need to preserve collective ministerial responsibility, which means that civil servants must not tell committees what advice they have given to their ministers, or about inter-departmental consultations, or about the nature and work of Cabinet committees. The Memorandum also says that official witnesses should 'confine their evidence to questions of fact relating to existing Government policies and actions', and that they should avoid being drawn into discussion of alternative policy.

Despite these limitations, the 'open government' implications of extended select committee activity cannot lightly be dismissed.[48] A great deal more information about the private world of Whitehall departments is entering the public domain. Most of the oral and written evidence given to select committees comes from senior civil servants, some of whom in consequence have become public figures. This amounts to a small dent in the minister's personal monopoly of departmental accountability, and requires us to modify some of the conventional dogma about ministerial responsibility. It would be surprising if civil servants whose traditional role has been to protect ministers from political attack did not have also, while still accepting that role as overwhelmingly the dominant one, a heightened consciousness of the legitimate claims of parliamentary scrutiny.

The Civil Service and Pressure Groups

It would be misleading to view government departments as organizations in which civil servants, and ministers, make and administer government policy in complete isolation from the outside world. On the contrary, there is close (some would say too close) contact between civil servants and pressure groups. We use the term 'pressure group', even though, as Finer has observed, it is slightly misleading in that it implies that such groups have to use some kind of sanction to get inside government departments whereas, as we shall see, the door is often wide open.[49]

Consultation between civil servants and pressure groups is a major feature of the day-to-day life of government departments. Indeed, as we saw in chapter 7, the need to consult with outside interests is one of the major constraints within which civil servants operate. The two sides are brought together by two main factors: functional necessity, and cultural norms which encourage consultation.[50] As government has become more technical and complex, departments have become increasingly dependent on pressure groups for information and expertise. As one writer on this area reminds us, except for the scientific civil service, British central government has no tradition of 'concentrated expertise', and civil servants go to those *outside* government with the necessary expertise.[51] As Blondel puts it, if pressure groups were to starve the civil service of information, 'the administration of the country would come to a halt'.[52] Civil servants also need the acquiescence of pressure groups in the implementation of government policy, and the integration of such groups in the policy process makes it more likely that policies will be implemented. An oft-cited example is the National Health Service, where central government is dependent on the co-operation of the medical profession in general, and the British Medical Association in particular. Some pressure groups actually administer legislation on behalf of government: a notable example being the Law Society, which administers the legal aid scheme.

What Jordan and Richardson refer to as the 'functional logic' of consultation and negotiation is reinforced by cultural norms.[53] It is felt that pressure groups, in Beer's words, 'have a "right" to take part in making policy' related to their sector of activity.[54] The British political culture is characterized by what another American scholar refers to as a 'persistent corporatism', which ensures that the representation of pressure groups is not only tolerated, but even insisted upon.[55] The relationship is not, of course, one-sided: pressure groups also benefit from close contact with government departments. The opportunity to exert influence at an early stage of the policy process, the exchange of information and the conferring of public recognition and legitimacy are all advantages for the groups.

Consultation between civil servants and groups takes place through a variety of channels, ranging from statutory obligations to consult pressure groups to more informal contacts. Certain groups are engaged in a continuous process of consultation with civil servants on every issue of importance from legislation and subordinate legislation to departmental circulars. In some cases, the requirement for consultation is given statutory form. Probably the best known example is the 1947 Agriculture Act, which requires ministers to consult 'such bodies of persons who appear to them to represent the interests of producers in the agricultural industry'. In practice, this has meant the National Farmers Union and, since 1978, the Farmers Union of Wales.

Another interface between civil servants and pressure groups is the extensive system of advisory committees, which provide departments with expert information and act as forums for discussion between civil servants and pressure group representatives. Thus representatives of the BMA, the Royal Colleges and the Royal College of Nursing serve on such DHSS advisory committees as the Standing Medical Advisory Committee, the Standing Nursing and Midwifery Committee and the Joint Consultants Committee. The NFU is represented on a wide range of Ministry of Agriculture, Fisheries and Food advisory committees, from the Bee Diseases Advisory Committee to the Myxomatosis Advisory Committee.

There is also a convention of prior consultation with certain pressure groups before the introduction of new policy. Dorothy Johnstone cites the example of the process of consultation on the introduction of value added tax, in which over 400 associations received consultation papers from the Customs and Excise.[56] At the other end of the consultation spectrum, there are often informal contacts between civil servants and pressure group officials, who continually call one another on the telephone, and lunch together. The head of Britain's biggest steel union in the 1970s even played squash regularly with the under secretary in charge of the Department of Industry's Iron and Steel Divison.[57]

It is this practice of consultation, and the relationships which develop within them, which have led Richardson and Jordan to describe the British policy process as being built around 'policy communities' made up of departments and pressure groups. It is a system in which policy-making has become compartmentalized, and in which the 'normal' policy style is one of 'bureaucratic accommodation', in which consultation and negotiation with groups is the 'standard operating procedure'.[58]

As we saw earlier, this close relationship has obvious benefits for civil servants (and the pressure groups with which they identify). Another advantage from the point of view of government is that pressure groups act as surrogates for the 'public interest': defined by one senior civil servant as 'the balance of organised pressure at any given time'.[59] But is the system of consultation which has grown up between civil servants and pressure group officials in the public interest? One concern is that departments are sometimes *too* close to a particular group, and in danger of accepting their advice too uncritically, and hence being 'captured' by them. The relationship between MAFF and the NFU has often been seen in this light: in the view of one former Cabinet minister, 'MAFF is not a good department for determining the public interest: it is a very good department for determining the agricultural interest, not always the same thing.'[60]

The relationship betweeen civil service and pressure groups is not only a close one, but a closed one. The key to unlocking what Richardson and Jordan refer to as 'the door of influence' is to get on the department's consultation list, but, as they observe, the very nature of the consultation process excludes certain groups.[61] As Ryan demonstrates in his study of the penal lobby, some groups are 'acceptable' and others are not.[62] Not all pressure groups are part of policy communities. The consultation process tends to be dominated by producer groups like employers' associations, trade unions and professional associations, who are well organized. The consumers of public goods and services are often not organized at all, and are therefore excluded from the consultation process.

The Civil Service and the Private Sector

One response to the criticism that the civil service is too isolated is the growing interchange of staff between the civil service and outside organizations. This interchange is intended 'to provide opportunities for civil servants to gain business experience outside Whitehall, and to enable Departments to benefit from the knowledge and expertise of staff on secondment from industry and commerce'.[63] The potential benefits of interchange were endorsed by the Fulton Committee, which was critical of the small numbers involved in the 1960s, and asked for 'determined efforts' to be made to promote such exchanges on a much larger scale.[64] A formal exchange scheme was set up in 1968, and a new initiative launched in

1977 increased the number of secondments, which trebled between 1977 and 1985 (see table 9.1).

The interchange scheme is aimed at staff with potential at any level from junior management upwards, and is usually for a period up to two years. A significant proportion of those seconded from the civil service are at about principal level, including many staff in specialist grades. Over 170 companies were involved in the scheme in 1985, including Boots plc, Ferranti plc, GEC, Midland Bank plc, W. H. Smith and Sons and Unilever plc. Since 1984, the scheme has been supplemented by the 'Whitehall and Industry Scheme', which enables civil servants, generally at assistant secretary level, to spend short periods of ten to 15 days on attachment to companies in the private sector. In 1985 over 20 'high-fliers' were seconded under this scheme. Arrangements also exist whereby civil servants at assistant secretary level and above are appointed as unpaid non-executive directors or observers at board meetings of private sector companies. Between 1978 and 1985 more than 30 companies were involved in these arrangements.

TABLE 9.1   *Interchange of staff between civil service and industry and commerce, 1977–85*

Year	Secondments from civil service	Secondments to civil service	Total
1977	63	60	123
1978	127	74	201
1979	131	82	213
1980	143	67	210
1981	140	64	204
1982	152	92	244
1983	189	104	293
1984	186	116	302
1985	229	157	386

Source: Management and Personnel Office, *Interchange of Staff between the Civil Service and Other Organisations: 1985 Report*

Secondments also take place between the civil service and non-commercial bodies. Some 520 such secondments were in operation in 1985, many of them between departments and organizations with which they have functional links. Thus the Department of the

Environment seconds officials to local authorities, a notable example being the exchange arrangements made in 1983 between an under secretary in charge of the Inner Cities Directorate and the chief executive of the London Borough of Hounslow.

A more controversial link between the civil service and the world of industry and commerce is the appointment of top civil servants to positions in the private sector after retirement. In France it is called 'changing slippers' (*pantouflage*), in the USA 'the revolving door', and in Japan 'the golden parachute'. In recent years, there has been a growing number of senior civil servants leaving Whitehall at the retirement age of 60, or earlier, and moving into top boardroom jobs with salaries two or three times the figure they earned in the civil service. The former Cabinet Secretary, Lord Hunt, became a director of Prudential Assurance, Unilever and the London subsidiary of the Banque Nationale de Paris after his retirement in 1979. His colleague, Lord Bancroft, Head of the Home Civil Service, 1978–81, became a non-executive director of Bass, Rugby Portland Cement, Grindlays Bank and Sun Life Assurance. Sir Douglas Wass, Permanent Secretary of the Treasury, 1974–83, became a non-executive director of De La Rue Co., Equity and Law Life Assurance and Barclays Bank. The former Permanent Secretary at the MOD, 1976–83, Sir Frank Cooper, became chairman of United Scientific Holdings, and a director of Babcock International, N. M. Rothschild and Sons, Morgan Crucible and Westland. Cooper's appointment at United Scientific Holdings, a major defence contractor, was particularly well publicized because the man he replaced, Peter Levene, was appointed to Cooper's old department as Chief of Defence Procurement, an example of the 'revolving door' moving someone in as well as out (see chapter 5).

Defenders of the migration of senior civil servants from the corridors of Whitehall to the boardrooms of the City argue that civil servants should be no less free than others to use their talents after retirement from their main careers, and that such movements contribute to the economic life and well-being of the country. The acceptance of outside business appointments, it is argued, also helps to break down what some see as a cultural barrier between the private and public sectors.[65] Critics, on the other hand, argue that there is a danger that in order to obtain a particular private sector post, a civil servant could bestow favours on his prospective employers and, after his move, use his knowledge of the department's affairs, and his contacts, to secure unfair advantages for his new employer. What has concerned some critics is that such appointments can lead to what one Conservative MP has described as the danger of 'subliminal corruption'.[66] The difficulties that such appointments can raise were recorded by Richard Crossman whose Permanent Secretary at the DHSS, Sir Clifford Jarrett, told him, in the middle of a 'battle royal' with the private pensions consultants, that upon retirement he hoped to be given permission to accept a post as President of the Corporation of the Society of Pension Consultants. Crossman observed: 'I am sure there is nothing dishonest about it . . . but it seems to me that if my top civil servant has without my knowledge been talking to the pension consultants about a job with them, in any other country that would be thought to be an improper relationship.'[67]

The danger of abuse of such appointments has long been recognized, and rules governing acceptance of outside business appointments were introduced as long ago as 1937, and were substantially revised in 1975. Senior civil servants of the rank of under secretary and above, taking up posts within two years of leaving the civil service, must obtain prior permission from the government. In the case of applications from permanent secretaries, the Prime Minister is advised by an Advisory Committee of persons from outside the civil service. Responsibility for decisions in all other cases rests with departmental ministers. In practice, however, permission is rarely refused and, even if it were, has no legal effect. In the period 1979–83, of 1,809 applications from civil servants and officers in seven major government departments (1,404 of them from the MOD, over half of which involved jobs in the defence industry) only 15 were rejected.[68]

Despite such rules, the business appointments of former senior civil servants have attracted increasingly critical attention, notably from the Treasury and Civil Service Committee of the House of Commons, which published reports on the subject in 1980 and 1984.[69] The 1984 report recommended new safeguards, including a delay of up to five years before civil servants of the rank of under secretary and above could take up a post in the private sector, the follow up of links between ex-civil servants and their former departments to ensure that conditions are being complied with, and sanctions (including loss of inflation proof pensions) against those who breach these controls, all of which were rejected by the government in 1985.[70] The government's rejection was premised on the principle of minimizing the obstacles to freedom of movement between the public sector and other sectors of national life, and the fact that the committee had found no evidence of impropriety.

Advocates of reform, however, would argue that it is equally important that civil servants should be seen to be above any suspicion of impropriety, and that a tighter code of conduct is required to prevent the erosion of public confidence in the traditional independence and impartiality of the civil service, especially in a world where the public and private sectors increasingly inter-penetrate.

Dropping the Mask

One factor which has helped to diminish the 'facelessness' of the civil service has been the increasing tendency for senior civil servants to be publicly identified by the mass media. Senior civil servants are regularly named, and sometimes profiled, by the Whitehall corre-spondents of the quality newspapers. On occasion, serving officials have also dropped their masks and discussed their work with the media. Civil servants have appeared on radio programmes like the BBC's *Talking Politics* series, and described their work and role.[71] The myth of a 'faceless' civil service has been further undermined by the participation of senior civil servants (including five permanent secretaries) in the BBC Radio 4 series, *No, Minister*, in which senior officials discussed such controversial issues as the relationship be-tween ministers and civil servants, the size of the civil service, and its competence and accountability. Some officials have even expressed their personal opinions on such policy issues as membership of the European Community.[72]

More controversially, some civil servants have been publicly associated with particular governments: for example, Sir William Armstrong, the then Head of the Home Civil Service, allowed himself to become publicly associated with the Heath government in the early 1970s. Armstrong appeared at press conferences with the Prime Minister, and was the only other person with Heath when the Prime Minister attempted to negotiate with Joe Gormley, the Presi-dent of the National Union of Mineworkers, over the miners' pay claim in 1973. Sir William, who earned the nickname of 'the deputy Prime Minister', was regarded by some observers as having stepped over the line between political adviser and politically neutral civil servant, perhaps compromising his ability to serve a government of a different complexion.

More recently, Armstrong's namesake, Sir Robert Armstrong, not only Head of the Home Civil Service but also Cabinet Secretary, has put his head above the parapet, and become closely associated with the Thatcher government. Sir Robert was called upon twice in 1986 to rescue the government from political difficulties: first over the Westland affair, where he, in effect, spoke for the Prime Minister and the Cabinet when giving oral evidence to the Defence Select Committee of the House of Commons; and later in the year, when he was the government's chief witness during the hearings in the New South Wales Supreme Court, in the government's attempts to prevent the publication in Australia of the memoirs of the former MI5 officer, Peter Wright (see Prologue).

The 1980s have also seen an increasing tendency for retired civil servants to 'come out of the closet' and pronounce publicly on various issues. One of the former permanent secretaries who have, in Peter Hennessy's words, 'trod the boards as never before', is the former Cabinet Secretary, Lord Hunt, who has criticized the deficiencies of the machinery of Cabinet government, observing that there is 'a hole in the centre of government', a problem which, in his opinion, has not been entirely solved.[73] The same metaphor was used by Sir Frank Cooper, a former Permanent Secretary at the Ministry of Defence, who argued in a public lecture that there was 'a defence hole at the centre of government', with a need for adequate machinery to look at security in 'the fullest and roundest sense'.[74]

Other recently retired officials have spoken out critically on government policies. Sir Leo Pliatzky, a former Permanent Secretary at the Department of Trade, has been critical of the conduct of economic policy.[75] And Lord Bancroft, a former Head of the Home Civil Service, has been critical of the Conservative government's attitude towards the civil service. In a House of Lords debate on the Civil Service in 1986, Bancroft said that the permanent, non-political civil service which had been built up over a century and a quarter could be destroyed in a decade by ministerial hostility, misuse and indifference; and he feared that this was happening. He argued that, in his view, the government's record as an employer was seen by most civil servants as 'callous opportunism'.[76]

Bancroft's criticisms have reinforced the pronouncements of Sir Douglas Wass, former Permanent Secretary to the Treasury and Joint Head of the Home Civil Service, in the 1983 BBC Reith Lectures.[77] In what one commentator has described as 'the politest of attacks on Thatcherism', Wass defended the concept of a permanent, politically neutral civil service (see also chapter 8), and made coded criticisms of the Thatcher government's reductions in the size of the civil service.[78] Wass has also become publicly identified, along with other retired permanent secretaries, with the campaign for more open government, acting as an adviser to the 1984 Campaign for Freedom of Information, a reversal of roles described by one newspaper as comparable to 'a retired reverend mother becoming a chorus girl'.[79]

Thus several former senior officials who once occupied what Peter Hennessy describes as the 'ringside seats in the stadium of British government', have broken the rules of a lifetime to comment, sometimes controversially, on public issues.[80] For some commentators this trend is partly a consequence of changes in the culture of British society.[81] It can also be interpreted as a manifestation of the deteriorating relationship between the civil service and the Thatcher government.

Postscript

The much criticized Section 2 of the 1911 Official Secrets Act was replaced by a new Official Secrets Act in 1989. The new legislation narrows the scope of the former Act by making it a criminal offence to disclose specific categories of information: defence, security and intelligence, international relations and law enforcement matters. Although described by the then Home Secretary as a 'liberalising' measure, critics argue that the new Act represents a tightening of the law, pointing to the omission of a public interest defence (cf. the Ponting affair) or a defence of prior publication (cf. the *Spycatcher* case).[82]

The Armstrong Memorandum issued in the wake of the Ponting affair was revised in 1987 in order to allow for the possibility of a civil servant being able to appeal to the Head of the Home Civil Service in the event of receiving instructions from ministers or other officials which they believe to be unlawful, improper, unethical or which raise 'a fundamental issue of conscience'.[83] As we saw in the postscript to chapter 6, the government subsequently agreed that this new right of appeal be written into the CSPCSC.

The TCSC report which prompted the government to amend the CSPCSC also reiterated its predecessor committee's concern that some government press officer posts should be filled by political appointments rather than career civil servants.[84] Mrs Thatcher's press secretary, Bernard Ingham, at the centre of so much controversy in the 1980s, left his post soon after the prime minister's resignation in December 1990.[85]

10

Slimmer and Fitter: the Quest for Efficiency and Effectiveness

When Northcote and Trevelyan presented their famous report on the civil service in 1853, central government was largely confined to defence, foreign and colonial affairs, the maintenance of law and order, the regulation of overseas trade and the collection of taxes (see chapter 2). The size of the civil service reflected this essentially regulatory state, totalling less then 40,000 civil servants in 1851. But the nature of central government's tasks has changed dramatically since the nightwatchman era of the mid-nineteenth century. The period since Northcote–Trevelyan has witnessed the evolution from a regulatory to a collectivist state, and today there are few areas of society with which central government cannot be said to be involved. Central government's regulatory functions have expanded, and it has taken on vast new functions, notably the range of policies and services covered by the welfare state, and responsibility for managing the economy. A hundred years after Northcote–Trevelyan, the civil service had expanded twentyfold.

Within this framework of 'big government', departments, and the civil servants who staff them, carry out a wide range of activities. For example, in 1986 over 170,000 civil servants in the Ministry of Defence supported the armed forces, many of them working in defence establishments like the Royal Naval Dockyards. Over 90,000 staff worked in the Department of Health and Social Security, a large proportion of them paying out more than 30 different types of benefit equivalent to nearly one-third of total public expenditure. In the Inland Revenue, 70,000 civil servants were employed assessing and collecting taxes. Nearly 55,000 worked for the Department of Employment Group, paying out unemployment benefit, running job centres and so on. These and other executive activities were run by a civil service which numbered nearly 600,000, and which, in 1985–6, had gross running costs of £12.3 billion, about 3.4 per cent of gross national product.[1]

Given the range of central government activity, the number of people employed and the sums of money involved, it is hardly surprising that the efficiency and effectiveness of the central administrative machine is a matter of recurrent political and public debate. There has long been a popular view which associates the civil service (and other bureaucracies) with inefficiency, 'red tape', proliferation of badly worded forms and unnecessary duplication of effort. The growth of the civil service has been ridiculed in Parkinson's Law, which holds that 'work expands so as to fill the time available for its completion'.[2] Such questions have come to dominate political debate about the civil service in the 1980s.

But before we come to discuss the main themes of the debate on the efficiency of the civil service, we need to be clear about the terms involved. What do we mean by 'efficiency'? What do we mean by 'effectiveness'? The differences between the two concepts have been defined by the Treasury and Civil Service Committee:

> an *efficient* programme is one where the target is being achieved with the least possible use of resources and instruments. Similarly, on the way to achieving the target, the actual output of a programme should be secured with the least use of resources. An *effective* programme is one where the intention of the programme is being achieved.[3]

There are, however, considerable difficulties in finding adequate measures of outputs in government departments, although the inputs, chiefly staff costs, can usually be measured. Measures for assessing the progress made towards achievement of intentions are even harder to find. Thus the MOD has put forward as a measure of the effectiveness of a strategy of nuclear deterrence the fact that there has been no major war for over 30 years.[4] It is also difficult to disentangle the impact of a particular government policy from other factors that may be at work.

Despite such problems, the quest for efficiency and effectiveness has dominated political debate since the 1960s, and has been a central feature of the Thatcher government's attitude towards the civil service. Before we discuss the Thatcher government's attempts to create a 'slimmer and fitter' civil service, however, we need to look back at developments before the 1979 election.

From Fulton to Thatcher

For many years the British civil service was regarded by most observers as 'the best in the world'. By the early 1960s, however, there was increasing criticism that the civil service was amateurish and incapable of dealing with the problems of an increasingly complex and technologically advanced society.[5] Concern about the managerial competence of the civil service was voiced in 1961 by the Plowden Committee on the Control of Public Expenditure, which found that senior civil servants did not devote enough time to management compared with policy advice.[6] But criticism of the management inadequacies of the civil service reached its height in the Report of the Fulton Committee in 1968. A key theme of the Committee's findings was the promotion of efficiency in the civil service, and the Report was highly critical of the fact that too few civil servants were skilled managers, arguing that the higher civil service in particular tended 'to think of themselves as advisers on policy to people above them, rather than as managers of the administrative machine below them'.[7] Fulton has been described as the 'high-water mark of managerialism', and as being imbued with 'a business–managerial philosophy'.[8]

What, then, did Fulton have to say about efficiency in the civil service? Fulton argued that to function efficiently, large organizations, including government departments, need a structure in which units and individual members have clearly defined authority and responsibilities for which they can be held accountable. Fulton concluded that there was scope for organizing executive activities in such a way that the principle of 'accountable management' (a concept developed at General Motors in the USA) could be applied within departments. Its achievement was seen to depend upon identifying or establishing accountable units within departments: defined as 'units where outputs can be measured against costs or other criteria, and where individuals can be held personally responsible for their performance'.[9]

Where measures of achievement could be established in quantitative or financial terms, and individuals held responsible for output and costs, Fulton recommended that accountable units should be set up. Work of this kind should be organized into separate 'commands', and the managers of each command should be given clear-cut responsibilities and commensurate authority and be held accountable for performance against budgets, standards of achievement and other tests. In those areas of administrative work where performance could not be assessed in terms of measurable output, Fulton recommended the application of the concept of management by objectives (MBO), whereby the head of a branch agrees with his superiors and subordinates a programme of objectives, with priorities and dates for completion.[10]

Some of the evidence to the Fulton Committee argued that accountable management could be most effectively introduced where an activity was separately established outside a government department, by 'hiving off' to boards and corporations which would be wholly responsible in their own fields within the powers delegated to them.[11] Although such bodies would be outside the day-to-day control of ministers and the scrutiny of Parliament, ministers would retain powers to give them directions when necessary. Fulton was impressed by the system of 'hiving off' operating in Sweden, and observed that there was a wide variety of activities in the UK to which it might be possible to apply the principle. The Committee recommended an early and thorough review of the whole question.[12]

The general thrust of the Fulton recommendations was accepted by the then Labour government, and the idea of accountable management was taken up as part of the 'new style of government' introduced by the Conservative government under Mr Heath in 1970. The 1970 White Paper, *The Reorganisation of Central Government* which, as we saw in chapter 4, had expounded the rationale of giant departments, promised 'a sustained effort to ensure that . . . executive blocks of work will be delegated to accountable units of management, thus lessening the load on the departmental top management'.[13] The concept was subsequently reflected in the development of what were known as departmental agencies: identifiable units within a government department under the direction of a minister accountable to Parliament, but with an executive head who is also an accounting officer, with a large degree of freedom in personnel matters. The Defence Procurement Executive was created as an agency within the MOD in 1971, responsible for providing defence equipment. The following year, the Property Services Agency (PSA), responsible for the management of government property, the provision of equipment and the maintenance of government buildings, was set up as an agency within the Department of the Environment. The year 1972 also saw the creation of the Employment Services Agency and the Training Services Agency, both within the Department of Employment (and both later to be 'hived off' to form part of the Manpower Services Commission). The concept of accountable management was also applied to quasi-commercial activities in the civil service, with the Royal Ordnance Factories (1974) and the Royal Mint (1975) being given their own separate trading funds.[14]

Despite such developments, the House of Commons Expenditure Committee, which reported on the progress of the Fulton recommendations in 1977, concluded that there had not been a determined effort to implement the recommendations on accountable management, observing that it did not believe that the proposals had 'been taken sufficiently seriously' by the civil service.[15] In its response, the Labour government pointed out that the objectives of government departments were 'complex and interrelated in a way and to an extent' which limited the number of tasks to which this approach could successfully be applied.[16] The evidence of the Civil Service Department to the Expenditure Committee also pointed to drawbacks in the progress made on MBO. By 1974 the CSD had undertaken a trial of MBO involving 45 projects, but progress had apparently 'stopped at about this point'.[17] The CSD reported that in some cases MBO had proved over-elaborate and costly to install, and that the staff side had been worried about the 'unfair pressure' put on individuals by aspects of reviewing and recording performance.[18]

The area in which the concept of 'hiving off' could be applied also proved to be limited. Few government activities met the detailed criteria set by the Conservative government in the early 1970s, in particular that the activity should be largely self-financing; that it did not require regular ministerial involvement; that quantitative performance measures could be adopted; and that adequate career opportunities could be provided for staff.[19] Nevertheless, a few activities were found suitable for hiving off. In 1971 a major part of the Department of Trade and Industry was hived off to form the Civil Aviation Authority, and in 1974 the Manpower Services Commission was formed from part of the Department of Employment. The process of hiving off from Employment was continued by the Labour government in 1974 with the creation of the Health and Safety Commission and the Advisory Conciliation and Arbitration Service (ACAS). Interestingly, the lack of career opportunities for staff in the hived-off Manpower Services Commission was a factor in the reclassification of its personnel as civil servants in 1976.

Another important strand in the Heath government's attempts to introduce a new style of government in 1970 was a greater emphasis on policy analysis, with the introduction of a system of regular reviews of policy designed to 'provide Ministers with an opportunity to identify and discuss alternative policy options'.[20] Attempts to evaluate and review government programmes had been attempted in the 1960s, when a few departments had developed feasibility studies in PPBS (Programme, Planning and Budgeting System: originally introduced in the American Department of Defense), but policy evaluation remained basically experimental.[21] The system introduced by the Heath government was called Programme Analysis and Review (PAR), and was seen as a necessary complement to the PESC cycle developed in the early 1960s following the criticisms in the Plowden Report. PARs were intended to assess the effectiveness of current departmental programmes in achieving their aims and to review other available options.

Some important PARs were carried out in the early 1970s, but this particular experiment in policy analysis petered out after 1973. In their survey of the experiment, Gray and Jenkins argue that PAR was unable to satisfy the technical, organizational and political preconditions for effective analysis.[22] Not only was there no systematic idea of how PARs would operate from the initiation stage to implementation, but the system also lacked any coherent strong central organization, with departments being left to organize their PARs in very much their own way. Politically, there was little evidence that PAR received ministerial backing: 'depth analysis was unimportant and ministers preferred superficiality'.[23] The Labour government of 1974 was suspicious of PAR as part of 'an alien ideology', closely associated with the Heath government; and with the 'crisis of control' in public expenditure of the mid-1970s PAR became increasingly irrelevant. It was formally abandoned by the Thatcher government soon after the 1979 election.

The Thatcher Years

The abolition of PAR was just one manifestation of the Thatcher government's shift of emphasis from effectiveness to efficiency. Elected on a manifesto which promised to reduce public expenditure and the role of the state, the government's policy towards the public sector was to make substantial economies by reducing waste, bureaucracy and 'over-government'.[24] As we saw in chapter 8, the Thatcher government was also critical of the lack of managerial skills in the higher civil service. Echoing the Plowden and Fulton Committees of the 1960s, it maintained that senior officials spent too much time on policy-making and too little on the efficient management of government departments. The election of the Conservatives marked a turning-point in the debate about efficiency and effectiveness in the civil service. The gospel became, in the words of Gray and Jenkins, 'that of managerialism couched in the language of the health farm: organisations are fat and need to be slimmer'.[25] Since 1979 the government's commitment to greater efficiency has led to a series of initiatives designed to create a 'slimmer and fitter civil service'.

TABLE 10.1 *Industrial and non-industrial staff in the civil service, 1979–88 (full-time equivalents in thousands)*

Year	Industrial	Non-industrial	Total
1979	166	566	732
1980	157	547	704
1981	150	540	690
1982	138	528	666
1983	130	519	649
1984	120	504	624
1985	101	498	599
1986	96	498	594
1987	90	507	598
1988	73	507	580

Source: Civil Service Statistics, 1988–89

The first part of the Thatcher government's programme for achieving efficiency in the civil service was the imposition of strict limits on the number of civil servants. The total size of the civil service when the Conservative government came to office in May 1979 was 732,000 and, following a review, the government set a target of 630,000 by April 1984.[26] As table 10.1 shows, the total was actually down to 624,000 by that date. By April 1988, the total size of the civil service was 580,000, which represents a 20 per cent reduction since 1979.

Whilst the size of the civil service has contracted dramatically since the election of the Thatcher government, not all departments have been equally affected. As table 10.2 shows, the DOE (including the PSA) has declined at more than twice the rate of the service as a whole, and in some departments numbers have actually increased because of the pressures on the services they provide. Thus the staff of the Home Office prison service increased in response to a growing prison population. The staff of the Department of Employment has also grown partly because of the need to meet increased workload as a result of rising unemployment. Indeed, the extra workload carried by the Department of Employment and the DHSS in 1986 led to the government agreeing to *increase* the total of civil servants by nearly 9,000 for the remainder of the 1986–7 financial year, although the size of the civil service will continue to be reduced in later years.[27]

TABLE 10.2   *Civil service staff: by ministerial responsibility (thousands)[a]*

	1979	1986	1988
Agriculture, Fisheries and Food	14.5	11.7	11.1
Chancellor of the Exchequer's departments			
Customs and Excise	28.8	25.1	26.3
Inland Revenue	84.6	69.3	66.6
Department for National Savings	10.8	7.8	7.4
Treasury and others	4.0	8.8	8.3
Defence	247.7	169.5	143.4
Education and Science	3.7	2.4	2.5
Employment Group[b]	53.6	55.7	58.3
Energy	1.3	1.0	1.0
Environment (including PSA)	56.0	34.9	33.0
Foreign and Commonwealth	12.1	9.6	9.6
Health and Social Services	100.9	94.9	102.3
Home	33.5	37.5	39.2
Scotland[c]	13.7	12.9	13.0
Trade and Industry[d]	19.1	14.8	14.6
Transport	13.9	14.7	14.1
Welsh Office	2.6	2.3	2.2
Other departments	31.4	21.5	26.7
Total all departments	732.3	594.4	579.6

[a] As at 1 April.
[b] Department of Employment; Health and Safety Executive; Advisory Conciliation and Arbitration Service; Manpower Services Commission; Employment Services Agency; and Training Services Agency.
[c] Departments of the Secretary of State for Scotland and the Lord Advocate.
[d] In 1979 Industry (9.5 thousand staff) and Trade (9.6 thousand staff) were separate departments. In June 1983 they were combined as the Department of Trade and Industry.

Sources: Social Trends, 1986; Annual Abstract of Statistics, 1990

Reductions in civil service staff have been achieved in a number of ways. Some functions have been dropped or materially curtailed (e.g. the collection of certain statistics). There have been changes in the scope of departmental work: thus the Inland Revenue removed a special band of income tax and thereby saved some 1,000 staff. Some departments have reduced staff by more efficient methods and general streamlining: the Ministry of Agriculture, Fisheries and Food saved 700 staff by streamlining the regulations and simplifying its arrangements for the payment of capital grants to farmers. Reductions have also been achieved by 'contracting out' (e.g. cleaning services in the MOD) and by 'hiving off' functions (e.g. about 250 staff in the Royal Botanic Gardens were excluded from the MAFF manpower count in 1984).

The size of the civil service in 1986 was down to 594,000, smaller than at any time since the Second World War. Thus, in numerical terms, the Thatcher government's programme for civil service cuts has been very successful. But, to paraphrase the late Professor Joad, 'it all depends what you mean by' the civil service. The cuts since 1979 are partly cosmetic. The staff of the Royal Botanic Gardens may no longer be classified as civil servants, but they are still performing the same jobs that they were carrying out before they were removed from the MAFF. The reductions in civil service manpower have also occurred disproportionately in the industrial civil service, which stood at 96,000 in 1986 as compared with 615,000 in 1945. The non-industrial civil service, however, was about the same as it was in 1945.[28]

The second part of the Thatcher government's programme for promoting efficiency in the civil service has been to ensure value for money, a theme highlighted by the revelations of Leslie Chapman, a former senior civil servant in the PSA.[29] A central plank of this policy has been the continuous programme of efficiency scrutinies of specific activities in departments initiated by Sir Derek (now Lord) Rayner, the then joint managing director of Marks and Spencer, who was appointed by the Prime Minister immediately after the 1979 election to advise her on ways of improving efficiency and eliminating waste in central government. Rayner was familiar with the corridors of Whitehall, having served as a member of the Business Team which advised Edward Heath in 1969–70, and as chief executive of the MOD's Defence Procurement Executive from 1971–3. At Marks and Spencer he had spearheaded a small team of executives who had reduced staff costs by 5 per cent through the implementation of such measures as simplifying stock control and the abolition of forms.[30] Although Rayner was only appointed on a part-time basis, he was supported by a small unit of about six civil servants (known as the Rayner Unit) based in the Prime Minister's Private Office. He was succeeded in 1983 by Sir Robin Ibbs, an executive director of Imperial Chemical Industies and a former head of the Central Policy Review Staff, when the Efficiency Unit, as it is now called, was also absorbed into the Management and Personnel Office.

Some observers saw in the Rayner approach a variant of what PAR had been intended to achieve in the 1970s, but whereas the latter was concerned with policy analysis and, hence, effectiveness, the efficiency scrutinies are concerned with reducing inputs, and therefore with efficiency in the narrow sense. They ask three simple questions about the activity under investigation: 'what is it for, what does it cost and what value does it add?'[31]

The Rayner technique has been described as that of 'the laser beam rather than the arc light'.[32] The scrutinies look in great detail at particular aspects of civil service work. The choice of scrutiny topics is the responsibility of the minister in charge of the department, but under the oversight of the Efficiency Unit which is consulted on the choice of the subject. Each scrutiny is generally carried out by an examining officer of the affected department, who is usually a high-flier marked out for promotion, normally of principal rank, and completed within 90 working days. Paradoxically, the career of Clive Ponting underwent a marked advance following favourable notice by Mrs Thatcher of his cost-saving proposals put forward as part of a Rayner exercise.[33]

The scope of the efficiency scrutinies has been wide ranging and has included such diverse topics as withdrawal arrangements for National Savings Certificates, the organization of MOT tests, and the forensic science service of the Home Office. The scrutinies have also included a number of service-wide or multi-departmental reviews, such as the government's statistical services across 22 departments, and a review of official forms.

The efficiency scrutinies have unearthed a number of administrative inefficiencies, ranging from the maintenance of tax files for PAYE taxpayers, to the government laboratory breeding rats at a cost of £30 each when they could have been purchased on the open market for £2 each. But whilst many proposals have been accepted, a large proportion have not been implemented. A survey by the National Audit Office in 1986 found that less than half of the economies identified by the efficiency scrutinies in four selected departments were expected to be achieved.[34] Even a study which had the backing of the Prime Minister, the review of DHSS arrangements for paying social security benefits, was not totally implemented. The review, which suggested reducing the frequency of benefit payments and making payments direct to bank accounts, led to howls of protest from pensioners' organizations and sub-postmasters, and the actual saving in DHSS administrative costs was only £29 million per year, as opposed to the original estimate of £66 million.[35]

Despite such setbacks, the efficiency scrutinies have resulted in substantial savings. Between 1979 and 1983 (when Rayner's appointment ended) departments had completed 155 scrutinies, not including multi-departmental reviews. It was calculated in 1986 that the scrutinies had produced annual savings of £300 million, and cumulative savings of £950 million.[36] But the savings are small compared with the total cost of the civil service, and in the words of one commentator, the scrutinies have been 'more a delicate duster than a new broom'.[37]

Defenders of the scrutinies argue, however, that the main success of the scrutiny programme has been not so much in the individual savings identified, but in their impact on influencing the 'management conventions' of ministers and civil servants, and in making them recognize that it is possible to improve efficiency. Thus Metcalfe and Richards argue that at the individual level the carrying out of scrutinies has had a 'Smirnoff effect' in that, like drinkers of the well-known vodka, scrutineers are 'never quite the same again', and their experience produces a change of attitude and outlook.[38] Whether this will lead to lasting changes in the culture of Whitehall as a whole is a question to which we shall return later in the chapter.

MINIS and the FMI

One of the early Rayner scrutinies was a study of the provision of management information for ministers in the DOE. The study was initiated by the then Secretary of State, Michael Heseltine, who was concerned at the absence of a 'management ethos' in government departments. According to a report in *The Financial Times*, when Heseltine was appointed to the DOE:

he could not untangle the chains of responsibility within the department. It was impossible to figure out who was doing what, or why, or whether it needed doing at all. There appeared to be duplication of effort and conflicting estimates of costing. It was very rare to be able to find one person easily identifiable as being responsible.[39]

The result of the Rayner study was the setting up in early 1980 of the DOE system known as Management Information System for Ministers (MINIS), which is designed to enable the secretary of state to explore 'who does what, why and what does it cost?' Its purpose is to 'bring together information about activities, past performance and future plans for each part of the Department'.[40] The system shows how the work of the Department is organized and who is responsible for each area of its activity. Great claims have been made about MINIS: not only has it revealed substantial scope for economies (Heseltine has said that MINIS directly enabled him to cut staff at the DOE in a way that would otherwise not have been possible), but it has also enabled ministers to ensure that resources are allocated in accordance with their priorities.[41] Heseltine subsequently introduced MINIS when he took over the MOD in 1983, where it was responsible for discovering, *inter alia*, that the Department had three separate units each ordering false teeth for the three different armed services.[42] In 1983, following another Rayner study (referred to as the Joubert study, after its examining officer), MINIS was complemented in the DOE by a computerized cost centre accounting and budgeting system, known as MAXIS, delegating responsibility for running costs to line managers.

Despite Heseltine's claim that MINIS had improved both the efficiency and effectiveness of the DOE, there was general scepticism in the rest of Whitehall about whether a development which was very much the creation of one particular minister was transferable to other departments. There was also little ministerial interest in MINIS, a presentation to Cabinet in 1982 being reported to have been an occasion which 'met with a less than enthusiastic response'.[43] One group which was favourably impressed with MINIS, and unimpressed with the reasons offered by other departments for not adopting such systems themselves, was the Treasury and Civil Service Committee of the House of Commons in its 1982 Report on *Efficiency and Effectiveness in the Civil Service*. The Committee was highly critical of the absence of any clear orientation towards the achievement of efficiency and effectiveness at the higher levels of the civil service, and of the limited attempts to set operational objectives, measure outputs and results, and thus to guide the proper use of resources. The Committee put forward a series of recommendations to improve the management of government departments, including the introduction of MINIS, or its equivalent, in all departments, and the need for more, and more clearly defined, responsibilities to be assigned to managers.

The Committee was, of course, pushing at an open door, and the government's response to its report was outlined in a 1982 White Paper, which announced the Financial Management Initiative (FMI), emphasizing the need for a general and co-ordinated drive to improve financial management in departments.[44] The FMI had been formally launched in May 1982 through the circulation of a prime ministerial paper to ministers in charge of departments. The Initiative called for radical changes in the organization and style of management, involving moves towards devolved authority and accountable management. The aims were:

to promote in each department an organisation and system in which managers at all levels have:

(a) a clear view of their objectives and means to assess and, wherever possible, measure outputs or performance in relation to those objectives;

(b) well-defined responsibility for making the best use of their resources, including a critical scrutiny of output and value for money; and

(c) the information (particularly about costs), the training and the access to expert advice that they need to exercise their responsibilities effectively.[45]

Following the launching of the Initiative, 31 departments were required to examine the way in which they arranged all aspects of their programmes and to develop a programme of work for improving their financial management. They were assisted in this exercise by a special unit of civil servants and outside consultants, the Financial Management Unit (FMU), set up jointly by the MPO and the Treasury. Following a review in 1984, the FMU was replaced by a Joint Management Unit (JMU).

Progress reports on the FMI are set out in two White Papers published in 1983 and 1984.[46] As Gray and Jenkins observe, the aim of the Initiative represents a general approach rather than a single strategy, and a variety of different management systems has emerged.[47] A lot of activity has gone into the development within departments of management information systems similar to that pioneered at the DOE, and MINIS has been joined by such systems as MINIM (MAFF), DEMIS (Department of Energy) and ARM (DTI). Progress has also been made towards the development of a more decentralized style of budgetary control by dividing departments into appropriate blocks and into 'cost centres' within each block, with their managers accountable for the management of the costs under their control and for the results they achieve. The DHSS, for example, has over 800 cost centres with managers responsible for keeping expenditure within their budget for supplies and services over which they can exercise control. Improvements have also been made in the management of departments' own programme expenditure.

Better information for ministers and top officials, and plans for a more decentralized style of budget control, are of little value without a new breed of skilled manager. Consequently, FMI is being complemented by a set of improvements in personnel management, based in part on the Cassells Report of 1983, including improved career management and training for those with the potential to rise to senior positions.[48] In 1985, a new course was introduced for those at under secretary level to include the opportunity for senior civil servants to think collectively about management problems. The same year saw the start of a three-year trial for performance-related pay (as recommended by the Megaw Committee in 1982, see chapter 6) for all staff in grades 3 to 7.[49] A new 'productivity' scheme was subsequently approved, under which officials at the levels of deputy secretary and under secretary would be offered the chance to compete for special discretionary payments of up to £2,000 for good performance.[50]

Thus a series of developments has taken place in the systems and procedures of departments, and in the policies for career management and training, in an attempt to encourage cost-consciousness and to allow civil servants to have a clearer view of their policy objectives. According to some, the FMI will ultimately be seen as a watershed in the civil service's approach to management.[51] For others, however, lasting reforms in the management of government departments mean more than the introduction of new systems and new techniques. As Metcalfe and Richards observe, lasting reforms depend upon substantial changes in the Whitehall culture: 'the, often unspoken, set of assumptions about their role within which senior civil servants think and act'. It is a culture which is sceptical of the value of managerial change and the importance of business methods in the civil service, and within which 'writing a well constructed ministerial brief on a topical subject or steering a Bill through Parliament has higher value . . . than implementing a new policy or improving the administration of an existing policy.'[52] In the words of an ex-permanent secretary, the Whitehall culture is characterized by a gentlemen–players view, in which the former make policy and the latter implement it.[53]

Efficiency Audit

In addition to changes in the management procedures and budgetary systems of government departments, the early 1980s have also seen significant changes in the machinery of central government audit. The word 'audit' tends to conjure up images of dusty ledgers, receipts and volumes of figures. In public administration, however, the ramifications of audit processes go far wider than this and are central to the whole process of evaluating the efficiency of government programmes.

The central figure in the audit process is the Comptroller and Auditor-General (CAG), an office set up by the Exchequer and Audit Departments Act of 1866 (which was slightly amended in 1921 by an Act of the same title) to verify the regularity of departmental expenditure by auditing the books of government departments. The CAG's findings are reported to the Public Accounts Committee of the House of Commons, set up five years before the CAG. In the words of Sir Edward (later Lord) Bridges, the CAG 'puts up a lot of game for the Committee to have a shot at'.[54] Always chaired by a leading member of the opposition, who is normally an ex-Treasury minister (past chairmen have included Harold Wilson, Edward du Cann and Joel Barnett), the Committee summons before it the permanent secretaries of government departments, in their capacity as accounting officers, to answer points raised in the CAG's reports. Notwithstanding the doctrine of individual ministerial responsibility, permanent secretaries are in this context, and in this context only, personally responsible for ensuring the legality of departmental spending. As such, they can state in writing to the minister their disagreement with proposals which they consider they would have difficulty in defending before the PAC. The second permanent secretary at the Department of Industry, Peter Carey, submitted an accounting officer's minute relating to the financial propriety of Tony Benn's decision to provide funds for the Kirkby Workers' Co-operative in 1975.[55]

The Committee has an enviable reputation as the one select committee before which even the most exalted permanent secretary can be made to tremble. Indeed, the appearance of the then chief executive of the Property Services Agency before the Committee in 1984, in his capacity as accounting officer, to answer questions about the 1983 Wardale Report on fraud and corruption in the PSA, was followed a fortnight later by the announcement that his appointment had been terminated by mutual agreement.[56] In the words of a current member of the PAC, the Committee's reports can have 'seismic effects throughout Whitehall'.[57]

Although the Gladstonian concept of audit focused on the narrowly technical concern with legality and regularity, ensuring that expenditure had been upon approved services and in accordance with statutory authority, the CAG was encouraged by the PAC to extend his remit into broader questions of economy and efficiency – value for money (VFM) or 'efficiency audit' – in administration, a process facilitated by the vagueness of the Exchequer and Audit Departments Acts when it came to explaining what is actually meant by 'audit'. More recently, the CAG's investigations have broadened even further to include 'effectiveness audit', seeking 'to assess how successful particular programmes have been in meeting the policy objectives of Government'.[58]

As the CAG has delved more deeply into these issues, so the role of the PAC has also developed far beyond the narrow concern with legality and regularity. For example, the Committee drew attention in the session 1972–3 to the inadequacy of financial arrangements for securing the government a share of profits from the exploitation of North Sea oil and gas.[59] In a completely different area, the Committee pointed in its Fourth Report for the session 1974–5 to the inadequate costs and staff estimates of the new centralized Vehicle and Driver Licensing Office at Swansea, revealing that the estimated cost of the office at the time of the Committee's report had risen from £146 million to £350 million, and that the estimated staff requirements were expected to be nearly 50 per cent higher than forecast.[60] In 1985 the Committee also provided a valuable service in drawing attention to the high costs of the development of the MOD's torpedo projects and the poor value for money which appeared to have been obtained.[61]

Although the CAG's role developed beyond a concern with regularity, it did so without explicit legislative authority. The lack of independence of the CAG from the Executive – the holder of the office and his department being subject to Treasury oversight – was seen as further evidence of the ambiguity and untidiness of the system of central audit. Important changes in the statutory basis of audit were made by the National Audit Act 1983, which had its origins in the proposals put forward in 1981 by the PAC, and comprehensively rejected in a government White Paper the same year.[62]

The Committee recommended that the CAG should be empowered to carry out full VFM audits and studies of the effectiveness of government programmes. The centrepiece of the Committee's recommendations, however, was its proposal for the creation of a National Audit Office, headed by the CAG, to have responsibility for the external audit of all government authorities and health authorities, and for advising Parliament on the efficiency with which public money is invested in non-departmental bodies, in nationalized industries and other public corporations, and in privately owned companies. In the face of government procrastination, Norman St John Stevas, a former Leader of the House of Commons, introduced a Private Members' Bill to implement the PAC Report. The subsequent Act (watered down at the government's insistence) failed to extend the CAG's jurisdiction to nationalized industries, but under the Act a revamped Exchequer and Audit Department was transformed into the National Audit Office, and the CAG became an officer of the House of Commons, separate from the Treasury. The Act also gve a statutory basis to the CAG's role in carrying out VFM audit by enabling him to carry out examinations into 'the economy, efficiency and effectiveness' in the use of resources by government departments and other public bodies subject to his audit.

According to one review, the stage 'is thus set for an extension of rigorous questioning of the efficiency and effectiveness with which civil servants perform their duties'.[63] The National Audit Act certainly effects a welcome up-dating of the statutory basis of central audit, but Britain still lags a long way behind countries such as the USA and Sweden in its arrangements for central audit, especially in its lack of emphasis on regular evaluation of the effectiveness of government programmes.[64]

Information Technology

As we were reminded by our discussion in chapter 6 of the civil service industrial dispute of 1981, government is increasingly dependent on computers and the personnel who operate them. Information technology is a development which has enormous potential for improving the efficiency and effectiveness of government departments. Central government is the country's major user of information technology, operating a wide range of computers, telecommunication networks, word processors and other systems. In 1985, there were 450 central government computer installations in use or on order for general and administrative purposes, and it has been estimated that the number of communicating computer terminals in administrative government will be 100,000 by 1992: one terminal for every five or six civil servants.[65]

Many operations of central government depend upon computer-based systems: the payment of social security benefits and pensions; the issue of driver and vehicle licences; the collection of taxes; even the selection of winning Premium Bonds by ERNIE; and there are plans to develop computerization even further. The DHSS's computer system at its Central Office in Newcastle is among the largest in the world, and the Department's operational strategy for computerization of the social security system has proposed the planned development of a national network of computer centres linking local and central offices. Information technology is also playing a significant role in the computerization of the PAYE system, with the Inland Revenue planning to set up 12 regional computer centres, with all of its 600 local tax offices being assigned to one of these centres to form the biggest on-line system in Europe. Indeed, computerization of the PAYE system is regarded as essential to implementing reforms in the structure of personal taxation.[66]

The actual and potential benefits of information technology for improving the efficiency and effectiveness of the civil service are great. It offers the prospect of substantial savings in staffing and other administrative costs: it is hoped that by 1995 the operational strategy will have reduced DHSS staff by 25,000, with a net saving of £1,900 million gross. Information technology also offers benefits in the saving of routine clerical work and in the accuracy and speed with which information can be processed. Information technology is also seen as a development which will provide a better quality of service to the public: thus computerization of the PAYE system is intended to improve the standard of service and cut down on error rates. The DHSS's operational strategy is seen as facilitating the development of 'the whole person concept', whereby an individual's entitlements can be examined in a comprehensive manner. It also provides the possibility of a cashpoint-type system from which clients would be able to draw their entitlements.[67]

Despite these benefits, information technology also has costs. It is seen by many as a potential threat to the privacy of the individual, and as a development which paves the way for the creation of the type of nightmare state foreshadowed by Orwell's *1984*. Three features of information technology have been singled out as providing opportunities for misuse: the huge storage capacity of computers allied to their ability to collate data instantly and produce what is stored; the ease with which data storage systems can communicate with each other; and the extensive means available for the rapid dissemination and presentation of information.[68]

The dangers to individual liberty and privacy posed by the development of information technology have long been recognized, and are an important part of the wider debate about freedom of information which was discussed in chapter 9. The Lindop Committee of 1978, which stressed the need to protect the citizen against the misuse of computer data, was followed three years later by the British government's signing of the European Convention on Data Protection, and, in 1984, by the Data Protection Act, which came into operation in 1986.[69] The 1984 Act created a legally enforceable right for people to discover what information is held about themselves on computer data banks (including those of central government), and to demand its correction or erasure where appropriate. Although the Act does convey substantial protection, it suffers from several defects, notably the failure to cover information held on manual records, and the discretionary powers given to the Home Secretary to forbid access to information concerning health and social work records, and other data which he believes ought to remain confidential.[70]

A major problem of information technology is to reconcile the protection of civil liberties with the administrative benefits associated with the new technology.[71] For many commentators, the balance has not been struck, and it is argued that stronger measures are needed to protect the rights of the individual: possibly the appointment of an Information Technology 'Ombudsman' to investigate complaints that data are being misused.[72]

An 'Efficiency Revolution'?

The efficiency scrutinies, MINIS and the FMI are the latest developments in a long line of attempts to improve efficiency and effectiveness in the civil service, stretching back to the early 1960s. Are such innovations merely a variation on some familiar themes, or do they add up to an 'efficiency revolution'? In many ways, recent developments are evolutionary rather than revolutionary. As Lee reminds us, 'the holy grail' of accountable management which has been introduced via the FMI was discussed long ago by the Fulton Report.[73] But, nearly 20 years on from Fulton, there has been a change of emphasis. The developments of the 1980s are primarily concerned with efficiency, with the major focus on costs, rather than with the more elusive concept of effectiveness. There has been a shift of emphasis from what one civil servant has termed 'grand schemes' like PAR to ones which are predominantly management exercises.[74] This shift reflects the changed context of civil service reform: the presence of a government committed to scaling down 'big government' and to reducing public expenditure.

The initiatives of the Thatcher government also differ from those of the post-Fulton era in the degree of political commitment. Recent developments are supported by the determination and personal support of the Prime Minister herself. In the oft-quoted words of one civil servant: 'we tried before, but without the clout'.[75] The 'efficiency strategy' of the 1980s is reinforced by a strong political commitment, at least on the part of the Prime Minister, a commitment which can be contrasted with the lack of political clout of government in the immediate post-Fulton period.

The developments of the 1980s have been described by Gray and Jenkins as 'a world where bureaucrats (and ministers) are redefined as *accountable managers*, public sector operations subdivided into *businesses*, and the public seen as the *customer*'.[76] But how far can private sector management techniques be transplanted into the public sector? Whilst the objective of most private sector organizations is to make a profit, government departments (as we saw in chapter 7) operate in a milieu in which civil servants are constrained by the need to act fairly, reasonably and equitably.

There are often other, more political, considerations. As Sir Kenneth Clucas, a former permanent secretary, puts it:

To achieve a least-cost deployment of resources may be only one of a number of objectives ... Other factors such as compatibility with the ideology of the Government of the day, the attitude of important interest groups, acceptability to government backbenchers, effect on individual geographical areas, are all perfectly proper considerations for Ministers to take into account when deciding for or against any particular step. There will thus frequently be a clash between considerations of efficiency and other political priorities.[77]

Recent developments have also been criticized as being based on too narrow a concept of performance, preoccupied with a narrow concept of efficiency and value for money, with little concern for the quality or impact of public services or customer satisfaction.[78] Consequently, it is argued, the current approach often results in lower standards of public service, particularly in those parts of government where civil servants come face to face with the public.

Consider, for example, the effect of staffing constraints on the quality of the operation of the DHSS's social security system which was reported in November 1986 to be 'facing breakdown', and in need of a 10,000 increase in local staff.[79] In November 1986, there were 170,000 items of post waiting to be looked at; 140,000 outstanding claims for supplementary benefit; 160,000 claims for single payments; 217,000 other claims, and 22,500 appeals waiting to be processed. Manpower reductions have also taken their toll on civil service morale, with several disputes being triggered by changes in staffing levels and workloads. In the most serious cases, social security offices in Birmingham and Oxford were closed for almost five months.[80]

The relationship between resource constraints and lower standards has also been the subject of comment by the Parliamentary Commissioner for Administration who, in three investigations in the early 1980s, found delays in dealing with applications due to a combination of increases in workload and constraints on manpower resources. The Commissioner concluded that he had no doubt that other departments were also feeling the strain of having to operate a system of priorities in fulfilling their responsibilities.[81]

Such evidence shows that while the 1980s may be characterized as the 'language of the health farm', as any competent family doctor will warn someone going on a diet, slimming can be bad for your health. The civil service, like the human body, is a system. Human systems, like bureaucratic ones, are goal-orientated. Goals can be jeopardized when forcible dieting results in wasted muscles as well as in loss of fat.

Postscript

Despite the misgivings expressed about the impact of the developments of the 1980s on the quality of public services, others argued that these developments did not go far enough and had only scratched the surface of the civil service's management problems. Disappointment with the slow progress of FMI and other reforms led the Efficiency Unit (apparently prompted by the prime minister) to undertake an efficiency scrutiny of the progress made in improving management in the civil service. This scrutiny was to result in a major new initiative, known as the Next Steps programme. We will discuss this important initiative in chapter 12.

11

Conclusion: the Civil Service at the Crossroads?

In writing this book we have had to contend from the outset with the amorphous and elusive character of public bureaucracy, having noted (especially in chapters 1 and 4) the absence of agreed definitions both of 'civil servants' and of the 'departments' in which they work. The blurred nature of the definitional and functional boundaries of the British civil service is a by-product of its complex history, some important aspects of which we have tried to unravel in chapter 2. And the civil service is in any case just one important part of a vast network of public and semi-public institutions whose definitional complexity has in recent years been highlighted by debates about 'privatization' and 'hiving off' and about the rationality or otherwise of the Thatcher government's antipathy towards quangos. To compound our difficulties, the subject of this book has been constantly in motion even as we have tried to pin it down. Choosing a title like *The Civil Service Today* is hazardous in so far as the civil service, like all institutions, is a product of yesterday, and will not be quite the same tomorrow. A major theme of this, our concluding chapter, must be the diagnosis and prognosis of 'change' in the context of changing constitutional precepts and new, perhaps transient, political preoccupations.

At the same time, we must not exaggerate either the elusiveness or the novelty of the subject, nor must we fall into the error of telescoping our perception of change into too narrow and too artificial a time-span. It is tempting, for instance, to think of the Thatcher era – cuts in civil service numbers, suspension of the Pay Research Unit, the Rayner efficiency reviews, the Financial Management Initiative, GCHQ, 'deprivileging', 'politicization', increased militancy of civil service unions etc. – as being of revolutionary significance, not just for the civil service as such but also for the British constitution as a whole. Commentators (including, no doubt, the present authors) often inadvertently encourage this view by over-dramatizing ephemeral novelty, focusing attention on current headlines and speculating incautiously about the future on the basis of recent events.

This is not in itself a matter for criticism or self-criticism (students quickly and understandably complain if journal articles and text-books are 'out of date'), but it does mean that we must be on our guard against the danger of adopting too short a time-perspective. Many of the events of the Thatcher era have been, by any standards, of major significance for the civil service; but many of them are a continuation of earlier trends, and even the most novel of in-novations must be interpreted, not just in its own immediate context, but also in the light of recent history and wider circumstances. Can we be sure that textbooks written 20 years hence will not say that the Wilson era in the late 1960s (the age of Fulton) or the Heath era in the early 1970s (the age of CPRS, PAR, and 'giant departments') were every bit as significant in the modern history of the civil service as is the era of Mrs Thatcher?

Keeping these caveats in mind, we end this book by reflecting, briefly, on five main areas in which change has been particularly evident. To put it another way, had we been writing, say, two decades ago, we might have identified five major features of the civil service – political neutrality, permanency, centralization, ministerial responsibility, the dominance of a generalist tradition – as being, apparently, more or less immutable. But writing as we are now, in the late 1980s, we can be much less confident about the centrality or the durability of any of them.

Political Neutrality

Civil servants owe loyalty to the government of the day, of whatever party, and must therefore steer clear of overt expressions of party political commitment. But real life is not quite so simple: readers will recall the debate about 'loyalty' in the context of the Ponting case, and the controversy about the role of information officers in the Westland affair. Could a Cabinet Secretary like Sir Robert Armstrong, called upon on more than one occasion to rescue the Thatcher government from political difficulty, expect to have the automatic confidence of a Labour administration?

In this context we recall the inconclusive debate about 'politic-ization', discussed in chapter 8. This emotionally charged word turns out, on closer inspection, to be compounded of an amorphous mixture of quite disparate things. It includes such matters as active prime ministerial involvement in top appointments; the recruitment and 'inward secondment' of staff holding posts outside the civil service; the desirability or otherwise of extending the use of temporary political advisers to ministers. One particularly obvious and worrying aspect of 'politicization' arises in the sphere of industrial relations, with the increased militancy of civil service unions, as discussed in chapter 6. Can civil servants be expected to submit passively to, let alone to connive in, policies designed expressly to 'deprivilege' them?

There is little overt evidence that the Thatcher government, any more than its predecessors, is trying consciously to subvert the traditional neutrality of the civil service, though sometimes, like its predecessors, it wants things both ways. At the same time, however, we also accept that absolute neutrality has probably become an unrealistic aspiration in an age of increasingly polarized party politics. Governments that want to change things do not *want* to be advised by ideologically innocent fence-sitters. New governments do not want to be advised by officials who have risen to the top of the civil service apparently because they have displayed, not just loyalty but also enthusiasm for the previous government's programme. We would broadly echo the view of the Treasury and Civil Service Committee in 1986 that politicization is now a fact of life and that governments should openly acknowledge that this is so. We should not fear politicization in itself (though we should always try to be clear in our minds what exactly we are talking about), but we should insist that it be brought out in the open so that we can all see how it operates.

We also note, in passing, the view of some commentators that the role of the civil service may have substantially to be reappraised in the event of a hung Parliament. However, such a contingency would not, in itself, necessarily make the civil service any more or less 'neutral'. Civil servants would continue to serve their designated minister, appointed by a constitutional monarch (whose own 'neutrality' might be even more significantly threatened by the persistence of a no-majority Parliament); they might have to learn to cope with divisions between the component parts of a coalition (though coalitions are nothing new in Britain, and single-party governments are themselves often significantly divided); they might even have to carry on Her Majesty's Government during an uncertain period of post-election coalition-building. Here, as with other aspects of change, we will just have to wait and see.

Permanency

This aspect of the subject overlaps with the previous one. Political neutrality is predicated upon the existence of a career civil service which owes allegiance to any duly elected government, and upon the preservation of the sharp dividing line established at the beginning of the nineteenth century (see chapter 2) between parliamentary/ministerial and permanent/non-ministerial servants of the Crown. The Civil Service Commission remains the principal gate-keeper in this context, though it has had to devote more and more of its time to the rather introspective task of securing cost-effectiveness in the recruitment process, and has increasingly devolved to departments responsibility for recruiting staff in the lower and middle grades of the civil service hierarchy. It has also had to contend (see chapter 5) with more 'inward secondments', particularly at senior levels (cf. the Levene affair). Although this still happens only on a modest scale, it may become a more prominent and enduring feature of the civil service, particularly if the present-day emphasis on financial–managerial criteria of efficiency and effectiveness (see chapter 10) is maintained while salaries (see chapter 6) remain insufficient to attract personnel with highly marketable expertise in management (and indeed in other valued specialisms) to embark upon permanent careers in the civil service.

Other related issues include the continuing debate about the role of temporary ministerial advisers (see above), the need for an independent or semi-independent 'think tank' to undertake long-term and non-departmental studies of policy (the Central Policy Review Staff having been abolished in 1983), and about the proposal, recently renewed by the Treasury and Civil Service Committee, for some kind of ministerial policy unit (cf. the French *cabinet du ministre*), staffed by 'outsiders' as well as 'insiders'. Our own view is that the abolition of the CPRS was a mistake, and that departmental policy units would at least do something to reinforce the inadequate capacity of ministers, supposedly responsible for policy, to be masters in their own departments. If this is seen as the thin end of the wedge for introducing a 'spoils' system for top civil service jobs, perhaps on lines similar *mutatis mutandis* to the American system, then we would regard this as no bad thing, provided – as in the case of 'politicization' – that it is brought about positively, following rational and open discussion, rather than covertly and/or by accident.

Centralization

'Whitehall' is not a legitimate synonym for the British civil service. Only a small fraction of civil servants works in London, let alone in one busy thoroughfare in SW1. The wide dispersal of government jobs has been in part a consequence of the twentieth-century growth of an interventionist state, in which services are delivered more or less to the citizen's doorstep via decentralized agencies (including ones such as local government and the National Health Service, which are not staffed by civil servants). Any shrinkage in the welfare state and any steps to privatize or hive off government functions can affect the scope of such decentralized activity. In the first edition, we envisaged a situation (reminiscent of administrative arrangements in Sweden) in which a much smaller civil service, situated mainly in London, became responsible exclusively for policy formulation under the guidance of ministers, while the *delivery* and the *administration* of policy was entrusted to other agencies. This is now coming about as a result of the Next Steps programme (see chapter 12).

There has in recent years been a good deal of discussion (particularly in the wake of the Hardman Report of 1973) about job dispersal, and a significant and deliberate shift of civil service jobs out of the capital. But administrative decentralization does nothing to compromise the *constitutional* centralism of the civil service. In a unitary state, with a unified civil service, it is inevitable that top advisory posts will have to be located close to ministers and to Parliament. Federal systems necessarily have more than one layer of bureaucracy. Thus the centralized character of the civil service is a consequence of our present constitutional arrangements, and any substantial change in the position of the civil service is predicated upon constitutional reform, i.e. devolution of power away from the centre of government.

The indivisibility of the civil service in the United Kingdom has already been breached in the case of Northern Ireland; and the issue of devolution of power to Scotland and Wales has featured prominently on the agenda of political debate, particularly in the 1970s. Future prospects for change in this area are uncertain (the more so given the Labour Party's painful memories); but the Alliance parties are heavily committed to decentralization policies which may have substantial implications for the future unity of the civil service. It is not inconceivable that, one day, there will be not just one 'civil service', but several – all owing ultimate loyalty to the Crown, but via the medium of devolved, sub-national institutions of government.

The subject also has an international dimension. 'Home' civil servants nowadays spend a lot of their time 'away', liaising with international institutions, particularly those of the EEC. The sovereignty of Parliament has been compromised by commitment to the Treaty of Rome, and civil servants' lives have had to adjust to a new environment of international, sometimes supra-national, institutions. The notion of a constitutionally centralized service needs to be adapted to take account of both the regional and the international complexity of modern government.

Ministerial Responsibility

The decline of ministerial responsibility, designed in an era where ministers' portfolios were within the compass of their knowledge and understanding, has been a recurrent theme in the modern literature of public administration. Ministers, by themselves, are manifestly too narrow a conduit through which to secure adequate public accountability for large and complex government departments; many important institutional areas of government and quasi-government (public corporations, local authorities, quangos) are barely under even the nominal control of government ministers.

So far as civil servants are concerned, we have noted a number of developments in the past few decades. Complaints about official maladministration can be investigated by the Parliamentary Commissioner for Administration, who has direct access to civil servants and their files; parliamentary select committees have grown in number and scope in the past few years, and increasingly summon civil servants to give evidence to them (albeit within the limits set by the Osmotherly Rules); there has been a lively debate, dating back at least to the Fulton Report, about the desirability of more 'open government'; we noted in chapter 9 the increasing tendency of retired senior civil servants like Sir Douglas Wass to 'go public' and pronounce openly on all manner of issues, including open government. The *internal* accountability of civil servants has been enhanced by the development of devolved budgeting machinery (notably FMI, discussed in chapter 10), which has increased the pressure for improvements in *external* accountability and has brought some useful information about the machinery of government into the public domain.

Governments cling resolutely onto ministerial responsibility as a convenient constitutional fiction; civil servants are torn by anxiety to maintain it as a protective umbrella and by frustration both about the unpredictability of its application and about its inhibiting effects on their working lives. Not all civil servants relish their position as anonymous, neutral minions of ministers, though this remains the central tenet of their professional ethic.

There has been much discussion in recent years about redefining the role of civil servants to take account of modern constitutional realities, e.g. by drafting a comprehensive code of civil service conduct. This ties up with points made earlier about the future survival of the long-established principle of 'neutrality' in the civil service. And some of the recent developments, mentioned above, may yet proceed further. The debate about openness in government (fuelled by almost universal execration of Section 2 of the Official Secrets Act 1911, see chapter 9 and the discussion of the Ponting and Wright cases in the Prologue) shows no signs of abating. Even if the recent growth of select committees were to be halted, or even reversed, MPs will surely never be content with the conventional workings of ministerial responsibility, via antique procedural rituals like question time, as their sole means of access to goings-on in government departments.

Meanwhile, *collective* ministerial responsibility has taken its share of knocks in recent years: many would regard the Westland affair as just the tip of the iceberg in this context. Does collective responsibility mean collective decision-making, or does it mean ministers closing ranks behind a Prime Minister, come what may – or does the truth lie somewhere between these positions? If Cabinet government really is giving way to prime ministerial government, as some commentators have suggested, are civil servants nowadays adequately doing their job merely by 'knowing their minister's mind', or do they have all the time also to be guessing whether their minister's mind accords with that of the Prime Minister?

The 'Cult of the Amateur'

The central message of the Fulton Report was that the dominant position of the generalist civil servant was no longer appropriate to the needs of twentieth-century government. The precious skills of specialist civil servants had been seriously undervalued and were being inefficiently deployed. Some general progress has been made in this area in the 20 years since Fulton, though the impact of remedial devices like the open structure, recently extended to embrace the top seven grades of the civil service, has been more symbolic than real. The same can probably be said of post-Fulton improvements in civil service training.

However, since the election of Mrs Thatcher's government, the generalist has been compelled to learn new managerial and budgeting skills; the computer (requiring specialist expertise to run it) has become a pervasive feature of the government machine. Perhaps the age of the specialist has now dawned; not the age of the scientifically trained specialist of Harold Wilson's technological revolution but the age of the management consultant and of the accountant.

The metaphor of a civil service 'at the crossroads' used in the title of this chapter perhaps does not adequately accommodate the fact that the service is *already* following new and unfamiliar routes. These new paths have not, by and large, been of the civil service's own choosing, and it may not like some of the prospects that can be seen on the horizon. Some observers may regard the recent and continuing developments described in this chapter as reflecting dangerous constitutional heresies. This will always be a matter for debate. Meanwhile, the fact remains that the Fulton Committee's rhetoric about today's civil service being 'fundamentally the product of the nineteenth-century philosophy of the Northcote–Trevelyan Report' was a misleading half-truth even 20 years ago; and developments in the 1970s and, more particularly, the 1980s, have now rendered that interpretation wholly out of date.

12

Beyond the Crossroads: the Next Steps Programme[1]

The end of the 1980s – destined, as matters turned out, to be the last years of Mrs Thatcher's long period in office – saw the launch of a package of reforms that could well turn out to be, in the words of the Treasury and Civil Service Committee, 'the most far-reaching since the Northcote–Trevelyan reforms in the nineteenth century'.[2] These reforms, dubbed the 'Next Steps', promise a transformation of the structure and culture of the civil service, and will make a substantial impact upon the organizational arrangements of government departments. The radical declared aim of the authors of this programme is, put simply, 'to establish a quite different way of conducting the business of government':[3] given the Thatcher government's emphasis upon the introduction of more businesslike practices into government, use of the word 'business' in this context has a special resonance.

Although the government has insisted that existing constitutional principles (particularly those relating to ministerial responsibility) will remain undisturbed, it seems inevitable that the Next Steps must have substantial implications for the relationships between civil servants and ministers and between ministers and Parliament. In a nutshell, the Next Steps programme promises eventually to transfer most of the functions of government departments that involve delivering services to the public (as distinct from the traditional 'higher civil service' functions of policy-making and ministerial advice) to semi-autonomous agencies. Such agencies will continue to be staffed (at least for the time being) by civil servants, and will be headed by chief executives, generally appointed by open competition, on fixed-term contracts – many of whom have been and will be appointed from outside the civil service. Those managing the agencies will enjoy a good deal of day-to-day freedom from ministerial and departmental supervision and interference, but will operate within the terms of published framework documents, which will define agency goals and set performance targets. It is envisaged that about three-quarters of the civil service will be working in agencies by the end of the 1990s. Even in the early years of that decade a great many civil servants already *do* work in agencies.

The Next Steps has an important bearing on a great many of the themes already explored in earlier chapters. For instance (looking back at those chapters, more or less in sequence):

1 The definition of a 'civil servant' (chapter 1) and hence the statistical profile of the service (chapter 3). Will Next Steps eventually result in the emergence of two distinct categories of civil servant, the majority who are employed in agencies, and the minority who work in the 'core departments', formulating policy and advising ministers?

2 The definition and organizational form of government departments, and the relationships between them (chapter 4). Next Steps looks set to add further layers of difficulty to the already difficult problem of defining government departments, and delineating the boundaries of departments and the quasi-governmental and non-departmental public bodies associated with them.

3 Civil service recruitment and training (chapter 5) and conditions of service (chapter 6). The autonomy enjoyed by agencies will extend increasingly into matters like staff recruitment and training. It is perhaps worth noting that two early additions to the ever-growing list of agencies were the Civil Service College and the Civil Service Commission (renamed the Recruitment Agency). As the programme gains momentum, we are bound to see substantial erosion of the traditional adherence to nationally negotiated pay scales, common to any given grade ('grades', in their present form, may well largely disappear), and moves (already evident even before the launch of Next Steps) away from automatic annual salary increments and towards performance-related pay. The management of civil service careers may be complicated by the development, *de facto*, of a two-tier service (see above) – or by the perceived necessity of managing careers so as to minimize the likelihood of such a division developing.

4 The internal arrangements of most departments (chapter 7) will be transformed. A set of new organizational arrangements will have to be developed to encompass the relationship between the inner core and an orbiting array of agencies. The functions of agencies will tend

to be quite specialized, and relevant specialist skills may receive enhanced recognition in an agency context. Will the traditional generalist hegemony survive in its traditional form?

5   What of the relationship between agencies on the one hand and ministers, supported and advised by civil servants in the 'core' departments, on the other (chapter 8)? The rationale of Next Steps is to institutionalize the functional separation between policy advice and service delivery. The latter will be managed at arm's length (a familiar, and perhaps slightly ominous, phrase to those who have studied the history of the nationalized industries) from ministers. Yet the latter, according to declared government policy, are to retain ultimate constitutional responsibility to Parliament for agencies. How can managerial freedom logically and practically be reconciled with continuing ministerial responsibility? This is a crucial issue to which we will return later in this chapter.

6   Given that the Next Steps programme places particular emphasis upon quality of service, will the creation of agencies, in practice, help to improve the 'public face of private government' (chapter 9)? Will it contribute to 'open government'; will it give select committees (for instance, via published framework documents) new opportunities to hold departments and ministers to account in public for their performance – and for their mistakes? Will there be more interchange of ideas and personnel between the civil service and the private sector?

7   'Efficiency and effectiveness' (chapter 10). Is the Next Steps something fundamentally new, or is it just an incremental, perhaps even a mere cosmetic change? The Next Steps is, as we shall see, the produce of a report by the Efficiency Unit. It has much affinity with some of the ideas put forward, twenty years earlier, in the Fulton Report; it represents an evolutionary progression from such developments as the Financial Management Initiative. Just how innovatory is it?

We cannot hope to address here and now, let alone convincingly answer, all these questions. The Next Steps programme itself will take many years to come to full maturity. Judgments about impact, and *a fortiori* about 'success' or 'failure' must be hedged around with caution. As we shall see, the early momentum has been impressive, but its continuation cannot simply be taken for granted. This chapter seeks merely to explain the nature of this important – indeed, potentially momentous – programme, and to offer some cautious comments upon several of the more interesting and problematical aspects of it.

Origins of the Next Steps

Soon after Mrs Thatcher's third successive election victory in 1987 – around the time when the first edition of this book was being completed – stories began to appear in the press about the existence of a highly confidential and controversial report by the Cabinet Office Efficiency Unit, then headed by Sir Robin Ibbs. The report, said to have been submitted to the Prime Minister just prior to the election, recommended a major shake-up in the structure and configuration of central government departments.[4] The original version of the Ibbs Report was said to envisage the eventual division of the civil service into a small inner core, concerned exclusively with policy advice, while the bulk of departmental functions and civil service jobs, concerned with the delivery of public services, should be assigned to semi-autonomous (but not fully privatized) agencies – an arrangement reminiscent of the Swedish administrative model. There were further rumours about a good deal of Whitehall infighting over the proposals; the Treasury, for example was apparently worried about the possible weakening of central financial discipline and the fragmentation of pay scales.

Nearly twenty years earlier the Fulton Report[5] had explored the concept of accountable management and had also been sufficiently impressed by its observation of Swedish administration to call for a review of the issue of 'hiving off'. The Committee had noted the potential dangers of separating policy-making from execution, but saw 'no reason to believe that the dividing line between activities for which Ministers are directly responsible and those for which they are not, is necessarily drawn in the right place today'.[6] However, it had gone on to observe that, 'the creation of further autonomous bodies, and the drawing of the line between them and central government, would raise parliamentary and constitutional issues, especially if they effected the answerability for sensitive matters such as the social and education services.' In 1977, the Eleventh Report of the Expenditure Committee on *The Civil Service*[7] had taken a less sanguine view of the matter. 'Hiving off', it said, 'is only viable in limited areas of government . . . and should be approached with caution'. And it went on to say, again focussing on the crucial problem of accountability, that 'hiving off necessarily involves a diminution in the area of ministerial control'.[8]

The Ibbs proposals themselves were from the outset clearly identifiable as an extension of the Thatcher government's long-standing preoccupation with efficiency and effectiveness in government – reflected, in particular, in the devolved budgeting principles of the Financial Management Initiative, introduced in 1982 – see chapter 10.

The Next Steps

A published version of the Ibbs Report, entitled *Improving Management in Government: The Next Steps*, appeared in February 1988.[9] It was based on more than 150 interviews with civil servants (including 26 permanent secretaries) and ministers. The Report revealed that, 'the management and staff concerned with the delivery of government services (some 95 per cent of the Civil Service) were generally convinced that the developments towards more clearly defined and budgeted management [here they had particularly in mind the FMI] are positive and helpful'.[10] However, it also noted some concern that senior civil service management 'is dominated by people whose skills are in policy formulation and who have relatively little experience of managing or working where services are actually being delivered'.[11] A senior grade 2 officer was quoted as saying that 'the golden road to the top is through policy and not through management'.[12]

The Report also cast doubts upon the time-honoured notion of a unified civil service:

In our discussions it was clear that the advantages which a unified Civil Service are intended to bring are seen as outweighed by the practical disadvantages, particularly beyond Whitehall itself. We were told that the advantages of an all-embracing pay-structure are breaking down, that the uniformity of grading frequently inhibits effective management and that the concept of a career in a unified Civil Service has little relevance for most civil servants, whose horizons are bounded by their local office or, at most, by their department.[13]

The core recommendation was that agencies be established to carry out the executive functions of government within a policy and resources framework set by the relevant department:

The aim should be to establish a quite different way of conducting the business of government. The central Civil Service should consist of a relatively small core engaged in the function of servicing Ministers and managing departments, who will be the 'sponsors' of particular government policies and services. Responding to these departments will be a range of agencies employing their own staff, who may or may not have the status of Crown servants, and concentrating on the delivery of their particular service, with clearly defined responsibilities between the Secretary of State and the Permanent Secretary on the one hand and the Chairmen or Chief Executives of the agencies on the other. Both departments and their agencies should have a more open and simplified structure.[14]

The Report acknowledged that the size and organizational definition of agencies would necessarily vary from case to case. The main strategic control would lie with the Minister and the permanent secretary:

But once the policy objectives within the framework are set, the management of the agency should then have as much independence as possible in deciding how those objectives are met. A crucial element in the relationship would be a formal understanding with Ministers about the handling of sensitive issues and the lines of accountability in a crisis. The presumption must be that, provided management is operating within the strategic direction set by Ministers, it must be left as free as possible to manage within that framework.[15]

The authors of *The Next Steps* expressed their belief in the feasibility of Parliament 'through ministers' treating managers 'as directly responsible for operational matters'.[16]

On the day of publication, Mrs Thatcher made a House of Commons statement[17] endorsing the recommendations. She said that the new agencies would 'generally be within the Civil Service, and their staff will continue to be civil servants'; she later conceded that the word 'generally' did admit the possibility of their being set up outside the civil service in appropriate cases.[18] She also said that there would be 'no change in the arrangements for accountability;'[19] the work of departmentally related select committees, the Public Accounts Committee and the Parliamentary Commissioner would not be affected. The Prime Minister announced the appointment of Mr Peter Kemp, former deputy secretary in the Treasury, now promoted to be second permanent secretary in the Office of the Minister for the Civil Service (OMCS), to act as project officer, to oversee the implementation of the programme. Twelve organizational units – employing in total some 70,000 civil servants – were initially identified as particularly promising candidates for agency status.

Inquiries by the Treasury and Civil Service Committee

Soon after these announcements, the Sub-committee of the Commons Treasury and Civil Service Committee embarked on the first of what has become a regular series of inquiries into the progress of the Next Steps programme.[20] This was a logical sequel to its earlier substantial inquiries into the FMI proposals[21] and into *Civil Servants and Ministers: Duties and Responsibilities*.[22] In its Report, based on this inquiry,[23] the Treasury and Civil Service Committee expressed criticisms of *The Next Steps* on the grounds of its vagueness and lack of novelty. But it was generally supportive in principle of the proposals – a position that it has adhered to in its subsequent reports.

The Report stressed the need for a greater sense of urgency in the search for enhanced efficiency, and underlined 'the need to change the culture and attitudes of the civil service'.[24] Among other things, the Committee called for adequate investment in training;[25] and stressed the need for promotion policy to reward management skills as well as traditional policy work.[26] The Report also stressed the importance of performance-related pay[27] – likely to be an increasingly important product of the Next Steps initiative. The delicate issue of accountability was addressed at some length by the Committee, which called for a debate on the subject.[28] The basic problem is quite simply stated but not at all easily resolved. How can ministers credibly cling to their virtual monopoly of accountability to Parliament, via traditional models of ministerial responsibility that (according to Mrs Thatcher) were to remain unaltered by *The Next Steps*, in respect of agencies whose chief executives are expected to take managerial initiatives at arm's length from ministerial control?

Is it conceivable in sensitive areas like social security benefits payments (where every client thinks he or she is entitled to more), tax collection (where every client thinks that he or she should be paying less), the issuing of passports (where holidays and business trips can be ruined by delays), or perhaps even weather forecasting (where the Meteorological Office sometimes finds itself branded as the scapegoat for unexpected storms) that an arm's-length relationship can be maintained? 'Sensitive' often means *politically* sensitive. Angry members of the public may complain to the agency Chief Executive, who will no doubt do his best to explain and mollify. Some customers may indeed be mollified; but some of those who are not (particularly any who have studied the doctrine of ministerial responsibility) may write to their MPs, who may then write to the Minister. The latter seeks an explanation from the Chief Executive and leans hard on him to find an answer that will deflect the mounting prospect – a dreadful one to ministers and their civil servants – of a serious parliamentary row. The Chief Executive, on a three- or five-year contract, is uneasily aware that he cannot afford to fall out with his minister.

Is this a problem? The architects of the Next Steps programme would argue that the situation is little different from, and certainly no worse than, that which would have prevailed anyway in pre-agency days. A lot of services have long been delivered, in practice, at arm's length from day to day ministerial control (tax collection is a special instance of this). On the contrary, they would point out that the situation should be *better* for the consumer of a public service, in so far as the agency system encourages direct access by customers, with recourse to ministers still in place as a fallback position. MPs on select committees can get their questions answered, at first hand, from the horse's mouth – the Chief Executive – rather than at second-hand via ministers, who know nothing of the agency's day-to-day business. And what is wrong with a minister 'leaning' on a Chief Executive, whose salary, after all, comes from the taxpayer's pocket, in the cause of improving efficiency and the quality of public service? They may well be right (we need more experience of the Next Steps programme in action before we can be sure one way or the other); and the agencies themselves, and the services for which they are responsible, vary so much that generalized criticisms are hazardous. But a lingering question mark remains – particularly in respect of sensitive services of the kind just referred to. With the old constitutional ground rules still firmly in place, and in the absence of a fully fledged system of administrative law (such as can be found in Sweden) is Next Steps, for all the talk about managers being given more freedom to manage, merely a re-packaging exercise?

One obvious parallel that comes to mind is the old problem about the relationship between ministers and nationalized industries, albeit with the added complication here that the chief executives and staff of the new agencies have retained their status as civil servants. As already noted, one long-term by-product of *The Next Steps* may be a further erosion of the already blurred definitional boundary that separates those who are 'civil servants' from those who are not.[29]

For its part, the Treasury and Civil Service Committee implicitly recognized the nature and magnitude of the problem:

Ministers will, and must, remain clearly accountable on the Floor of the House for . . . [matters of policy, strategy, etc.], just as they will remain answerable to Select Committees. We believe, however, that there is a dilemma in the case of matters for which the Chief Executive is responsible. The House needs to assess the risk that Chief Executives' freedom of manœuvre – their ability to improve efficiency and the quality of service – will be constrained if Ministers continue to answer questions in great detail about the activities which are to become the responsibilities of agencies themselves. Where decisions are made which affect individuals, such as the withdrawal of benefit or refusal to grant a passport, there will always be cases which need to be raised with the Minister, whether because of an anomaly in the rules or for some other reason. This does not represent a constraint upon managerial freedom, but an essential check on possible abuse.[30]

The Committee said that it shared the government's hope that most problems of this sort could be resolved without reference to ministers by dealing directly with those responsible.[31] Given that much of the problem of accountability to Parliament revolves around the adequacy of information, the Select Committee welcomed the stated intention that agency policy and resources frameworks would normally be published. In its reply to the Committee's 1988 Report, the Government reaffirmed (in line with Mrs Thatcher's statement, quoted earlier) that it did not envisage that setting up agencies 'will result in changes to the existing constitutional arrangements'.[32] However, it pointed to the fact both that framework documents were to be published, and that MPs might often wish to deal directly with chief executives on operational matters, as signalling 'some developments in the way in which external accountability is discharged'.

What about the role in this context of investigatory select committees? According to the government's reply to the Committee's Report, chief executives giving evidence to select committees would, 'as a general rule', do so on behalf of their ministers (compare our earlier discussion of the Osmotherly Rules);[33] but, 'in practice, where a select committee's interest is confined to the day-to-day operation of an agency, ministers will normally regard the chief executive as being the person best placed to answer on their behalf'. It is the view of the present writers that framework documents, used as the basis for cross-examining chief executives, provide potentially a very important weapon in the hands of select committees in monitoring the service delivery functions of government. Moreover, it will be a great pity of the departmentally related committees fail to make good use of this opportunity.

In its second inquiry into Next Steps, in 1989 – by which time the programme had made substantial progress – the Sub-committee asked the chief executives of the Companies House Agency and the Vehicle Inspectorate Agency how much difference the creation of agencies had made to their dealings with Parliament:

They told us that they now dealt more directly with Members, rather than corresponding with them via Ministers, and furthermore, Members were dealing directly with the lower grades of staff such as district managers. This procedure is spelt out in several Agency Framework Documents [for example, those of the Vehicle Inspectorate Agency, and of the Employment Service – see below] and would seem, if anything, to increase the ability of Members to pursue questions about the operations of a particular Department (e.g. a constituent's wrongly calculated benefit claim).[34]

The Committee expressed itself 'satisfied that, to date, no problems have arisen over the accountability of Chief Executives';[35] however, it also noted that the agencies created to date (i.e. by the summer of 1989) had been small, the largest being HMSO, with just 3,000 staff. Mr Kemp had acknowledged that the creation of a Social Security Benefits Agency (with some 70,000 staff) would involve 'some interesting questions of accountability'.[36]

Thought had also to be given to the position of accounting officers entrusted with the task of giving evidence to the Public Accounts Committee.[37] Senior official witnesses appearing before the TCSC in its 1988 inquiry said firmly in evidence that this important role should remain with permanent secretaries. However, the Committee argued that chief executives should be allowed to appear before the PAC as accounting officers on behalf of their agencies.[38] The government later conceded significant ground on this. The position now is that chief executives whose agencies are covered by a complete Vote in the annual Estimates will be the accounting officers; if their agency is encompassed by only part of a Vote they will be 'agency accounting officers', appearing alongside their permanent secretary.

Progress with the Next Steps

In a report published in October 1989, the Public Accounts Committee noted that 'initial progress has been slower than planned', and warned that the ten-year time-scale envisaged by the OMCS (see below) 'does carry the risk of a loss of impetus which, if the initiative is successful, will need to be maintained'.[39] In its 1989 Report, the TCSC noted that 'departments have varying track records in implementing the Next Steps programme' and that 'in some cases . . . progress was not as fast as it might have been'.[40]

The point about possible loss of impetus is an important one. The Next Steps programme was, at its inception, very much a product of the Thatcher–Rayner–Ibbs era. Although Mrs Thatcher's prime ministerial successor pledged his continuing support for the programme, and although the Labour Party has not opposed it, it is always hard to sustain ministerial interest in, and political momentum for, anything over a period as long as ten years: and Next Steps is hardly a politically glamorous subject. Although on the face of it, Whitehall seems to have buckled down willingly to the task of implementing the programme, one cannot help wondering if there is a danger that more traditional departmental values may not – in the absence of sustained ministerial backing – reassert themselves, particularly given the Treasury's scepticism about some of the original proposals.

However, the Next Steps team remains optimistic. In his evidence to the Treasury and Civil Service Committee in 1988, Mr Kemp accepted a suggestion that, in ten years, he hoped that at least three quarters of the civil service would be working in agencies.[41] He reiterated this view when the Sub-committee returned to the subject of Next Steps in the following session,[42] and again in his evidence to the Sub-committee the following year.[43] In the latter context, he estimated that about half the civil service would be in agencies by the end of 1991 (by which time the giant Social Security Benefits Agency – employing around 13 per cent of non-industrial civil servants, would be up and running). We suspect in any case that a ratchet effect applies here. Any attempt to dismantle the Next Steps programme – which has received a good deal of cross-party support, and seems generally attractive to civil service managers – would now be seen by many people (inclding the Treasury and Civil Service Committee) as a retrograde step. It would cause as much, if not more, disruption to dismantle agencies than was involved in setting them up in the first place. Calling the programme to a halt with some agencies in place and others not, would leave the central machinery of government looking very lopsided.

The overall picture changes almost by the minute. By 5 January 1991, 34 agencies had been established, employing a total of 79,720 civil servants (out of a total of around 570,000) – ranging from 50 (National Weights and Measures Laboratory) to 33,800 (the Employment Service). Thirty activities had been announced as being 'under consideration' for agency status. Full details are given in the lists appended to this chapter (see tables 12.1 and 12.2). These lists of agencies and candidate agencies included by far the most ambitious part of the programme to date – the decision, announced in May 1989, to adopt the agency model for most of the operational tasks of the Department of Social Security.[44] The Resettlement Agency, with 530 staff, had already been set up in May 1989 to administer DSS resettlement units, offering help to particularly disadvantaged people. An Information Technology Services Agency, with about 3,000 staff, based in Lytham St Anne's, came into being in April 1990 to handle computing and communications technology for the Department and its other agencies. The massive Social Security Benefits system, with nearly 70,000 civil servants employed in around 500 local offices, and with a budget of around £50bn a year, was to become an agency in April 1991. It is an understatement to say that running an agency of this size (containing about one-seventh of the total non-industrial civil service) is a challenging prospect – one that presents major potential problems both of internal management and of external accountability. A Social Security Contributions Agency, with 6,200 staff, is to be responsible for the administration of National Insurance contributions.

Identifying Agencies – Privatization by Stealth?

The procedure for identifying agencies has varied from department to department. Rejection of a candidate does not preclude reconsideration at a later date. Having identified a candidate, the department consults with the Next Steps team and the Treasury to discuss operational details, work out the terms of a framework agreement and decide upon a timetable. The Department must of course demonstrate that the agency will have a sound managerial and financial structure. The particularly demanding and important task of constructing the framework agreement 'involves the selection of a range of performance indicators which will enable the Department to judge productivity, financial performance, quality of service and so on'.[45]

It has been repeatedly affirmed from the outset, in response to suspicious Opposition questions about whether Next Steps might be a deliberate first step towards privatization, that by the time an agency has been identified, privatization will already have been considered, and ruled out, as the appropriate short-run strategy. To quote Mrs Thatcher:

Before an agency is established, alternative options, including contracting out the work and privatisation will be examined. 'Next Steps' is primarily about those operations which are to remain within Government. I cannot rule out, however, that after a period of years agencies, like other Government activities, may be suitable for privatisation. Where there is a firm intention of privatisation when an agency is being set up, this should be made clear.[46]

A Divided Civil Service?

If three-quarters of the civil service is destined to be working in agencies by 1998, what of the other quarter, who will remain at work in the 'core departments'? In its 1989 inquiry, the Sub-committee of the Treasury and Civil Service Committee discussed the relationship between agencies and departments with Mr Kemp, who said that departments would have to learn to trust the chief executives and to adopt a 'hands-off' approach.[47]

In its 1988 Report, the Committee had said that 'the golden route to the top' for civil servants in the Next Steps era should combine management experience in agencies with policy experience in the core departments.[48] The government had accepted this in its reply to the Committee's Report,[49] and the Committee received a lot of further evidence, supportive of this position, in its 1989 inquiry.[50] The 1989 Report repeated the earlier recommendation 'that those reaching the highest ranks of the Civil Service in the core departments should have experience both of management and policy work'.[51] But some observers have expressed reservations about the realism of this prescription. The president of the First Division Association, for instance, drew attention to a major dilemma:

The more the chief executives are encouraged . . . to develop management structures and pay and grading arrangements that are uniquely appropriate

TABLE 12.1 *Executive agencies established by 5 January 1991*

Agency	Staff[a]
Building Research Establishment	680
Central Office of Information	740
Central Veterinary Laboratory	560
Civil Service College	200
Companies House	1,100
Driver and Vehicle Licensing Agency	5,300
Driving Standards Agency	2,100
Employment Service	33,800
Historic Royal Palaces	330
HMSO	3,200
Hydrographic Office[b]	890
Information Technology Services Agency	2,900
Insolvency Service	1,400
Intervention Board	860
Laboratory of the Government Chemists	320
Land Registry	10,800
Meteorological Office	2,250
National Engineering Laboratory	520
National Physical Laboratory	830
National Weights and Measures Laboratory	50
Natural Resources Institute	330
Occupational Health Service	100
Ordnance Survey	2,550
Patent Office	1,150
QEII Conference Centre	60
Radiocommunications Agency	460
Registers of Scotland	1,000
Resettlement Agency	530
Royal Mint	970
Training and Employment Agency (Northern Ireland)	1,700
Vehicle Certification Agency	70
Vehicle Inspectorate	1,600
Veterinary Medicines Directorate	70
Warren Spring Laboratory	300

34 in number

Total 79,720

[a] As at 1 April 1990.
[b] A Defence Support Agency. Figure does not include service personnel.

Source: Adapted from information provided by the Office of the Minister for the Civil Service

TABLE 12.2 *Next Steps: Activities under consideration
on 5 January 1991*

Activity	Staff[a]
Cadw (Welsh Historic Monuments)	220
Central Science Laboratory	400
Central Statistical Office	1,000
Chessington Computer Centre	430
Child Support Agency	n.a.
Civil Service Commission (the Recruitment Agency)	340
Defence Research Agency	11,700
Directorate General of Defence Accounts[b]	2,100
Farm and Countryside Service	2,550
Fisheries Protection Services	170
Forensic Science Service	580
Fuel Suppliers Branch	30
Historic Scotland	570
Military Survey[b]	850
NHS Estates	130
Passport Office	1,200
Planning Inspectorate	550
Pollution Inspectorate	210
Property Holdings	1,600
RAF Training[b]	2,500
Royal Parks	570
Service Children's Schools[b]	1,000
Social Security Benefits Agency	68,200
Social Security Contributions Unit	6,200
Teachers Pensions Branch	390
Valuation Office	5,700
Youth Treatment Service	220
Ordnance Survey (Northern Ireland)	200
Rating Division (Northern Ireland)	270
Social Security Operations (Northern Ireland)	5,000
30 in number	
Customs and Excise[c]	26,900
Inland Revenue (excluding Valuation Office)[c]	60,400
Total	202,180

[a]   As at 1 April 1990.

Notes to table cont.
b   A Defence Support Agency. Figure does not include service personnel.
c   Moving towards operating fully on Next Steps lines, as set out in the
     Chancellor of the Exchequer's statement of 25 July 1990.
Note: Many other areas of Government are under consideration including
     prisons, and other parts of the Ministry of Defence.
Source: Adapted from information provided by the Office of the Minister
     for the Civil Service

to their own operations the more difficult it will become to organise a
regular interchange of people between the agencies and the centre. No
guidance is available as to how the departmental responsibility for the
career development of individuals will be reconciled with the operational
autonomy of the chief executive; and no-one knows how it will be possible
to tempt civil servants back to the centre if pay in the agencies is determined
on commercial criteria whilst political considerations still dominate pay
rates at the centre.[52]

This is another variant of the problem, already discussed, of how an
arm's length relationship between the centre and the agencies is to be
reconciled with ministerial responsibility to Parliament.

When the Treasury and Civil Service Sub-committee considered
the future of the unified UK civil service in the context of the Next
Steps programme,[53] the Cabinet Secretary, Sir Robin Butler, used the
cunning phrase 'unified but not uniform' to describe his vision of the
future shape of the civil service.[54] In reply to a request for elucidation
by the Sub-committee, Mr Kemp provided, in a written memorandum, the following:

The heart of Next Steps is a recognition that the Civil Service has a large and
varied range of functions. . . . In practice since the primary objective in my
view is to give Agencies the specific tools and facilities they need to carry out
their own immensely varied tasks, there must in my view be a continuing
and increasing reduction in uniformity as between Agencies in all manner of
their features. This however must be within the backstop [*sic*] of a general
unifying framework which, as Sir Robin Butler said in a speech to the
[Institute of Personnel Management] in September 1988, will include such
matters as 'requirements of equity, accountability, impartiality and a wide
view of the public interest'.[55]

Clearly all kinds of implications arise from the managerial freedoms
envisaged – further erosion, almost certainly, of nationally standardized pay and grading, perhaps also of the principle (for most officials,

more theoretical than real) of transferability within the service. The Treasury and Civil Service Committee, in its 1989 Report, expressed a belief that it should be possible to maintain the national character of the civil service while recognizing the diversity of its functions.[56] We must wait and see.

Meanwhile, one by-product of the Next Steps programme has been the generation of a lot of paper – framework documents, agency reports and publicity material, select committee reports, etc. In October 1990 – two and a half years into the Next Steps programme – the government published the first in a series of annual reports on Next Steps, containing useful short accounts of the nature and the objectives of the agencies established so far.[57] This evident concern to expose agencies to public scrutiny is one of two particularly welcome features of the programme. The other is the declared primary aim of the programme itself – to improve the management of public services, and to sensitize civil servants working in the field of service delivery to the needs of their customers.

Notes

Prologue: Some Crises of the 1980s

1 See, for example, Brian Chapman, *British Government Observed* (Allen and Unwin, London, 1963); *The Administrators: the Reform of the Civil Service*, Fabian Tract 355 (The Fabian Society, London, 1964); Peter Shore, *Entitled to Know* (MacGibbon and Kee, London, 1966).

2 Hugh Thomas (ed.) *Crisis in the Civil Service* (Anthony Blond, London, 1968).

3 *Report of the Committee on the Civil Service 1966–68* (Chairman, Lord Fulton), Cmnd 3638 (HMSO, London, 1968), hereafter referred to as the Fulton Report. For a comprehensive bibliography of the Report and its numerous accompanying volumes of evidence, memoranda, etc. see R.A. Chapman, *The Higher Civil Service in Britain* (Constable, London, 1970), pp. 174–84.

4 See Richard Norton-Taylor, *The Ponting Affair* (Cecil Woolf, London, 1985). Clive Ponting told his own story of the affair in the *The Right to Know* (Sphere Books, London, 1985).

5 Ponting, *The Right to Know*, p. 171.

6 Norton-Taylor, *The Ponting Affair*, pp. 102–3.

7 HC Deb., 18 February 1985, cols 737ff.

8 Reproduced as Annex A to the memorandum submitted by the Cabinet Office (MPO) to the Treasury and Civil Service Committee, 1985–6, HC 92–II, pp. 7–9.

9 A detailed chronology of events can be found in the Fourth Report from the Defence Committee, 1985–86: *Westland plc: the Government's Decision-Making*, HC 519 (HMSO, London, 1986). See also Dawn Oliver and Rodney Austin, 'Political and constitutional aspects of the Westland affair', *Parliamentary Affairs*, 40 (1987) pp. 20–40; and Magnus Linklater and David Leigh, *Not with Honour* (Sphere Books, London, 1986).

10 Fourth Report from the Defence Committee, 1985–86, para. 60.

11 Third Report from the Defence Committee, 1985–86: *The Defence*

Implications of the Future of Westland plc, HC 518 (HMSO, London, 1986).

12 Fourth Report from the Defence Committee, 1985–86.

13 Ibid., para. 213.

14 Seventh Report from the Treasury and Civil Service Committee, 1985–86: *Civil Servants and Ministers: Duties and Responsibilities*, vol. 1, Report, HC 92–I (HMSO, London, 1986).

15 *Civil Servants and Ministers: Duties and Responsibilites*: Government Response to the Seventh Report from the Treasury and Civil Service Committee, Cmnd 9841 (HMSO, London, 1986).

16 *Westland plc*: Government Reponse to the Third and Fourth Reports from the Defence Committee, Cmnd 9916 (HMSO, London, 1986).

17 First Report from the Treasury and Civil Service Committee, 1986–87: *Ministers and Civil Servants*, HC 62 (HMSO, London, 1986).

18 First Report from the Liaison Committee, 1986–87: *Accountability of Ministers and Civil Servants*, HC 100 (HMSO, London 1986).

19 *Accountability of Ministers and Civil Servants*: Government Response to the First Report from the Treasury and Civil Service Committee, and to the First Report from the Liaison Committee, Cm 78 (HMSO, London, 1987).

20 *Guardian*, 26 July 1986.

21 The proceedings ran from 18 November to 19 December 1986, and were extensively reported in the quality newspapers.

22 *Guardian*, 14 March 1987.

23 Ibid.

24 *Attorney General* v *Observer, etc, The Times*, 14 August 1987.

Chapter 1 Charting the Territory

1 See, for instance, M. Albrow, *Bureaucracy* (Macmillan, London, 1970); A. Dunsire, *Administration: The Word and the Science* (Martin Robertson, London, 1973), ch. 5.

2 Phrase attributed to Harold Laski.

3 *Guardian*, 29 September 1982. Lady Young's comments were made with reference to publication of the White Paper, *Efficiency and Effectiveness in the Civil Service*, Cmnd 8616 (HMSO, London, 1982).

4 C. Hood, 'Keeping the centre small: explanations of agency type', *Political Studies*, 26 (1978), pp. 30–46.

5 See G. Drewry, 'Quelling the quango', *Public Law* (1982), pp. 384–9; A. Barker (ed.) *Quangos in Britain* (Macmillan, London, 1982).

6 *Report of the Royal Commission on the Civil Service, 1929–31* (Chairman, Lord Tomlin), Cmd 3909 (HMSO, London, 1931), para. 9.

7 Henry Parris, *Constitutional Bureaucracy* (Allen and Unwin, London, 1969), ch. 1.

8 R. A. Chapman and J. R. Greenaway, *The Dynamics of Administrative Reform* (Croom Helm, London, 1980), p. 53.

9 W. J. M. Mackenzie and J. W. Grove, *Central Administration in Britain* (Longman, London, 1957), p. 10.

10 Loopholes in the post–1870 principles of open competition are noted by, among others, E. W. Cohen, *The Growth of the British Civil Service 1780–1939* (Frank Cass, London, 1941), pp. 165–6; Sir J. Craig, *A History of Red Tape* (MacDonald and Evans, London, 1955), p. 188. The subject of recruitment is discussed in ch. 5.

11 See Parris, *Constitutional Bureaucracy*, pp. 39–40; he distinguishes this usage from the more modern sense of the adjective 'civil', employed to distinguish between the civil service and the political or parliamentary service of the Crown.

12 The phrase 'administration of justice' to embrace both judicial functions and the running of the courts (e.g. by civil servants in the Lord Chancellor's Department) may sometimes cause confusion here.

13 See Drewry, 'Quelling the quango'; Barker (ed.) *Quangos in Britain*.

14 J. Lynn and A. Jay (eds) *Yes, Minister*, vol. 1 (BBC, London, 1981), p. 12.

15 K. B. Smellie, *A Hundred Years of English Government*, 2nd edn (Duckworth, London, 1950), p. 57.

16 Sir E. Troup, *The Home Office* (Putnams, London, 1925), ch. 2.

17 Craig, *A History of Red Tape*, p. 57.

18 Ibid., p. 59.

19 Parris, *Constitutional Bureaucracy*, p. 42.

20 H. E. Dale, *The Higher Civil Service of Great Britain* (Oxford University Press, London, 1941); cf. R. K. Kelsall, *Higher Civil Servants in Britain* (Routledge and Kegan Paul, London, 1955); Chapman, *The Higher Civil Service in Britain*. See also *Report of the Royal Commission on the Civil Service, 1953–55* (Chairman, Sir Raymond Priestley), Cmd 9613 (HMSO, London, 1955).

21 Dale, *The Higher Civil Service*, p. 17.

22 The Fulton Report, vol. 1.

23 Ibid., para. 209.

24 Recent official reports on the subject of overseas representation include: *Report of the Committee on Representational Services Overseas* (Chairman, Lord Plowden), Cmnd 2276 (HMSO, London, 1964); *Report of the Review Committee on Overseas Representation* (Chairman, S. Duncan), Cmnd 4107 (HMSO, London, 1969); Central Policy Review Staff, *Review of Overseas Representation* (HMSO, London, 1977); Second Report from the Foreign Affairs Committee, 1979–80: *Foreign and Commonwealth Office Organisation*, HC 511 (HMSO, London, 1980).

Chapter 2 How Things Came to Be

1 The Fulton Report, vol. 1, para. 1.
2 A. L. Lowell, *The Government of England* (Macmillan, London, 1908), vol. 1., p. 145.
3 Smellie, *A Hundred Years of English Government*, p. 56; cf. Chapman and Greenaway, *The Dynamics of Administrative Reform*, pp. 16–17.
4 J. P. W. Mallalieu, *Passed to You, Please* (Victor Gollancz, London, 1942), p. 18.
5 Parris, *Constitutional Bureaucracy*, p. 22.
6 Cohen, *The Growth of the British Civil Service*, p. 52.
7 Parris, *Constitutional Bureaucracy*, p. 49.
8 Lord Bridges, *The Treasury* (Allen and Unwin, London, 1964), pp. 108–10.
9 Ibid., p. 110.
10 Smellie, *A Hundred Years of English Government*, p. 69.
11 Ibid., p. 165.
12 *Reports of the Royal Commission on the Civil Service, 1912–15*, (Chairman, Lord MacDonnell), various Cd numbers (HMSO, London); *Report of the Machinery of Government Committee* (Chairman, Lord Haldane), Cd 9230 (HMSO, London, 1918); *Final Report of the Committee Appointed to Inquire into the Organisation and Staffing of Government Offices* (Chairman, Sir John Bradbury), Cmd 62 (HMSO, London, 1919).
13 H. Roseveare, *The Treasury: The Evolution of a British Institution* (Allen Lane, London, 1969), p. 248.
14 *Report on the Organisation of the Permanent Civil Service*, reproduced as Appendix B of the Fulton Report, vol. 1.
15 Chapman and Greenaway, *The Dynamics of Administrative Reform*, pp. 41–2.
16 Ibid., p. 48.
17 Cohen, *The Growth of the British Civil Service*, pp. 167–74.
18 *First Report of the Commission of Inquiry on the Selection, Transfer and Grading of Civil Servants* (Chairman, Lyon Playfair), C. 1113 (HMSO, London, 1875).
19 *Second Report of the Royal Commission on the Civil Service* (Chairman, Sir Matthew Ridley), C. 5545 (HMSO, London, 1888).
20 C. H. Sisson, *The Spirit of British Administration* (Faber and Faber, London, 1959), p. 39.
21 Cohen, *The Growth of the British Civil Service*, p. 209.
22 Mackenzie and Grove, *Central Administration in Britain*, p. 64.
23 V. M. Subramaniam, 'The relative status of specialists and generalists: an attempt at a comparative historical explanation', *Public Administration*, 46 (1968), pp. 331–40; cf. Smellie, *A Hundred Years of English Government*, p. 70. See also Sir Ernest Barker, *The Develop-*

ment of Public Services in Western Europe 1660–1930 (Oxford University Press, London, 1944).

24 W. H. Greenleaf, *The British Political Tradition*, vol. 1 (Methuen, London, 1983), pp. 40–1; S. A. Walkland, *The Legislative Process in Great Britain* (Allen and Unwin, London, 1968), ch. 1; G. Drewry, 'Public General Acts – now and a hundred years ago', *Statute Law Review* (1985), pp. 152–61.

25 J. Pellew, *The Home Office 1848–1914: From Clerks to Bureaucrats* (Heinemann, London, 1982), p. 181.

26 List taken from David Butler and Gareth Butler, *British Political Facts, 1900–1985* (Macmillan, London, 1986), pp. 70–80.

27 Eleventh Report from the Expenditure Committee, 1976–77: *The Civil Service*, HC 535 (HMSO, London, 1977), together with separate volumes of Evidence and Appendices.

28 For a discussion of the impact of Fulton, see 'Symposium: Fulton 20 years on', *Contemporary Record*, 2, 2 (1988), pp. 44–55.

Chapter 3 Some Facts and Figures

1 F. M. G. Willson, 'Coping with administrative growth: super-departments and the ministerial cadre, 1957–77', in David Butler and A. H. Halsey (eds) *Policy and Politics* (Macmillan, London, 1978), p. 37.

2 For a discussion of this area, see Christopher Hood, 'Government bodies and government growth', in Barker (ed.), *Quangos in Britain*, pp. 44–68.

3 *The Dispersal of Government Work from London* (Hardman Report), Cmnd 5332 (HMSO, London, 1973).

4 HC Deb, 26 July 1979, cols 902–22.

5 Eleventh Report from the Expenditure Committee, 1976–77: *The Civil Service*, vol. I, Report, HC 535–I (HMSO, London, 1977), para. 31.

6 *The Employment of Women in the Civil Service*, Civil Service Department Management Studies No. 3 (HMSO, London, 1971).

7 Elizabeth Brimelow, 'Women in the civil service', *Public Administration*, 59 (1981), p. 323.

8 *Equal Opportunities for Women in the Civil Service: Programme of Action* (Cabinet Office/Management and Personnel Office, London, 1984).

Chapter 4 The Universal Department

1 C. Hood, A. Dunsire and K. S. Thompson, 'So you think you know what government departments are ... ?', *Public Administration Bulletin*, 27 (1978), pp. 20–32, at p. 23.

2 D. N. Chester and F. M. G. Willson, *The Organisation of British Central Government 1914–1964*, 2nd edn (Allen and Unwin, London, 1968), p. 17.

3 The principles are discussed in Chester and Willson, *The Organisation of British Central Government*. See also *Report of the Machinery of Government Committee* (Chairman, Lord Haldane), Cd 9230 (HSMO, London, 1918); C. Pollitt, *Manipulating the Machine: Changing the Pattern of Ministerial Departments, 1960–83* (Allen and Unwin, London, 1984).

4 A. H. Hanson and M. Walles, *Governing Britian: A Guidebook to Political Institutions*, 3rd edn (Fontana, London, 1980), p. 140.

5 For an interesting case study, see Sir Patrick Nairne, 'Managing the DHSS elephant; reflections on a giant department', *Political Quarterly*, 54 (1983), pp. 243–56.

6 *The Reorganisation of Central Government*, Cmnd 4506 (HMSO, London, 1970); cf. *Report of the Machinery of Government Committee*.

7 P. Norton, *Conservative Dissidents* (Maurice Temple Smith, London, 1978).

8 *Report of the Tribunal appointed to inquire into certain issues in relation to the circumstances leading up to the cessation of trading by the Vehicle and General Insurance Company Ltd*, HL 80, HC 133 (HMSO, London, 1972). See R. A. Chapman, 'The Vehicle and General affair; some reflections for public administration in Britain', *Public Administration*, 51 (1973), pp. 273–90.

9 *Report of the Tribunal*, paras. 60–2.

10 Ibid., p. 141, para. 7.

11 *Chain of Command Review: The Open Structure. Report of a team led by Sir Geoffrey Wardale* (Management and Personnel Office, London, 1981).

12 A. Sampson, *The Anatomy of Britain Today* (Hodder and Stoughton, London, 1965), pp. 171–2.

13 *The Reorganisation of Central Government*, para. 12(ii).

14 R. H. S. Crossman, *Inside View* (Jonathan Cape, London, 1972).

15 Hugo Young and Anne Sloman, *No, Minister: An Inquiry into the Civil Service* (BBC, London, 1982), p. 96.

16 H. Heclo and A. Wildavsky, *The Private Government of Public Money*, 2nd edn (Macmillan, London, 1979); J. Barnett, *Inside the Treasury* (André Deutsch, London, 1982); J. Bruce-Gardyne, *Ministers and Mandarins* (Sidgwick and Jackson, London, 1986).

17 R. H. S. Crossman, *The Diaries of a Cabinet Minister*, vol. 1 (Hamish Hamilton and Jonathan Cape, London, 1975), p. 25.

18 D. R. Miers and A. C. Page, *Legislation* (Sweet and Maxwell, London, 1982), pp. 25–9.

19 Barnett, *Inside the Treasury*, pp. 40–1.

20 The question of the Cabinet minutes was one of the matters disputed by Michael Heseltine in the Westland affair (see Prologue).

21 *The Reorganisation of Central Government*, para. 44.

22 See, in particular, Crossman's Introduction to Walter Bagehot, *The

English Constitution (Fontana, London, 1963); also his *Inside View*.

23 See Prime Minister's Questions, HC Deb., 11 November 1982.

24 *The Reorganisation of Central Government*, para. 45.

25 Ibid., para. 47.

26 Lord Rothschild, *Meditations of a Broomstick* (Collins, London, 1977). See also S. James, 'The Central Policy Review Staff, 1970–1983', *Political Studies*, 34 (1986), pp. 423–40.

27 For an assessment see A. Gray and B. Jenkins, 'Policy analysis in British central government: the experience of PAR', *Public Administration*, 60 (1982), pp. 429–50.

28 R. Norton-Taylor, *Guardian*, 27 September 1983. Cf. A. King (ed.) *The British Prime Minister*, 2nd edn (Macmillan, Basingstoke, 1985), pp. 114–18.

29 John le Carré, *The Honourable Schoolboy* (Pan Books, London, 1978), p. 54.

30 Heclo and Wildavsky, *The Private Government of Public Money*.

31 Ibid., p. 76.

32 William Plowden, quoted in D. Wilson (ed.) *The Secrets File* (Heinemann, London, 1984), p. 6.

33 Eleventh Report from the Expenditure Committee, 1976–77: *The Civil Service*. See *The Civil Service*: Government Observations on the Eleventh Report from the Expenditure Committee, Cmnd 7117 (HMSO, London, 1978).

34 Ibid., para. 88.

35 First Report from the Treasury and Civil Service Committee, 1980–81: *The Future of the Civil Service Department*, HC 54 (HMSO, London, 1980).

36 *The Future of the Civil Service Department:* Government Observations on the First Report from the Treasury and Civil Service Committee, Cmnd 8170 (HMSO, London, 1981), para. 9.

37 HC Deb., 12 November 1981, cols 658–66.

38 Seventh Report from the Treasury and Civil Service Committee, 1985–86: *Civil Servants and Ministers: Duties and Responsibilities*, vol. I, Report, HC 92–I, (HMSO, London, 1986), para. 5.44.

39 Ibid., vol II, Annexes, Minutes of Evidence and Appendices, HC 92–II, Q. 859.

40 Government Response to the Seventh Report from the Treasury and Civil Service Committee, Cmnd 9841 (HMSO, London, 1986), para. 38.

Chapter 5 Recruitment and Training

1 K. M. Reader, *The Civil Service Commission 1855–1975*, Civil Service Studies No. 5 (HMSO, London, 1981), pp. 35–6.

2 Kelsall, *Higher Civil Servants in Britain*, p. 77.

3　Mackenzie and Grove, *Central Administration in Britain*, p. 30.

4　P. Kellner and Lord Crowther-Hunt, *The Civil Servants: An Inquiry into Britain's Ruling Class* (Macdonald, London, 1980), p. 106.

5　Government Response to the Seventh Report from the Treasury and Civil Service Committee, para. 20.

6　*Civil Service Commission Annual Report 1985* (Civil Service Commission, Basingstoke, 1986), pp. 7–9.

7　Seventh Report from the Treasury and Civil Service Committee, 1985–86, para. 5.32.

8　Reader, *The Civil Service Commission 1855–1975*, p. 63.

9　*Report of the Committee of Inquiry on the Method II System of Selection* (Chairman, J. Davies), Cmnd 4156 (HMSO, London, 1969).

10　The Fulton Report, vol. 1., para. 95.

11　Eleventh Report from the Expenditure Committee, 1976–77, para. 20.

12　*Report of the Committee on the Selection Procedure for the Recruitment of Administration Trainees* (Chairman, F. H. Allen) (Civil Service Commission, Basingstoke, 1979). See G. K. Fry, *The Changing Civil Service* (Allen and Unwin, London, 1985), pp. 56–62.

13　*Selection of Fast Stream Graduate Entrants to the Home Civil Service [etc]: Report by Sir Alec Atkinson* (Management and Personnel Office, London, 1983).

14　A. P. Herbert, *Number Nine* (Methuen, London, 1951), p. 155.

15　Kellner and Crowther-Hunt, *The Civil Servants*, pp. 124–34.

16　*Civil Service Commission Annual Report 1984* (Civil Service Commission, Basingstoke, 1985), pp. 11–12.

17　*The Bulletin*, May 1985, p. 75.

18　The Fulton Report, vol. 1, pp. 134–6.

19　For example, A. Sampson, *The New Europeans*, rev. ed. (Panther Books, London, 1971), pp. 357–68.

20　Chapman and Greenaway, *The Dynamics of Administrative Reform*, pp. 143–58.

21　*Report of the Committee on the Training of Civil Servants* (Chairman, Ralph Assheton), Cmd 6525 (HMSO, London, 1944).

22　The Fulton Report, vol. 1., paras. 97–114.

23　Fry, *The Changing Civil Service*, pp. 68–9; see *Civil Service College. Programme, April 1986–March 1987* (Civil Service College, Basingstoke, 1986), p. 155.

24　N. E. A. Moore, 'The Civil Service College: what it is and what it is not', *Management in Government*, 39 (1984), pp. 96–103, at p. 98.

25　*The Bulletin*, May 1985, pp. 74–5.

Chapter 6 Conditions of Service

1　*Report of the Royal Commission on the Civil Service, 1953–55* (Chairman, Sir Raymond Priestley), Cmd 9613 (HMSO, London, 1955).

2   Fry, *The Changing Civil Service*, p. 101.
3   Ibid., p. 104.
4   *Report of the Committee on the Value of Pensions* (Chairman, Sir Bernard Scott), Cmnd 8417 (HMSO, London, 1981).
5   Salary scales, though, are adjusted to meet part of the cost.
6   P. Hennessy, *The Times*, 5 March 1981.
7   Reported in *The Times*, 20 April 1982.
8   *Report of an Inquiry into the principles and the system by which the remuneration of the non-industrial Civil Service should be determined* (Chairman, Sir John Megaw), Cmnd 8590 (HMSO, London, 1982).
9   Reported in *The Sunday Times*, 17 March 1985.
10 Fry, *The Changing Civil Service*, p. 123.
11 Mackenzie and Grove, *Central Administration in Britain*, ch. 9.
12 Chapman and Greenaway, *The Dynamics of Administrative Reform*, p. 89.
13 L. D. White, *Whitley Councils in the British Civil Service* (University of Chicago Press, Chicago, 1933); H. Parris, *Staff Relations in the Civil Service. Fifty Years of Whitleyism* (Allen and Unwin, London, 1973); F. Stack, 'Civil service associations and the Whitley Report of 1917', *Political Quarterly*, 40 (1969), pp. 283–95; Chapman and Greenaway, *The Dynamics of Administrative Reform*, pp. 85–100.
14 P. B. Beaumont, *Government as Employer – Setting an Example* (Royal Institute of Public Administration, London, 1981), p. 23.
15 Chapman and Greenaway, *The Dynamics of Administrative Reform*, p. 99.
16 Fry, *The Changing Civil Service*, p. 137. See also C. Painter, 'Civil service staff militancy: joining the mainstream of trade unionism', *Public Administration Bulletin*, 40 (1982), pp. 19–39.
17 See G. Drewry, 'The GCHQ case – a failure of government communications', *Parliamentary Affairs*, 38 (1985), pp. 371–86.
18 P. P. Craig, *Administrative Law* (Sweet and Maxwell, London, 1983), p. 606.
19 D. W. Logan, 'A civil servant and his pay', *Law Quarterly Review*, 61 (1945), p. 240 ff. See O. Hood Phillips and P. Jackson, *O. Hood Phillips' Constitutional and Administrative Law*, 6th edn (Sweet and Maxwell, London, 1978), pp. 341–5.
20 *Council of Civil Service Unions v. Minister for the Civil Service* [1984] All ER 957.
21 House of Commons Disqualification Act 1975; European Assembly Elections Act 1978.
22 *Report of the Committee on the Political Activities of Civil Servants* (Chairman, J. C. Masterman), Cmd 7718 (HMSO, London, 1949). *Report of the Committee on the Political Activities of Civil Servants* (Chairman, Sir Arthur Armitage), Cmnd 7057 (HMSO, London, 1978).
23 Armitage Report, para. 67.
24 Ibid., para. 69.

25 Reproduced as Annex B to the memorandum submitted by the Cabinet Office (MPO) to the Treasury and Civil Service Committee, 1985–86, HC 92-II, pp. 9–14.
26 Chapman, *The Higher Civil Service in Britain*, p. 115.
27 Quoted in ibid., p. 117.
28 C. K. Munro, *The Fountains in Trafalgar Square* (Heinemann, London, 1952), pp. 200–2. Quoted in Chapman, *The Higher Civil Service in Britain*, p. 120.
29 *Halsbury's Laws of England*, 4th edn (Butterworths, London, 1973), vol. 1, p. 1.
30 *Establishment Officer's Guide*, para. 4060.
31 *Civil Service Pay and Conditions of Service Code*, para. 9870.
32 *Establishment Officer's Guide*, para. 4062.
33 Report by a sub-committee of the First Division Association, 'Professional standards in the public service', *Public Administration*, 50 (1972), p. 171.
34 M. W. Wright, 'The professional conduct of civil servants', *Public Administration*, 51, (1973), pp. 3–4.
35 Ibid., p. 4.
36 First Division Association, 'Professional standards in the public service', p. 172.
37 Wright, 'The professional conduct of civil servants', pp. 7–11.
38 See J. Gapper, 'Unions get a sweet tooth for pay flexibility', *Financial Times*, 14 February 1989.
39 Fifth Report from the Treasury and Civil Service Committee, 1989–90: *The Civil Service Pay and Conditions of Service Code*, HC 260 (HMSO, London, 1990), para. 18.
40 Ibid., para. 38.
41 Fifth Special Report from the Treasury and Civil Service Committee, 1989–90: *The Civil Service Pay and Conditions of Service Code: The Government's Observations on the Fifth Report from the Committee in Session 1989–90*, HC 617 (HMSO, London, 1990).

Chapter 7 The Working Context

1 The Fulton Report, vol. 5 (2), Proposals and Opinions, pp. 1135–6.
2 D. C. Pitt and B. C. Smith, *Government Departments* (Routledge and Kegan Paul, London, 1981), p. 63.
3 P. Dunleavy, 'Bureaucrats, budgets and the growth of the state: reconstructing an instrumental model', *British Journal of Political Science*, 15 (1985), pp. 299–328.
4 For a survey of the regional offices of central government departments, see Brian W. Hogwood and Michael Keating (eds) *Regional Government in England* (Clarendon Press, Oxford, 1982).

5 See Michael Keating and Malcolm Rhodes, 'The status of regional government: an analysis of the West Midlands', in Hogwood and Keating (eds) *Regional Government in England*, pp. 51–73. Also see J. A. Cross, 'The regional decentralisation of British government departments', *Public Administration*, 48 (1970), pp. 423–41.

6 On the Northern Ireland Civil Service, see D. Birrell and A. Murie, *Policy and Government in Northern Ireland* (Gill and Macmillan, Dublin, 1980).

7 See J. G. Kellas and P. Madgwick, 'Territorial ministries: the Scottish and Welsh Offices', in Peter Madgwick and Richard Rose (eds) *The Territorial Dimension in United Kingdom Politics* (Macmillan, London, 1982), pp. 9–33. See also M. Keating and A. Midwinter, *The Government of Scotland* (Mainstream Publishing, Edinburgh, 1983).

8 See Kellas and Madgwick, 'Territorial ministries: the Scottish and Welsh Offices'.

9 Mackenzie and Grove, *Central Administration in Britain*, p. 222.

10 Reginald Bevins, *The Greasy Pole* (Hodder and Stoughton, London, 1965), p. 59.

11 The Fulton Report, vol. 1, para. 178.

12 Eleventh Report from the Expenditure Committee, 1976–77: *The Civil Service*, vol. II (I), Minutes of Evidence, HC 535-II, p. 25.

13 Dorothy Johnstone, *The Middle of Whitehall* (Bath University Centre for Fiscal Studies, Bath, 1984), p. 1.8.

14 *Chain of Command Review: The Open Structure. Report of a team led by Sir Geoffrey Wardale*, para. 5.19.

15 Kellner and Crowther-Hunt, *The Civil Servants*, p. 170.

16 M. Kogan (ed.), *The Politics of Education* (Penguin Books, Harmondsworth, 1971), p. 181.

17 D. Hencke, *Colleges in Crisis* (Penguin Books, Harmondsworth, 1978), p. 106.

18 Heclo and Wildavsky, *The Private Government of Public Money*, p. 118.

19 Kellner and Crowther-Hunt, *The Civil Servants*, p. 161.

20 Pitt and Smith, *Government Departments*, pp. 73–4.

21 Sir Basil Engholm, *Guardian*, 16 May 1977, quoted in Kellner and Crowther-Hunt, *The Civil Servants*, p. 34.

22 Sisson, *The Spirit of British Administration*, p. 16.

23 See, for example, the evidence of the ICPS to the Fulton Committee in the Fulton Report, vol. 5 (1).

24 L. A. Gunn, 'Ministers and civil servants: changes in Whitehall', *Public Administration* (Sydney), 26 (1967), p. 90.

25 The Fulton Report, vol. 1., paras 161, 162 and 235.

26 Eleventh Report from the Expenditure Committee, 1976–77, vol. II (II), pp. 556–64.

27 John Garrett, *Managing the Civil Service* (Heinemann, London, 1980), p. 65.

28 Eleventh Report from the Expenditure Committee, 1976–77, vol. II (I), p. 21.
29 Pitt and Smith, *Government Departments*, ch. 2.
30 Ibid., p. 24.
31 A. H. Birch, *Representative and Responsible Government*, (Allen and Unwin, London, 1964).
32 Ibid., pp. 148–9.
33 The Fulton Report, vol. 1, para. 146.
34 Fourth Report from the Home Affairs Committee, 1980–81: *The Prison Service*, vol. II, Minutes of Evidence, HC 412-II (HMSO, London, 1981), Q. 57.
35 Pitt and Smith, *Government Departments*, p. 28.
36 Mackenzie and Grove, *Central Administration in Britain*, p. 384.
37 See Louis Blom-Cooper, 'The new face of judicial review', *Public Law*, (1982), pp. 250–61; also Maurice Sunkin, 'What is happening to applications for judicial review?' *Modern Law Review*, 50 (1987), pp. 432–67.
38 *Congreve* v. *Home Office*, [1976] ALL ER 697.
39 *Legal Entitlements and Administrative Practices: A Report by Officials* (HMSO, London, 1979), especially paras 2–3.
40 Desmond Keeling, *Management in Government* (Allen and Unwin, London, 1972), p. 95.
41 Pitt and Smith, *Government Departments*, p. 34.
42 Ibid.
43 Ibid., p. 35.
44 See Frank Stacey, *Ombudsmen Compared* (Clarendon Press, Oxford, 1978).
45 Sir Edmund Compton, 'The administrative performance of government', *Public Administration*, 48 (1970), p. 6. Cecil Clothier, *The Ombudsman: Jurisdiction, Powers and Practice* (Manchester Statistical Society, Manchester, 1980), pp. 15–16.
46 Cecil Clothier, 'The value of an Ombudsman', *Public Law* (1986), p. 207.
47 See Roy Gregory and Peter Hutchesson, *The Parliamentary Ombudsman* (Allen and Unwin, London, 1975), pp. 364–5.
48 Dennis Kavanagh, *British Politics: Continuities and Change* (Oxford University Press, Oxford, 1985), p. 46.
49 Ibid., p. 152.
50 See J. J. Richardson and A. G. Jordan, *Governing under Pressure* (Martin Robertson, Oxford, 1979).
51 See P. Dunleavy, 'The architecture of the British central state, Part I: Framework for analysis', *Public Administration*, 67 (1989), pp. 249–76; 'The architecture of the British central state, Part II: Empirical findings', *Public Administration*, 67 (1989), pp. 391–418. See also P. Dunleavy, 'Government at the centre', in P. Dunleavy, A. Gamble

and G. Peele (eds), *Developments in British Politics 3* (Macmillan, Basingstoke, 1990), pp. 96–125.

Chapter 8 Ministers and Civil Servants

1 A Sampson, *Anatomy of Britain*, (Hodder and Stoughton, London, 1962) p. 233.
2 Introduction to T. A. Critchley, *The Civil Service Today*, (Victor Gollancz, London, 1951), p. 10.
3 L. A. Gunn, 'The Fulton Report and its background', *Public Administration* (Sydney), 27 (1968), p. 311.
4 Sir Ivor Jennings, *The Law and the Constitution*, 5th edn (University of London Press, London, 1959), pp. 207–8.
5 Geoffrey Marshall, *Constitutional Conventions* (Clarendon Press, Oxford, 1984), p. 54.
6 Geoffrey Marshall, 'Police accountability revisited', in David Butler and A. H. Halsey (eds), *Policy and Politics* (Macmillan, London, 1978), pp. 61–2. See also Colin Turpin, 'Ministerial responsibility: myth or reality?', in Jeffrey Jowell and Dawn Oliver (eds), *The Changing Constitution* (Clarendon Press, Oxford, 1985), p. 52.
7 John P. Mackintosh, *The Government and Politics of Britain* (Hutchinson, London, 1970), p. 144.
8 L. A. Gunn, 'Ministers and civil servants: changes in Whitehall', p. 82.
9 See Annex 4 to the Seventh Report from the Treasury and Civil Service Committee, 1985–86: *Civil Servants and Ministers: Duties and Responsibilities*, vol. II, Annexes, Minutes of Evidence and Appendices, HC 92-II.
10 See Nevil Johnson, *State and Government in the Federal Republic of West Germany: The Executive at Work* (Pergamon Press, Oxford, 1983), pp. 188–96.
11 On Ministerial *cabinets*, see Ella Searls, 'French ministerial *cabinets*', Appendix to Report of a RIPA Working Group, *Top Jobs in Whitehall: Appointments and Promotions in the Senior Civil Service* (Royal Institute of Public Administration, London, 1987). See also Pauline Neville-Jones, 'The continental cabinet system: the effects of transferring it to the United Kingdom', *Political Quarterly*, 54 (1983), pp. 232–42.
12 F. F. Ridley, 'Political neutrality in the civil service', *Social Studies Review*, 1, 4 (1986), pp. 23–8.
13 Ibid., p. 23.
14 Seventh Report from the Treasury and Civil Service Committee, 1985–86, vol. II, pp. 7–9.
15 Ibid., p. 276.

16 S. E. Finer, 'The individual responsibility of ministers', *Public Administration*, 34 (1956), p. 393.

17 Peter Bromhead, *Britain's Developing Constitution* (Allen and Unwin, London, 1974), p. 70.

18 Robert Pyper, 'The F. O. resignations: individual ministerial responsibility revived?' *Teaching Politics*, 12 (1983), p. 207.

19 C. Turpin, *British Government and the Constitution* (Weidenfeld and Nicolson, London, 1985), pp. 357–60. See also *The Economist*, 4 February 1984.

20 HC Deb., 1 May 1972, col. 159.

21 Chapman, 'The Vehicle and General affair: some reflections for public administration in Britain', p. 289.

22 Turpin, *British Government and the Constitution*, p. 361.

23 See Gunn, 'Ministers and civil servants', pp. 78–79.

24 *Westland plc*: Government Response to the Third and Fourth Reports from the Defence Committee, Cmnd 9916 (HMSO, London, 1986). Seventh Report from the Treasury and Civil Service Committee, 1985–86, vol. I, Report, HC 92-I, para. 3.19. See Government Response, *Civil Servants and Ministers: Duties and Responsibilities*, Cmnd 9841 (HMSO, London, 1986), paras. 13–15.

25 Dawn Oliver and Rodney Austin, 'Political and constitutional aspects of the Westland affair', *Parliamentary Affairs*, 40 (1987), p. 36.

26 Quoted in H. Montgomery Hyde, *Carson, The Life of Sir Edward Carson* (Constable, London, 1974), p. 415.

27 Lord Strang, *The Foreign Office* (Allen and Unwin, London, 1955), p. 147. See also Sir John Tilley and Stephen Gaselee, *The Foreign Office* (Putnams, London, 1933), p. 3.

28 Anthony Crosland in Kogan (ed.), *The Politics of Education*, p. 179.

29 Ibid., p. 48.

30 R. G. S Brown and D. R. Steel, *The Administrative Process in Britain*, 2nd edn (Methuen, 1979), p. 129.

31 Bevins, *The Greasy Pole*, p. 57.

32 Crossman, *The Diaries of a Cabinet Minister*, vol. 3, p. 78.

33 Bruce Headey, *British Cabinet Ministers* (Allen and Unwin, London, 1974), p. 36.

34 Bruce-Gardyne, *Ministers and Mandarins*, p. 39.

35 Ernest Marples, 'A dog's life in the Ministry', in Richard Rose (ed.), *Policy-making in Britain* (Macmillan, London, 1969), pp. 128–31.

36 Brian Smith, *Policy Making in British Government* (Martin Robertson, Oxford, 1976), pp. 102–3. See also Headey, *British Cabinet Ministers*, ch. 4.

37 Headey, *British Cabinet Ministers*, p. 187.

38 G. K. Fry, *The Administrative 'Revolution' in Whitehall* (Croom Helm, London, 1981), p. 180.

39 Kogan (ed.), *The Politics of Education*. p. 42.

40 Shore, *Entitled to Know*, p. 153.

41 J. Lynn and A. Jay (eds), *The Complete Yes, Minister* (BBC, London, 1984).
42 Tony Benn, 'Manifestos and Mandarins', in *Policy and Practice: the Experience of Government* (Royal Institute of Public Administration, London, 1980), p. 62.
43 Tony Benn quoted in Young and Sloman (eds), *No, Minister*, p. 20.
44 Crossman, *The Diaries of a Cabinet Minister*, vol. 1; Michael Meacher, 'The men who block the corridors of power', *Guardian*, 14 June 1979.
45 Shirley Williams, 'The decision makers', and William Rodgers, 'Westminster and Whitehall: adapting to change', in *Policy and Practice*, pp. 79–102 and pp. 9–25.
46 Quoted in Young and Sloman (eds) *No, Minister*, p. 29.
47 See, for example, the comments of Denis Healey in Young and Sloman (eds), *No, Minister*, p. 25.
48 Heclo and Wildavsky, *The Private Government of Public Money*, p. 132.
49 Bruce-Gardyne, *Ministers and Mandarins*, p. 56.
50 See, for example, David Lipsey, 'Who's in charge in Whitehall?', *New Society*, 24 April 1980, pp. 155–7.
51 John Ward, 'Should it always be "Yes, Minister"?' Paper presented at the RIPA Conference, Brighton, 10–11 April 1981.
52 John Greenwood and David Wilson, *Public Administration in Britain* (Allen and Unwin, London, 1984), p. 84.
53 Ward, 'Should it always be "Yes, Minister"?'.
54 Gunn, 'The Fulton Report and its background', p. 315.
55 Barbara Castle, 'Mandarin power', *The Sunday Times*, 10 June 1973.
56 Malcolm Dean, 'Whitehall: the inside story', *Guardian*, 26 September 1979.
57 Nicholas Henderson, *The Private Office* (Weidenfeld and Nicolson, London, 1984), p. xviii.
58 Headey, *British Cabinet Ministers*, p. 128.
59 Dean, 'Whitehall: the inside story'.
60 Crossman, *The Diaries of a Cabinet Minister*, vol. 1, p. 385.
61 At the time of writing, 14 departments had four or more ministers.
62 Castle, 'Mandarin power'.
63 See, for example, David Lipsey (ed.), *Making Government Work*, Fabian Tract 480 (The Fabian Society, London, 1982).
64 Kevin Theakston, 'The use and abuse of junior ministers: increasing political influence in Whitehall', *Political Quarterly*, 57 (1986), p. 34.
65 See Gunn, 'Ministers and civil servants' for a discussion of this period.
66 Rudolf Klein and Janet Lewis, 'Advice and dissent in British government: the case of the special advisers', *Policy and Politics*, 6 (1977), pp. 1–25.
67 Seventh Report from the Treasury and Civil Service Committee, 1985–86, vol. I, para. 5.22.

68 Young and Sloman (eds), *No, Minister*, p. 90.
69 J. R. Greenaway, 'Bureaucrats under pressure: the Thatcher government and the mandarin elite', *Teaching Politics*, 13 (1984), p. 67. Hugo Young and Anne Sloman (eds), *The Thatcher Phenomenon* (BBC Publications, London, 1986), p. 48.
70 Greenaway, 'Bureaucrats under pressure', p. 69. See also F. F Ridley, 'The British civil service and politics: principles in question and traditions in flux', *Parliamentary Affairs*, 36 (1983), pp. 28–48.
71 Geoffrey K. Fry, 'The development of the Thatcher government's "grand strategy" for the civil service: a public policy perspective', *Public Administration*, 62 (1984), p. 325.
72 Sir Antony Part quoted in D. Jessell, 'Mandarins and ministers', *The Listener*, 11 December 1980, p. 775.
73 See Fry, *The Changing Civil Service*, p. 106.
74 Quoted in Patrick Cosgrave, *Thatcher: The First Term* (Bodley Head, London, 1985), p. 169.
75 Ridley, 'The British civil service and politics', p. 45.
76 Sir John Hoskyns, 'Whitehall and Westminster: an outsider's view', *Parliamentary Affairs*, 36 (1983), pp. 145 and 142.
77 Quoted by Greenaway, 'Bureaucrats under pressure', p. 78.
78 Sir Douglas Wass, 'The public service in modern society', *Public Administration*, 61 (1983), p. 14.
79 Ibid., p. 13.
80 Sir Douglas Wass, *Government and the Governed* (Routledge and Kegan Paul, London, 1984), p. 57.
81 Wass, 'The public service in modern society', p. 13.
82 Wass, *Government and the Governed*, p. 56.
83 Wass, 'The public service in modern society', p. 13.
84 Geoffrey K. Fry, 'The attack on the civil service and the response of the insiders', *Parliamentary Affairs*, 37 (1984), p. 361.
85 The Fulton Report, vol. 5 (2), Proposals and Opinions, pp. 665–6; *Guardian*, 21 July 1986.
86 Seventh Report from the Treasury and Civil Service Committee, 1985–86, vol. II, Q. 655.
87 Ibid., vol. I, paras. 5.23 and 5.28–5.32.
88 Eleventh Report from the Expenditure Committee, 1976–77: *The Civil Service*, vol. I, Report, HC 535-I, para. 149.
89 *Civil Servants and Ministers: Duties and Responsibilities:* Government Response to the Seventh Report from the Treasury and Civil Service Committee, para. 35.
90 Report of a RIPA Working Group, *Top Jobs in Whitehall*.
91 Seventh Report from the Treasury and Civil Service Committee, 1985–86, vol. II, Q. 728.
92 Ibid., p. 154.
93 Seventh Report from the Treasury and Civil Service Committee, 1985–86, vol., I, para. 5.9.

94 Richard Norton-Taylor, 'When Thatcher lifts the knife mandarins fear for their skins', *Guardian*, 1 July 1983.
95 Hugo Young, 'Purging the devil's advocates', *The Sunday Times*, 24 October 1982.
96 Quoted in P. Hennessy, 'Why new masters could mean wholesale change', *The Independent*, 9 January 1989.
97 K. Theakston, 'Labour, Thatcher and the future of the civil service', *Public Policy and Administration*, 5 (1990), p. 47.
98 K. Theakston, 'The civil service: progress report 1988/89', *Contemporary Record*, 2, 6 (1989), p. 17.

Chapter 9 The Public Face of Private Government

1   Kellner and Crowther-Hunt, *The Civil Servants*, p. 19.
2   Heclo and Wildavsky, *The Private Government of Public Money*, p. 2.
3   William Plowden, *Newsweek*, BBC TV, 9 November 1978, quoted in Kellner and Crowther-Hunt, *The Civil Servants*, p. 272; Clive Ponting, *Whitehall: Tragedy and Farce*, (Hamish Hamilton, London, 1986) p. 92.
4   James Cornford, 'The right to know secrets', *The Listener*, 31 August 1978, pp. 258–9.
5   Lynn and Jay (eds), *The Complete Yes, Minister*, p. 21.
6   H. H. Gerth and C. Wright Mills (eds), *From Max Weber* (Routledge and Kegan Paul, London, 1948), p. 233.
7   James Michael, *The Politics of Secrecy* (Penguin Books, Harmondsworth, 1982), p. 9.
8   D. Thompson, 'The Committee of 100 and the Official Secrets Act 1911', *Public Law*, (1973), pp. 201–26. See also Michael, *The Politics of Secrecy*, pp. 50–9, for a discussion of the 'ABC' case.
9   C. M. Regan, 'Anonymity in the British civil service: facelessness diminished', *Parliamentary Affairs*, 39 (1986), p. 424.
10 *Report of the Departmental Committee on Section 2 of the Official Secrets Act 1911* (Chairman, Lord Franks), Cmnd 5104 (HMSO, London, 1972), vol. 3, Evidence, p. 320.
11 *Report of the Departmental Committee on Section 2 of the Official Secrets Act 1911*, vol. 1, Report, para. 88.
12 Andrew Boyle, *The Climate of Treason* (Hutchinson, London, 1979).
13 See, for example, *Open Government*, Cmnd 7520 (HMSO, London, 1979).
14 See, for example, Outer Circle Policy Unit, *Official Information Bill* (OCPU, London, 1978); Wilson (ed.), *The Secrets File*.
15 Heclo and Wildavsky, *The Private Government of Public Money*, p. 14.
16 *Report of the Departmental Committee on Section 2 of the Official Secrets Act 1911*, vol. 1, para. 58.
17 Kellner and Crowther-Hunt, *The Civil Servants*, p. 275.

18 Quoted in David Leigh, *The Frontiers of Secrecy* (Junction Books, London, 1980), p. 36.
19 Norton-Taylor, *The Ponting Affair*, p. 127.
20 Martin Gilbert, *Winston S. Churchill, Vol. 5, 1922–39* (Heinemann, London, 1976). See also Peter Kellner, 'Churchill, Mountbatten and the noble art of leaking', *New Statesman*, 31 August 1984.
21 Robert Pyper, 'Sarah Tisdall, Ian Willmore and the civil servant's "Right to Leak"', *Political Quarterly*, 56 (1985), p. 75.
22 Seventh Report from the Treasury and Civil Service Committee 1985–86, vol. II, Annexes, Minutes of Evidence and Appendices, HC 92-II, pp. 7–9.
23 Ibid., pp. 64–6.
24 Ibid., Q. 179.
25 *Report of the Departmental Committee on Section 2 of the Officials Secrets Act 1911*, vol. 4, Evidence, p. 187.
26 See Jeremy Tunstall, *The Westminster Lobby Correspondents* (Routledge and Kegan Paul, London, 1970).
27 Peter Kellner, 'The lobby, official secrets and good government', *Parliamentary Affairs*, 36 (1983), p. 275.
28 *The Independent*, 9 December 1986.
29 Anthony Howard, 'The role of the lobby correspondent', *The Listener*, 21 January 1965, p. 94.
30 Kellner, 'The lobby, official secrets and good government', pp. 276–7.
31 Ibid., p. 277.
32 *Guardian*, 25 November 1986.
33 Michael Cockerell, Peter Hennessy and David Walker, *Sources Close to the Prime Minister* (Macmillan, London, 1984), p. 144.
34 Henry James, 'The role of the Central Office of Information', in Annabelle May and Kathryn Rowan (eds), *Inside Information: British Government and the Media* (Constable, London, 1982), p. 188.
35 Crossman, *The Diaries of a Cabinet Minister*, vol. 1, p. 497. Quoted in May and Rowan (eds), *Inside Information*, p. 191.
36 Cockerell, Hennessy and Walker, *Sources Close to the Prime Minister*, p. 140.
37 *Guardian*, 26 February 1987.
38 Seventh Report from the Treasury and Civil Service Committee, 1985–86, vol. I, Report, HC 92-I, para. 5.20.
39 Mackenzie and Grove, *Central Administration in Britain*, p. v.
40 Ibid., p. 377.
41 Philip Norton, *The Commons in Perspective* (Martin Robertson, Oxford, 1982), p. 114.
42 Mackenzie and Grove, *Central Administration in Britain*, p. 379. See also Enid Russell-Smith, *Modern Bureaucracy: The Home Civil Service* (Longman, London, 1974), pp. 53–55.
43 Dale, *The Higher Civil Service*, p. 105.
44 Ponting, *Whitehall: Tragedy and Farce*, p. 151.

45 Kellner and Crowther-Hunt, *The Civil Servants*, p. 164.

46 Regan, 'Anonymity in the British Civil Service', p. 431.

47 CSD Gen 80/38, Civil Service Department, 1980.

48 Gavin Drewry (ed.), *The New Select Committees* (Oxford University Press, Oxford, 1985), p. 389.

49 S. E. Finer, *Anonymous Empire* (Pall Mall Press, London, 1958), pp. 3 and 21.

50 Grant Jordan and Jeremy Richardson, 'The British policy style or the logic of negotiation?', in Jeremy Richardson (ed.), *Policy Styles in Western Europe* (Allen and Unwin, London, 1982), p. 85. See also S. H. Beer, *Modern British Politics* (Faber and Faber, London, 1965), ch. 12.

51 Geoffrey Alderman, *Pressure Groups and Government in Great Britain* (Longman, London, 1984), p. 80.

52 Jean Blondel, *Voters, Parties and Leaders* (Pelican Books, Harmondsworth, 1963), p. 225.

53 Jordan and Richardson, 'The British policy style', p. 86.

54 Beer, *Modern British Politics*, p. 329.

55 H. Eckstein, *Pressure Group Politics* (Allen and Unwin, London, 1960), p. 24.

56 Dorothy Johnstone, *A Tax Shall be Charged*, Civil Service Studies No. 1 (HMSO, London, 1975).

57 A. Grant Jordan, 'Iron triangles, woolly corporatism, or elastic nets: images of the policy process', *Journal of Public Policy*, 1 (1981), pp. 120–1.

58 Jordan and Richardson, 'The British policy style', p. 81.

59 Richardson and Jordan, *Governing under Pressure*, p. 175.

60 Shirley Williams, 'The decision makers', p. 93.

61 Richardson and Jordan, *Governing under Pressure*, p. 174.

62 M. Ryan, *The Acceptable Pressure Group* (Saxon House, Farnborough, 1978).

63 Management and Personnel Office, *Interchange of Staff between the Civil Service and Other Organisations: 1985 Report.*

64 The Fulton Report, vol. 1, para. 128.

65 *Acceptance of Outside Appointments by Crown Servants*: Government Observations on the Eighth Report from the Treasury and Civil Service Committee, Cmnd 9465 (HMSO, London, 1985), para. 8.

66 Anthony Beaumont Dark MP, quoted in the *Guardian*, 21 September 1984.

67 Crossman, *The Diaries of a Cabinet Minister*, vol. 3, p. 732.

68 Eighth Report from the Treasury and Civil Service Committee, 1983–84: *Acceptance of Outside Appointments by Crown Servants*, HC 302 (HMSO, London, 1984).

69 Ibid., and Fourth Report from the Treasury and Civil Service Committee, 1980–81: *Acceptance of Outside Appointments by Crown Servants*, HC 216 (HMSO, London, 1981).

70 Government Observations on the Eighth Report from the Treasury and Civil Service Committee.
71 Anthony King and Anne Sloman (eds), *Westminster and Beyond* (Macmillan, London, 1973).
72 Young and Sloman (eds), *No, Minister*, p. 85.
73 Peter Hennessy, *Cabinet* (Basil Blackwell, Oxford, 1986), p. 188; Lord Hunt of Tanworth, 'Cabinet strategy and management', CIPFA/RIPA Conference, Eastbourne, 9 June 1983.
74 Sir Frank Cooper, 'Affordable defence: in search of a strategy', Lecture to the Royal United Services Institute, 9 October 1985.
75 Sir Leo Pliatzky, *Getting and Spending: Public Expenditure, Employment and Inflation* (Basil Blackwell, Oxford, 1982).
76 HL Deb., 26 February 1986, cols 1102–3.
77 Wass, *Government and the Governed*.
78 Grant Jordan, 'The 1983 Reith Lectures: forward to 1970', *Public Administration Bulletin*, 45 (August 1984), p. 37.
79 *The Times*, 5 March 1984.
80 Hennessy, *Cabinet*, p. 191.
81 F. F. Ridley, 'Political neutrality, the duty of silence and the right to publish in the civil service', *Parliamentary Affairs*, 39 (1986), p. 447.
82 See S. Palmer, 'Tightening secrecy law: the Official Secrets Act 1989', *Public Law* (1990), pp. 243–56.
83 Fifth Report from the Treasury and Civil Service Committee, 1989–90, para. 7. See also HC Deb., 2 December 1987, cols 572–75.
84 Fifth Report from the Treasury and Civil Service Committee, 1989–90, paras. 26–7.
85 Bernard Ingham's role as press secretary is discussed in Robert Harris, *Good and Faithful Servant: The Unauthorised Biography of Bernard Ingham* (Faber and Faber, London, 1990).

Chapter 10: Slimmer and Fitter: the Quest for Efficiency and Effectiveness

1 *Civil Service Statistics 1986* (HMSO, London, 1986), p. 4.
2 C. Northcote Parkinson, *Parkinson's Law, or the Pursuit of Progress* (John Murray, London, 1958), p. 4.
3 Third Report from the Treasury and Civil Service Committee, 1981–2: *Efficiency and Effectiveness in the Civil Service*, vol. I, Report. HC 236-I (HMSO, London, 1982), para. 52.
4 Ibid., para. 35.
5 See, for example, Chapman, *British Government Observed*; and Fabian Society, *The Administrators: the Reform of the Civil Service*.
6 *The Control of Public Expenditure* (Plowden Report), Cmnd 1432 (HMSO, London, 1961).
7 The Fulton Report, vol. 1, para. 18.

8   Pitt and Smith, *Government Departments*, p. 91; Brown and Steel, *The Administrative Process in Britain*, p. 12.

9   The Fulton Report, vol. 1, para. 150.

10 Ibid., paras. 153–6.

11 See, for example, the Fulton Report, vol. 5 (2), Proposals and Opinions, p. 507.

12 The Fulton Report, vol. 1, paras. 188–90.

13 *The Reorganisation of Central Government*, para. 14.

14 A survey of developments can be found in Garrett, *Managing the Civil Service*. See also Pollitt, *Manipulating the Machine*.

15 Eleventh Report from the Expenditure Committee, 1976–77: *The Civil Service*, vol. I, Report, HC 535-I, para. 94.

16 *The Civil Service*: Government Observations on the Eleventh Report from the Expenditure Committee, Cmnd 7117 (HMSO, London, 1978), para. 49.

17 Garrett, *Managing the Civil Service*, p. 135.

18 Eleventh Report from the Expenditure Committee, 1976–77, vol. II (I), Minutes of Evidence, HC 535-II, p. 23.

19 Sir Richard Meyjes, 'Development of government organisation' (unpublished paper, 1972), quoted in Pollitt, *Manipulating the Machine*, p. 102.

20 *The Reorganisation of Central Government*, para. 51.

21 Andrew Gray and Bill Jenkins (eds), *Policy Analysis and Evaluation in British Government* (Royal Institute of Public Administration, London, 1983), p. 12.

22 Gray and Jenkins, 'Policy analysis in British central government: the experience of PAR', pp. 429–50.

23 Ibid., p. 446.

24 *The Conservative Manifesto, 1979*, the full text of which can be found in *The Times Guide to the House of Commons, May 1979* (Times Books, London, 1979), pp. 282–94.

25 Andrew Gray and Bill Jenkins, 'Efficiency and the self-evaluating organisation – the central government experience', *Local Government Studies*, 8 (1982), p. 47.

26 *Efficiency in the Civil Service*, Cmnd 8293 (HMSO, London, 1981), para. 9.

27 *Guardian*, 15 January 1987.

28 *The Economist*, 2 March 1985, p. 45.

29 Leslie Chapman, *Your Disobedient Servant* (Chatto and Windus, London, 1978).

30 Peter Kellner, 'How Whitehall is learning the lessons of M & S', *The Sunday Times*, 24 August 1980.

31 David Allen, 'Raynerism: strengthening civil service management', *RIPA Report*, Winter 1981, p. 10.

32 Kellner, 'How Whitehall is learning the lessons of M & S'.

33 Ponting, *The Right to Know*, pp. 9–11.

34 National Audit Office, Report by the Comptroller and Auditor-

General, *The Rayner Scrutiny Programmes, 1979 to 1983*, HC 322, 1986.

35 Norman Warner, 'Raynerism in practice: anatomy of a Rayner scrutiny', *Public Administration*, 62 (1984), pp. 7–22.

36 Thirty-ninth Report from the Committee of Public Accounts, 1985–86: *The Rayner Scrutiny Programmes, 1979 to 1983*, HC 365 (HMSO, London, 1986), para. 13.

37 Peter Riddell, *The Thatcher Government* (Martin Robertson, London, 1983), p. 122.

38 L. Metcalfe and S. Richards, 'Raynerism and efficiency in government', in A. Hopwood and C. Tompkins (eds), *Issues in Public Sector Accounting* (Philip Allan, Oxford, 1984), p. 200.

39 R. Pauley, 'Heseltine uncovers a few home truths', *The Financial Times*, 18 November 1980, quoted in Andrew Likierman, 'Management information for ministers: the MINIS system in the Department of the Environment', *Public Administration*, 60 (1982), p. 129.

40 *Efficiency and Effectiveness in the Civil Service:* Government Observations on the Third Report from the Treasury and Civil Service Committee, Cmnd 8616 (HMSO, London, 1982), para. 27.

41 Appendix 5 (memorandum by Andrew Likierman) to the Third Report from the Treasury and Civil Service Committee, 1981–2, vol. III, Appendices, HC 236-III, p. 51. Also see Heseltine's own comments on MINIS in Michael Heseltine, *Where There's a Will* (Hutchinson, London, 1987), ch. 1.

42 Colin Hughes, 'Whitehall: the system strikes back', *The Times*, 24 March 1986.

43 Riddell, *The Thatcher Government*, p. 124.

44 Government Observations on the Third Report from the Treasury and Civil Service Committee.

45 Ibid., para. 13.

46 *Financial Management in Government Departments*, Cmnd 9058, (HMSO, London, 1983); *Progress in Financial Management in Government Departments*, Cmnd 9297 (HMSO, London, 1984).

47 Andrew Gray and William I. Jenkins, 'Accountable management in British central government: some reflections on the financial management initiative', *Financial Accountability and Management*, 2 (1986), p. 173.

48 *Review of Personnel Work in the Civil Service: Report to the Prime Minister by J. S. Cassells* (HMSO, London, 1982).

49 Cabinet Office (MPO), *The Civil Service Performance Bonus Scheme 1985*.

50 *The Times*, 29 January 1987.

51 J. S. Cassells, 'Civil servants and management', *Management in Government*, 38 (1983), p. 14.

52 Metcalfe and Richards, 'Raynerism and efficiency in government', pp. 199 and 201.

53 Sir Frank Cooper, 'Freedom to manage in government', RIPA Winter Lecture Series, March 1983, quoted in Metcalfe and Richards, 'Raynerism and efficiency in government', p. 209.

54 Quoted in G. Reid, *The Politics of Financial Control* (Hutchinson University Library, London, 1966), p. 114.

55 See Brian Sedgemore, *The Secret Constitution* (Hodder and Stoughton, London, 1980), pp. 138–9.

56 Twenty-sixth Report from the Committee of Public Accounts, 1983–84: *Fraud in the Property Services Agency*, HC 295 (HMSO, London, 1984).

57 Michael Latham, 'A watchdog with teeth: the Committee of Public Accounts', *Social Studies Review*, 1, 4 (1986), p. 41.

58 See Second Special Report from the Committee of Public Accounts, 1978–79: *The Work of the Committee of Public Accounts and the Status and Functions of the Comptroller and Auditor-General*, HC 330 (HMSO, London, 1979), p. xiv.

59 First Report from the Committee of Public Accounts, 1972–73: *North Sea Oil and Gas*, HC 122 (HMSO, London, 1973).

60 Fourth Report from the Committee of Public Accounts, 1974–75: *Miscellaneous Subjects*, HC 502 (HMSO, London, 1975).

61 Twenty-Eighth Report from the Committee of Public Accounts, 1984–85: *The Torpedo Programme*, HC 391 (HMSO, London, 1985).

62 See the notes by Gavin Drewry in *Public Law* (1981), pp. 304–10 and 478–80; (1982), pp. 564–9; and (1983), pp. 531–7.

63 *Financial Management in the Public Sector, A Review 1979–84* (Peat, Marwick, Mitchell & Co., London, 1984), p. 6.

64 J. J. Richardson, 'Programme evaluation in Britain and Sweden', *Parliamentary Affairs*, 35 (1982), pp. 160–80.

65 D. Campbell and S. Connor, *On the Record: Surveillance, Computers and Privacy* (Michael Joseph, London, 1986); E. Conn, 'The impact of information technology', *Management in Government*, 39 (1984), p. 111.

66 See S. Matheson, 'Computerisation of the Pay As You Earn System', in D. C. Pitt and B. C. Smith (eds), *The Computer Revolution in Public Administration* (Wheatsheaf Books, Brighton, 1984), pp. 91–104. See also the Green Paper, *The Reform of Personal Taxation*, Cmnd 9756 (HMSO, London, 1986).

67 DHSS, *Social Security Operational Strategy: A Framework for the Future* (HMSO, London, 1982); M. O'Higgins, 'Computerising the social security system: an operational strategy in lieu of a policy strategy', in Pitt and Smith (eds), *The Computer Revolution in Public Administration*, pp. 105–18.

68 Howard Elcock, 'Information technology: stopping Big Brother watching us', in Pitt and Smith (eds), *The Computer Revolution in Public Administration*, p. 178.

69 See *Committee on Data Protection* (Chairman, Sir Norman Lindop),

Cmnd 7341 (HMSO, London, 1978).

70 R. C. Austin, 'The Data Protection Act 1984: the public law implications', *Public Law* (1985), pp. 618–34.

71 C. Mellors and D. Pollitt, 'Legislating for privacy: data protection in Western Europe', *Parliamentary Affairs*, 37 (1984), pp. 199–215.

72 Elcock, 'Information technology: stopping Big Brother watching us'.

73 J. M. Lee 'Financial management and career service', *Public Administration*, 62 (1984), p. 2.

74 Quoted in Gray and Jenkins (eds), *Policy Analysis and Evaluation in British Government*, p. 51.

75 P. Nash, 'We tried before, but without the clout', *Management Services in Government*, 36 (1981), p. 138.

76 Gray and Jenkins, 'Accountable management in British central government', p. 171.

77 Sir Kenneth Clucas, 'Parliament and the civil service', in *Parliament and the Executive* (Royal Institute of Public Administration, London, 1982), p. 35.

78 See Christopher Pollitt, 'Beyond the managerial model: the case for broadening performance assessment in government and the public services', *Financial Accountability and Management*, 2 (1986), pp. 155–70.

79 Peter Hildrew, 'DHSS system "facing breakdown"', *Guardian*, 12 November 1986.

80 P. Lloyd and R. Blackwell, 'Manpower economies, management and industrial relations in the civil service', *Industrial Relations Journal*, 16 (1985), p. 31.

81 Annual Report of the Parliamentary Commissioner for Adminstration, 1981–82, HC 258 (HMSO, London, 1982), p. 14.

Chapter 12 Beyond the Crossroads: the Next Steps Programme

1 Parts of this chapter have been adapted from two items by Gavin Drewry, published in *Public Law*: 'Forward from FMI: the Next Steps', (1988), pp. 505–14; 'Next Steps: the pace falters', (1990), pp. 322–9.

2 Eighth Report from the Treasury and Civil Service Committee, 1987–88: *Civil Service Management Reform: the Next Steps*, HC 494 I–II (HMSO, London, 1988), para. 1.

3 See note 14 below.

4 See in particular articles in *The Guardian*, 7 September 1987 (R. Norton-Taylor) and 30 December 1987 (D. Henke).

5 See pp. 51–4 and 194–7, above.

6 The Fulton Report, vol. 1, 1968, para. 190.

7 Eleventh Report from the Expenditure Committee, 1976–77; and see above, pp. 196–7.

8   Ibid., para. 91.
9   Efficiency Unit, *Improving Management in Government: The Next Steps*, Report to the Prime Minister (HMSO, London, 1988).
10 Ibid., para. 3.
11 Ibid., para. 4.
12 Ibid.
13 Ibid., para. 12.
14 Ibid., para. 44.
15 Ibid., para. 21.
16 Ibid., para. 23.
17 HC Deb., 18 February 1988, cols 1149–56.
18 Ibid., col. 1150; (cf. HC Deb., 7 March 1988, col. 16, Richard Luce).
19 Ibid., col. 1151.
20 Eighth Report from the Treasury and Civil Service Committee, 1987–88; Government Reply, Cm. 524, (HMSO, London, 1988). Fifth Report from the Treasury and Civil Service Committee, 1988–89: *Developments in the Next Steps Programme*, HC 348 (HMSO, London, 1989); Government Reply, Cm. 841, (HMSO, London, 1989). Eighth Report from the Treasury and Civil Service Committee, 1989–90: *Progress in the Next Steps Initiative*, HC 481 (HMSO, London, 1990); Government Reply, Cm. 1263, (HMSO, London, 1990).
21 Third Report, 1981–82, HC 236. See p. 204 above.
22 Seventh Report, 1985–86, HC 92. See p. 95, above.
23 Eighth Report, 1987–88.
24 Ibid., para. 19.
25 Ibid., paras. 24–5.
26 Ibid., para. 26.
27 Ibid., para. 29.
28 Ibid., para. 51.
29 See pp. 13–17 and 28–30, above.
30 Eighth Report, 1987–88, paras. 43–4.
31 Ibid., para. 44.
32 Cm. 524, 1988, p. 9.
33 See p. 183, above.
34 Fifth Report, 1988–89, para. 62.
35 Ibid., para. 63.
36 Ibid., Evidence, Q. 10.
37 See pp. 207–9, above.
38 Eighth Report, 1987–88, para. 49.
39 Thirty-Eighth Report from the Committee of Public Accounts, 1988–89: *The Next Steps Initiative*, HC 420, (HMSO, London, 1989), para. 11.
40 Fifth Report, 1988–89, paras. 10 and 11.
41 Eighth Report, 1987–88, Evidence, QQ 23–4.
42 Fifth Report, 1988–89, Evidence, Q. 5.
43 Eighth Report, 1989–90, Evidence, Q. 8.

44 See HC Deb., 17 May 1989, cols 320–3. The decision followed a study initiated in July 1988, and subsequently published as the Hickey Report.

45 Fifth Report, 1988–89, para. 66; Evidence, Q. 272.

46 HC Deb., 24 October 1988, col. 14 (W. A.).

47 Fifth Report, 1988–89, para. 68; Evidence, Q. 32.

48 Eighth Report, 1987–88, para. 26.

49 Cm. 524, 1988, p. 5.

50 Fifth Report, 1988–89, para. 69.

51 Ibid.

52 P. Stokes, 'The agency challenge', *FDA News*, May 1990, p. 24.

53 Fifth Report, 1988–89, paras. 55–8.

54 Ibid. Evidence, Q. 320.

55 Eighth Report, 1989–90, p. 84, para. 2.

56 Fifth Report, 1988–89, para. 58.

57 *Improving Management in Government – the Next Steps Agencies. Review 1990*, Cm. 1261, (HMSO, London, 1990).

Select Bibliography

Books and Articles

General Works on the Civil Service

Brown, R. G. S. and Steel, D. R., *The Administrative Process in Britain*, 2nd edn (Methuen, London, 1979).

Campbell, G. A., *The Civil Service in Britain*, 2nd edn (Duckworth, London, 1965).

Chapman, R. A., *The Higher Civil Service in Britain* (Constable, London, 1970).

Fry, G. K., *The Changing Civil Service* (Allen and Unwin, London, 1985).

Garrett, J., *Managing the Civil Service* (Heinemann, London, 1980).

Hennessy, P., *Whitehall* (Fontana Press, London, 1990).

Kellner, P. and Crowther-Hunt, Lord, *The Civil Servants: An Inquiry into Britain's Ruling Class* (Macdonald, London, 1980).

Mackenzie, W. J. M. and Grove, J. W., *Central Administration in Britain* (Longman, London, 1957).

Part, A., *The Making of a Mandarin* (André Deutsch, London, 1990).

Ponting, C., *Whitehall: Tragedy and Farce* (Hamish Hamilton, London, 1986).

Ridley, F. F., *Specialists and Generalists* (Allen and Unwin, London, 1968).

Sisson, C. H., *The Spirit of British Administration* (Faber and Faber, London, 1959).

Government Departments

Barnett, J., *Inside the Treasury* (André Deutsch, London, 1982).

Chester, D. N. and Willson, F. M. G., *The Organisation of British Central Government 1914–1964*, 2nd edn (Allen and Unwin, London, 1968).

Dunleavy, P., 'The architecture of the British central state, Part I: Framework for analysis', *Public Administration*, 67 (1989), pp. 249–76.

Dunleavy, P., 'The architecture of the British central state, Part II, Empirical findings', *Public Administration*, 67 (1989), pp. 391–418.

Heclo, H. and Wildavsky, A., *The Private Government of Public Money*, 2nd edn (Macmillan, London, 1979).

Hogwood, B. W. and Keating, M. (eds), *Regional Government in England* (Clarendon Press, Oxford, 1982).

Hood, C., Dunsire, A. and Thompson, K. S., 'So you think you know what government departments are . . . ?', *Public Administration Bulletin*, 27 (1978), pp. 20–32.

Madgwick, P. and Rose, R. (eds), *The Territorial Dimension in United Kingdom Politics* (Macmillan, London, 1982).

Pitt, D. C. and Smith, B. C., *Government Departments* (Routledge and Kegan Paul, London, 1981).

Pollitt, C., *Manipulating the Machine: Changing the Pattern of Ministerial Departments 1960–83* (Allen and Unwin, London, 1984).

History

Barker, Sir Ernest, *The Development of Public Services in Western Europe 1660–1930* (Oxford University Press, London, 1944).

Chapman, R. A. and Greenaway, J. R., *The Dynamics of Administrative Reform* (Croom Helm, London, 1980).

Cohen, E. W., *The Growth of the British Civil Service 1780–1939* (Frank Cass, London, 1941).

Craig, Sir John, *A History of Red Tape* (MacDonald and Evans, London, 1955).

Critchley, T. A., *The Civil Service Today* (Victor Gollancz, London, 1951).

Dale, H. E., *The Higher Civil Service of Great Britain* (Oxford University Press, London, 1941).

Dunhill, F., *The Civil Service: Some Human Aspects* (Allen and Unwin, London, 1956).

Fry, G. K., *Statesmen in Disguise: the Changing Role of the Administrative Class of the British Home Civil Service 1835–1966* (Macmillan, London, 1969).

Kelsall, R. K., *Higher Civil Servants in Britain* (Routledge and Kegan Paul, London, 1955).

Mallalieu, J. P. W., *Passed to You, Please* (Victor Gollancz, London, 1942).

Munro, C. K., *The Fountains in Trafalgar Square* (Heinemann, London, 1952).

Parris, H., *Constitutional Bureaucracy* (Allen and Unwin, London, 1969).

Pellow, J., *The Home Office 1848–1914: From Clerks to Bureaucrats* (Heinemann, London, 1982).

Roseveare, H., *The Treasury: The Evolution of a British Institution* (Allen Lane, London, 1969).

Sutherland, G. (ed.), *Studies in the Growth of Nineteenth Century Government* (Routledge and Kegan Paul, London, 1972).

Wright, M., *Treasury Control of the Civil Service, 1854–1874* (Clarendon Press, Oxford, 1969).

Recruitment, Training and Conditions of Service

Beaumont, P. B., *Government as Employer – Setting an Example* (Royal Institute of Public Administration, London, 1981).

Chapman, R. A., *Leadership in the British Civil Service: A Study of Sir Percival Waterfield and the Creation of the Civil Service Selection Board* (Croom Helm, London, 1984).

Gammon, G. J., 'The British higher civil service: recruitment and training', *Public Policy and Administration*, 4 (1989), pp. 28–40.

Moore, N. E. A., 'The Civil Service College: what it is and what it is not', *Management in Government*, 39 (1984), pp. 96–103.

Parris, H., *Staff Relations in the Civil Service: Fifty Years of Whitleyism* (Allen and Unwin, London, 1973).

Reader, K. M., *The Civil Service Commission 1855–1975*, Civil Service Studies No. 5 (HMSO, London, 1981).

Walker, N., *Morale in the Civil Service: A Study of the Desk Worker* (Edinburgh University Press, Edinburgh, 1961).

White, L. D., *Whitley Councils in the British Civil Service* (University of Chicago Press, Chicago, 1933).

Wright, M. W., 'The professional conduct of civil servants', *Public Administration*, 51 (1973), pp. 1–15.

See also 'Official Publications and Documents' below.

Ministers and Civil Servants

Bruce-Gardyne, J., *Ministers and Mandarins* (Sidgwick and Jackson, London, 1986).

Crossman, R. H. S., *The Diaries of a Cabinet Minister*, 3 vols. (Hamish Hamilton and Jonathan Cape, London, 1975–7).

Finer, S. E., 'The individual responsibility of ministers', *Public Administration*, 34 (1956), pp. 377–96.

Headey, B., *British Cabinet Ministers* (Allen and Unwin, London, 1974).

Hoskyns, Sir John, 'Whitehall and Westminster: an outsider's view', *Parliamentary Affairs*, 36 (1983), pp. 137–47.

Klein, R. and Lewis, J., 'Advice and dissent in British government: the case of the special advisers', *Policy and Politics*, 6 (1977), pp. 1–26.

Marshall, G., 'Ministers and their civil servants', *Public Policy and Administration*, 3 (1988), pp. 4–14.

Morrison, Lord, *Government and Parliament*, 3rd edn (Oxford University Press, Oxford, 1964).

Oliver, D., and Austin, R., 'Political and constitutional aspects of the Westland affair', *Parliamentary Affairs*, 40 (1987), pp. 20–40.

Ridley, F. F. 'The British civil service and politics: principles in question and traditions in flux', *Parliamentary Affairs* 36 (1983), pp. 28–48.

Robinson, A., Shepherd, R., Ridley, F. F., and Jones, G. W., 'Symposium on ministerial responsibility', *Public Administration*, 61 (1987), pp. 61–91.

Royal Institute of Public Administration, *Policy and Practice: the Experience of Government* (Royal Institute of Public Administration, London, 1980).

Theakston, K., 'The use and abuse of junior ministers: increasing political influence in Whitehall', *Political Quarterly*, 57 (1986), pp. 18–35.

Theakston, K., 'Labour, Thatcher and the future of the civil service', *Public Policy and Administration*, 5 (1990), pp. 44–57.

Turpin, C., 'Ministerial responsibility: myth or reality?', in J. Jowell and D. Oliver (eds), *The Changing Constitution*, 2nd edn (Clarendon Press, Oxford, 1989), pp. 53–85.

Wass, Sir Douglas, *Government and the Governed* (Routledge and Kegan Paul, London, 1984).

Young, H. and Sloman, A., *No, Minister: An Inquiry into the Civil Service* (BBC, London, 1982).

Civil Servants, Parliament and the Public

Chapman, R. A. and Hunt. M. (eds), *Open Government* (Croom Helm, London, 1987).

Clucas, Sir Kenneth, 'Parliament and the civil service', in *Parliament and the Executive* (Royal Institute of Public Administration, London, 1982), pp. 23–41.

Cockerell, M., Hennessy, P. and Walker, D., *Sources Close to the Prime Minister* (Macmillan, London, 1984).

Drewry, G. (ed.), *The New Select Committees*, 2nd edn (Oxford University Press, Oxford, 1989).

Englefield, D. (ed.), *Whitehall and Westminster: Government Informs Parliament: The Changing Scene* (Longman, London, 1986).

Gosling, R., and Nutley, S., *Bridging the Gap: Secondments between Government and Business* (Royal Institute of Public Administration, London, 1990).

Gregory, R. and Hutchesson, P., *The Parliamentary Ombudsman: A Study in the Control of Administrative Action* (Allen and Unwin, London, 1975).

Hooper, D., *Official Secrets: the Use and Abuse of the Act* (Secker and Warburg, London, 1987).

Michael, J., *The Politics of Secrecy* (Penguin Books, Harmondsworth, 1982).

Norton-Taylor, R., *The Ponting Affair* (Cecil Woolf, London, 1985).

Palmer, S., 'Tightening secrecy law: the Official Secrets Act 1989', *Public Law* (1990), pp. 243–56.

Pyper, R., 'Sarah Tisdall, Ian Willmore and the civil servant's "right to leak"', *Political Quarterly*, 56 (1985), pp. 72–81.

Richardson, J. J. and Jordan, A. G., *Governing Under Pressure* (Martin Robertson, Oxford, 1979).

Williams, D., *Not in the Public Interest* (Hutchinson, London, 1965).

Efficiency and Effectiveness

Chapman, L., *Your Disobedient Servant* (Chatto and Windus, London, 1978).

Fry, G. K., 'The development of the Thatcher government's "grand strategy'" for the civil service: a public policy perspective', *Public Administration*, 62 (1984), pp. 322–35.

Fry, G. K., 'The Thatcher government, the Financial Management Initiative and the "new civil service"', *Public Administration*, 66 (1988), pp. 1–20.

Gray, A. and Jenkins, B., 'Policy analysis in British central government: the experience of PAR', *Public Administration*, 60 (1982), pp. 429–50.

Gray, A. and Jenkins, B. (eds), *Policy Analysis and Evaluation in British Government* (Royal Institute of Public Administration, London, 1983).

Gray, A. and Jenkins, W. I., 'Accountable management in British central government: some reflections on the financial management initiative', *Financial Accountability and Management*, 2 (1986), pp. 171–85.

Likierman, A., 'Management information for ministers: the MINIS system in the Department of the Environment', *Public Administration*, 60 (1982), pp. 127–42.

Metcalfe, L. and Richards S., 'Raynerism and efficiency in government', in A. Hopwood and C. Tompkins (eds), *Issues in Public Sector Accounting* (Philip Allan, Oxford, 1984), pp. 188–211.

Peat Marwick/Royal Institute of Public Administration, *Developing the FMI Principles: Changes in Process and Culture* (Royal Institute of Public Administration, London, 1985).

Peat Marwick McLintock/Royal Institute of Public Administration; *Future Shape of Reform in Whitehall* (Royal Institute of Public Administration, London, 1988).

Pitt, D. C., and Smith, B. C. (eds), *The Computer Revolution in Public Administration* (Wheatsheaf Books, Brighton, 1984).

Pollitt, C., 'Beyond the managerial model: the case for broadening performance assessment in government and the public services', *Financial Accountability and Management*, 2 (1986), pp. 155–70.

The Next Steps

Chapman, R. A., 'The Next Steps: a review', *Public Policy and Administration*, 3 (1988), pp. 3–10.

Drewry, G., 'Forward from FMI: the Next Steps', *Public Law* (1988), pp. 505–14.

Drewry, G., 'Next Steps: the pace falters', *Public Law* (1990), pp. 322–9.

Flynn, A., Gray, A., and Jenkins, W., 'Taking the Next Steps: the changing management of government', *Parliamentary Affairs*, 43 (1989), pp. 154–78.

Fry, G., Flynn, A., Gray, A., Jenkins, W., and Rutherford, B., 'Symposium on Improving Management in Government', *Public Administration*, 66 (1988), pp. 429–45.

Kemp, P., 'Next Steps for the British civil service', *Governance*, 3 (1990), pp. 186–96.

Official Publications and Documents

This list is approximately in chronological order

Report on the Organisation of the Permanent Civil Service (Northcote–Trevelyan Report), C. 1713 (London, 1854).

First Report of the Commission of Inquiry on the Selection, Transfer and Grading of Civil Servants (Chairman, Lyon Playfair), C. 1113 (HMSO, London, 1875).

Second Report of the Royal Commission on the Civil Service (Chairman, Sir Matthew Ridley), C. 5545 (HMSO, London, 1888).

Reports of the Royal Commission on the Civil Service, 1912–15 (Chairman, Lord MacDonnell), various Cd numbers (HMSO, London).

Report of the Machinery of Government Committee (Chairman, Lord Haldane), Cd. 9230 (HMSO, London, 1918).

Final Report of the Committee Appointed to Inquire into the Organisation and Staffing of Government Offices (Chairman, Sir John Bradbury), Cmd. 62 (HMSO, London, 1919).

Report of the Royal Commission on the Civil Service, 1929–31 (Chairman, Lord Tomlin), Cmd. 3909 (HMSO, London, 1931).

Report of the Committee on the Training of Civil Servants (Chairman, Ralph Assheton), Cmd. 6525 (HMSO, London, 1944).

Report of the Committee on the Political Activities of Civil Servants (Chairman, J. C. Masterman), Cmd. 7718 (HMSO, London, 1949).

Report of the Royal Commission on the Civil Service, 1953–55 (Chairman, Sir Raymond Priestley), Cmd. 9613 (HMSO, London, 1955).

Control of Public Expenditure (Plowden Report), Cmd. 1432 (HMSO, London, 1961).

Sixth Report from the Estimates Committee, 1964–65: *Recruitment to the Civil Service*, HC 308 (HMSO, London, 1965).

Report of the Committee on the Civil Service, 1966–68 (Chairman, Lord Fulton), Cmnd 3638 (HMSO, London, 1968).
  Vol. 1, Report.
  Vol. 2, Report of a Management Consultancy Group.
  Vol. 3, Surveys and Investigations.
  Vol. 4, Factual, Statistical and Explanatory Papers.
  Vol. 5, Proposals and Opinions.

Report of the Committee of Inquiry on the Method II System of Selection (Chairman, J. Davies), Cmnd 4156 (HMSO, London, 1969).

The Reorganisation of Central Government, Cmnd 4506 (HMSO, London, 1970).

Report of the Tribunal appointed to inquire into certain issues in relation to the circumstances leading up to the cessation of trading by the Vehicle and General Insurance Company Ltd, HL 80, HC 133 (HMSO, London, 1972).

Report of the Departmental Committee on Section 2 of the Official Secrets Act 1911 (Chairman, Lord Franks), Cmnd 5104 (HMSO, London, 1972), together with separate volumes of Evidence.

The Dispersal of Government Work from London (Hardman Report), Cmnd 5332 (HMSO, London, 1973).

Eleventh Report from the Expenditure Committee, 1976–77: *The Civil Service*, HC 535 (HMSO, London, 1977), together with separate volumes of Evidence and Appendices.

Report of the Committee on the Political Activities of Civil Servants (Chairman, Sir Arthur Armitage), Cmnd 7057 (HMSO, London, 1978).

The Civil Service: Government Observations on the Eleventh Report from the Expenditure Committee, Cmnd 7117 (HMSO, London, 1978).

Report of the Committee on the Selection Procedure for the Recruitment of Administration Trainees (Chairman, F. H. Allen) (Civil Service Commission, Basingstoke, 1979).

Select Committees: Memorandum of Guidance for Officials (Osmotherly Rules) (Civil Service Department, London, 1980).

First Report from the Treasury and Civil Service Committee, 1980–81: *The Future of the Civil Service Department*, HC 54 (HMSO, London, 1980).

The Future of the Civil Service Department: Government Observations on the First Report from the Treasury and Civil Service Committee, Cmnd 8170 (HMSO, London, 1981).

Fourth Report from the Treasury and Civil Service Committee, 1980–81: *Acceptance of Outside Appointments by Crown Servants*, HC 216 (HMSO, London, 1981).

Chain of Command Review: The Open Structure. Report of a team led by Sir Geoffrey Wardale (Management and Personnel Office, London, 1981).

Efficiency in the Civil Service, Cmnd 8293 (HMSO, London, 1981).

Report of the Committee on the Value of Pensions (Chairman, Sir Bernard Scott), Cmnd 8417 (HMSO, London, 1981).

Third Report from the Treasury and Civil Service Committee, 1981–82: *Efficiency and Effectiveness in the Civil Service*, HC 236 (HMSO, London, 1982), together with volumes of Minutes of Evidence and Appendices.

Report of an Inquiry into the principles and the system by which the remuneration of the non-industrial Civil Service should be determined (Chairman, Sir John Megaw), Cmnd 8590 (HMSO, London, 1982).

Review of Personnel Work in the Civil Service: Report to the Prime Minister by J. S. Cassels (HMSO, London, 1982).

Efficiency and Effectiveness in the Civil Service: Government Observations on the Third Report from the Treasury and Civil Service Committee, Cmnd 8616 (HMSO, London, 1982).

Selection of Fast Stream Graduate Entrants to the Home Civil Service [etc.]: Report by Sir Alec Atkinson (Management and Personnel Office, London, 1983).

Financial Management in Government Departments, Cmnd 9058 (HMSO, London, 1983).

Progress in Financial Management in Government Departments, Cmnd 9297 (HMSO, London, 1984).

Eighth Report from the Treasury and Civil Service Committee, 1983–84: *Acceptance of Outside Appointments by Crown Servants*, HC 302 (HMSO, London, 1984).

Acceptance of Outside Appointments by Crown Servants: Government Observations on the Eighth Report from the Treasury and Civil Service Committee, Cmnd 9465 (HMSO, London, 1985).

Seventh Report from the Treasury and Civil Service Committee, 1985–86: *Civil Servants and Ministers: Duties and Responsibilities*, HC 92 (HMSO, London, 1986), together with separate volume of Annexes, Evidence and Appendices.

Thirty-ninth Report from the Committee of Public Accounts, 1985–86: *The Rayner Scrutiny Programmes, 1979 to 1983*, HC 365 (HMSO, London, 1986).

Civil Servants and Ministers: Duties and Responsibilities: Government Response to the Seventh Report from the Treasury and Civil Service Committee, Cmnd 9841 (HMSO, London, 1986).

Fourth Report from the Defence Committee, 1985–86: *Westland plc: The Government's Decision-Making*, HC 519 (HMSO, London, 1986).

Westland plc: Government Response to the Third and Fourth Reports from the Defence Committee, Cmnd 9916 (HMSO, London, 1986).

Report by the Comptroller and Auditor-General, 1985–86: The Financial Management Initiative, HC 588 (HMSO, London, 1986).

First Report from the Treasury and Civil Service Committee, 1986–87: *Ministers and Civil Servants*, HC 62 (HMSO, London, 1986).

First Report from the Liaison Committee, 1986–87: *Accountability of Ministers and Civil Servants*, HC 100 (HMSO, London, 1986).

Accountability of Ministers and Civil Servants: Government Response to the First Report from the Treasury and Civil Service Committee, and to the First Report from the Liaison Committee, Cm 78 (HMSO, London, 1987).

Efficiency Unit: *Improving Management in Government: The Next Steps*, Report to the Prime Minister (HMSO, London, 1988).

Reform of Section 2 of the Official Secrets Act 1911, Cm 408 (HMSO, London, 1988).

Eighth Report from the Treasury and Civil Service Committee, 1987–88: *Civil Service Management Reform: The Next Steps*, HC 494 I–II (HMSO, London, 1988).

Civil Service Management Reform: The Next Steps: Government Reply to the Eighth Report from the Treasury and Civil Service Committee, Cm 524 (HMSO, London, 1988).

Report by the Comptroller and Auditor General: *The Next Steps Initiative*, HC 410 (HMSO, London, 1989).

Fifth Report from the Treasury and Civil Service Committee, 1988–89: *Developments in the Next Steps Programme*, HC 348 (HMSO, London, 1989).

Developments in the Next Steps Programme: Government Reply to the Fifth Report from the Treasury and Civil Service Committee, Cm 841 (HMSO, London, 1989).

Thirty-Eighth Report from the Committee of Public Accounts, 1988–89: *The Next Steps Initiative*, HC 420 (HMSO, London, 1989).

The Financing and Accountability of Next Steps Agencies, Cm 914 (HMSO, London, 1989).

Fifth Report from the Treasury and Civil Service Committee, 1989–90: *The Civil Service Pay and Conditions of Service Code*, HC 260 (HMSO, London, 1990).

Eighth Report from the Treasury and Civil Service Committee, 1989–90: *Progress in the Next Steps Initiative*, HC 481 (HMSO, London, 1990).

Fifth Special Report from the Treasury and Civil Service Committee, 1989–90: *The Civil Service Pay and Conditions of Service Code: The Government's Observations on the Fifth Report from the Committee in Session 1989–90*, HC 617 (HMSO, London, 1990).

Improving Management in Government – The Next Steps Agencies: Review 1990, Cm 1261 (HMSO, London, 1990).

Progress in the Next Steps Initiative: Government Reply to the Eighth Report from the Treasury and Civil Service Committee, Cm 1263 (HMSO, London, 1990).

See also:

Establishment Officers' Guide.

Civil Service Pay and Conditions of Service Code.

Civil Service Statistics (annual) (HMSO, London).

Civil Service Commission Annual Reports (Civil Service Commission, London and Basingstoke).

Index

Index by Iris Walkland